ADVENTURERS IN THE NEW WORLD

ADVENTURERS IN THE NEW WORLD

THE SAGA OF THE COUREURS DES BOIS

GEORGES-HÉBERT GERMAIN

Scientific Director
JEAN-PIERRE HARDY

Original illustrations by
FRANCIS BACK

CANADIAN MUSEUM   MUSÉE CANADIEN
OF CIVILIZATION   DES CIVILISATIONS

CANADIAN MUSEUM   MUSÉE CANADIEN
OF CIVILIZATION   DES CIVILISATIONS

100 Laurier Street
Hull, Quebec, Canada J8X 4H2

© 2003 Éditions Libre Expression
© 2003 Canadian Museum of Civilization
for the English edition

Project Originator and Director
André Bastien

Senior Adviser – Publication and Illustration
Francis Back

Co-director
Jean-François Blanchette

Researchers
Francis Back, Denyse Beaugrand-Champagne,
Jim Hanson and Claude Paulette

Director of Illustration Research
Süzel Back-Drapeau

Contributors
Alain Beaulieu, Kathleen Brosseau, Nicole Denis,
Nathalie Guénette, Gilles Havard, David Keenlyside,
Janouk Murdock, Jean O'Neil and Frédéric Paradis

Photographers
Erwin and Peggy Bauer, Harry Foster,
Stephan Poulin and Merle Toole

Translator of fiction segments
Nora Alleyn

Translator of non-fiction segments
Janet Chapman

Copy Editor
Robert Lewis

Design
Lafond Legault

Digital Imaging
Film-O-progrès

Cover illustration
Canoes in a Fog, Lake Superior, 1869
(detail), Frances Ann Hopkins,
Collection of the Glenbow Museum,
Calgary, Canada

Les Éditions Libre Expression wishes to thank the
Canadian Museum of Civilization for its invaluable
collaboration, and also thanks the Department of
Canadian Heritage; the Canada Council for the Arts;
the Government of Quebec; and the Société de
développement des entreprises culturelles du Québec
(SODEC), which administers the Tax Credit for Book
Publishing.

Legal deposit, 4th quarter 2003
ISBN 0-660-19075-3
NM24-3/2003E

This work is translated from
Les Coureurs des bois : La Saga des Indiens blancs,
published by Éditions Libre Expression, 2003.
ISBN 2-7648-0060-6

Canadian Cataloguing in Publication Data

Germain, Georges-Hébert, 1944-
    Adventurers in the New World: The Saga of the Coureurs
    des Bois
    Translation of: Les Coureurs des bois
    Includes bibliographical references.

ISBN 0-660-19075-3

1. Fur traders – North America. 2. Indians of North America -
Mixed descent. 3. Trappers – North America. 4. Fur traders'
spouses – North America. 5. North America – History – Colonial
period, ca. 1600-1775. I. Hardy, Jean-Pierre, 1945-   . II. Canadian
Museum of Civilization. III. Title.

E46.G47 2003   970.03   C2003-941177-X

QUOTATIONS
The texts appearing under the chapter headings are excerpted
and translated from the following works: *Les Indiens blancs*,
Philippe Jacquin, pp. 11, 29, and 117; *Journal d'une campagne
au Canada à bord de la Sauvage, mars-juillet 1756*, Louis-
Guillaume Pascau Du Plessis, p. 47; *Lettres*, Jacques Duchesneau
de la Doussinière et d'Ambault, p. 69; *Un voyageur des pays
d'en haut*, Georges Dugas, p. 93; *Notes of a Sporting Expedition
in the Far West of Canada*, F.U. Graham, p. 141.

ILLUSTRATIONS
Many of the objects pictured in this book are from the
Canadian Museum of Civilization. Some of them were acquired
by the museum thanks to a contribution from the Government
of Canada's Emergency Purchase Fund.

TABLE OF CONTENTS

Part One
ODYSSEY INTO INDIAN COUNTRY   6

Chapter 1
ADVENTURERS IN THE NEW WORLD   10
Recruits for the New World   12
Jean Nicollet's Story   14
In the Service of God and King   16
A World of Freedom   18
The Land of Plenty   20
A Continent of Three Hundred Nations   22
Continental Trade   24
The White Tide   26

Chapter 2
CHILDREN OF THE COUNTRY   28
The Interpreters   30
Étienne Brûlé's Story   32
An Abundance of Fur-Bearing Animals   34
A Highly Coveted Commodity   36
The Beaver   38
Indian Hunting and Trapping Techniques   40
The Birchbark Canoe   42
An Outpost of Intercontinental Trade   44

Chapter 3
THE COUREURS DES BOIS   46
The Donnés   48
Guillaume Couture's Story   50
The Walking Dead   52
Pierre-Esprit Radisson's Story   54
The Iroquois Wife   56
The Coureurs des Bois   58
Nicolas Perrot's Story   60
Libertines and Debauchees   62

Part Two
ODYSSEY TO THE PAYS D'EN HAUT   64

Chapter 4
THE PORK EATERS   68
The Voyageurs   70
Jean-Baptiste Charbonneau's Story   72
The Voyageur's White Wife   74
The Voyageur's Country Wife   76
Marie-Anne Gaboury's Story   78
The Montreal Canoe   80
The Crew Members   82
The Outfitters   84
Capital of the Fur Country   86

Part Three
ODYSSEY TO THE COLD COUNTRY   88

Chapter 5
THE NORTH MEN   92
The Winterers   94
Joseph La France's Story   96
The Dogsled   98
Trade Goods   100
The Trading Companies   102
The Trading Posts   104
The Dutch Traders   106
When America Was French   108
New France   110

Part Four
ODYSSEY BEYOND THE MOUNTAINS   112

Chapter 6
THE WHITE INDIANS   116
The Trappers   118
The Trapper's Wife   120
Sacagawea's Story   122
The Trapper's Weapons and Equipment   124
The Horse   126
Trapping Techniques   128
The Rendezvous   130
The Mixed Bloods   132
Charles-Michel de Langlade's Story   134

Part Five
ODYSSEY INTO THE FAR WEST   136

Chapter 7
THE MÉTIS NATION   140
The Wagon Men   142
Gabriel Dumont's Story   144
Descendants of the English Traders   146
The Métis Wife   148
The Red River Cart   150
The Buffalo   152
The Hunting Expedition   154
The Buffalo Hunt   156

EPILOGUE
The Rebels   158

Most of those who set off
for the New World were young
bachelors with few ties,
like this young man
pictured in 1870.
They had little or no training
and their average age
was twenty-four.

Part One

ODYSSEY INTO INDIAN COUNTRY

The rain woke him up, a fine, fresh drizzle. It took him a while to realize that he was lying on his stomach by the river's edge, listening to, and feeling, the soft lapping of the waves at his feet. It was bright daylight, and that is what surprised him most.

"How did I fall asleep on the beach in plain daylight?"

He tried to stand so that he could move higher up into the rushes and dried grasses, but something was holding him down, like a huge weight on his back, and his arms and legs were so numb that he couldn't move them. His mind was so confused that he could only dwell on vague memories. He thought he was having a nightmare. Or that he had drunk too much wine at the fort with his friends. He dreamed that he was back at sea.

He heard movement farther up in the rushes: men's voices and laughter. They were not European voices. Nor was it the Algonquin language, which he was starting to understand fairly well. It resembled the Huron language, but with strange intonations, and it was much harder and more guttural and studded with unfamiliar words. That is how he realized that he had been made prisoner by the Indians, probably enemies of the French.

And then slowly it all came back to him. He and his friends had left to go hunting despite the warnings of those who knew the country well and who had often repeated to him that it was too dangerous to wander away from the fort unless accompanied by battle-hardened men. But he had insisted and had dragged his friends along with him. He wanted to go hunting ducks and Canada geese but also – and especially – needed to show, as usual, how courageous he was. In the last little while, he had developed a taste for danger. He wanted to see the landscapes and faces of this dangerous, forbidden, and entirely new world, which few men had dared to penetrate.

The strangers whose movements he had heard stopped talking. They approached and gathered around him. He could see their bare feet in the rushes and the butt of a musket planted on the ground near his face. "An English or a Dutch musket," he noted. A man stooped down and turned him over, very gently, onto his back. And then he saw them gathered around him, silhouetted against a whitish sky gorged with hot rain: the ferocious, the fascinating, Iroquois.

This Cree woman,
painted at Fort Union,
was the wife of a coureur des bois
named Deschamps
who worked as a hunter
for a fur trading company.

For a few years now, they had been waging guerrilla warfare in this area, where the French had organized a lucrative fur trade with the Huron and the Algonquin, the traditional enemies of the Iroquois.

He listened to the Iroquois warriors and tried to grasp what they were saying, what they intended to do with him. "Maybe they'll kill me!" And then he lost the thread of his thoughts. He could see himself once again on the ship that for days and days had pushed ever deeper into this vast country apparently empty of people, this wilderness with its water and skies he had never seen anywhere before. As they had sailed up the great river, its shores, covered with forests, had tightened around the ship as though the country itself wanted to grab and devour it, swallow it, with all its rigging, its passengers, its crew.

When he regained consciousness, it was still raining. The Indians were looking at him in silence. He couldn't make out their features against the light, their striped faces covered in red war paint. But he couldn't hold back an expression of horror when he saw, still oozing blood, the scalp of one of his companions, which an Iroquois was holding, nonchalantly, as if the blond hair were a scarf. The men burst out laughing when they saw the terror on his face. But they didn't harm him. On the contrary, one of them knelt down, felt his arms and legs, went off to find water, and upon returning helped him to drink from a birchbark container.

His inner voice was telling him: "It's happened, it's happened, I've finally achieved it." Despite the pain and the fear, he wanted to get up, to tell these men that he wanted to go with them, to live like them, to be one of them.

All summer long, he had mixed with the Algonquin, who were beginning to come to Trois Rivières to trade. He had spent many days with them, watching them build their great birchbark canoes, which the French had ordered. And he had learned a few words from them, hunting and trapping techniques, how to

Living in close contact with nature, the Indians had developed a distinctive material culture perfectly adapted to their environment.

hold a paddle, and how to walk in the forest soundlessly without leaving any tracks.

One day, in the middle of summer, he had gone on an expedition with the Huron, taking the fur trade route four or five days upriver from Ville Marie, past the Allumette Islands, to the extreme limit of the known world, where only a few dozen Europeans had ever dared to go. He and his companions had looked for the Iroquois along the way. The Huron wanted to instill fear in the Iroquois, or to impose peace, or at least to propose a truce.

But he soon realized that they were the fearful ones, with their muskets and iron hatchets and the crosses they wore around their necks. After a few days, so great and paralyzing was his fear that he wanted to retrace his steps, hoping they would never run into these awesome warriors, the Iroquois.

And then suddenly, without warning, there they were, around a bend in the river, in a clearing, looking impassive and indifferent, allowing themselves to be seen. That day he had sworn that the Iroquois village, as though by magic, had materialized out of the depths of the forest. And he would not have been surprised if it had disappeared again just as quickly, like a mirage.

He will never forget that scene engraved in his memory. It would change his life forever, mark him forever. The image kept returning as he lay on the cold pebbles, surrounded by the Iroquois.

That day, when they had arrived at the rough campsite, they could hardly make sense out of what they saw – the objects, the people, the whole scene. Everything was in such chaos that he was completely mystified. And then he had noticed, lying under a shelter made of branches, men, women, and children, relaxed, naked, side by side, some of them fast asleep, proof that no one was worried about the approach of the French. There was a dying fire whose smoke filled the shelter, but this didn't seem to bother them. Over another hearth, without a fire, hung a large copper pot filled with a black, nasty-smelling broth that had revolting stuff floating around in it. Farther on, to the right, two men were stretched out side by side. Both were seriously wounded, but nobody was paying any attention to them. Even they seemed indifferent to their fate, almost serene, despite the gaping wounds and burns that covered their bodies from head to toe. One of them was chanting in low, insistent tones.

The white leaders and Iroquois chiefs had negotiated for a long time. During their discussions, a child kept banging the copper pot with a tomahawk, non-stop, with all his strength, the noise growing louder or softer depending on where he hit the pot. And the dogs were howling. Shrill-voiced children were busy eviscerating the carcass of a bear in an advanced state of decomposition. The skin had been torn off and hung out to dry on a rough trellis made of branches.

The Iroquois seemed completely indifferent to the disorder and cacophony, the stink, the children's shouts, the clanging from the copper pot, the smoke, and even the presence of the French.

Gradually, he had felt his fear melt away. Amidst the chaos and the din, he had felt a

In trading with the Europeans, the Indians knew what they wanted and soon started asking for hardware, utensils, and other utilitarian items.

peace and a strength rise up and course through his arms and legs. He knew that he would never forget that moment, that scene, that new world infused with authentic feelings of joy, harmony, and vigour.

And there was that smile, that unforgettable smile that a young Iroquois woman, with naked breasts and shoulders, had tossed him, her dark eyes following him the whole time the French were in the campsite.

The Iroquois untied him so that he could stretch his limbs before getting into their canoe. They made him sit in the middle. At times he became delirious and would think of that beautiful woman and of how the Iroquois could look deep into your soul.

The rain had stopped when they made for shore, and they saw the sun set among the islands of the great river.

While his kidnappers prepared the campsite and the meal, he thought of his old life that might be slipping away, perhaps forever. He thought of his friends – lost or no doubt dead, while he was about to experience a brand new world that he had never seen before. At last!

"I've finally made it," he said, out loud. The Iroquois heard him. They laughed. They were with him. And he with them.

Chapter 1

ADVENTURERS IN THE NEW WORLD

Indian societies did not produce archives; the oral tradition has faded for such distant times. When it does resurface here and there, gathered and transcribed by a Jesuit or a voyageur, it is always fragmentary and inadequate. Frenchmen involved in the fur trade also had an oral culture, but they left no more traces than did the Indians. Yet all these men had spoken, thought, suffered, and struggled; the Canadian cold had nipped their flesh and the prairie wind had caressed their faces; their eyes had met those of the Huron or the Sioux; they had loved the country and its women. Their language, their feelings, their personal accounts are inaccessible; all that remains of their adventure are scattered scraps. They are the Men of the Wind.

Married men were advised to make the journey alone and to send for their wives and children once they were well established.

The St. Lawrence River basin covers a million square kilometres and contains a vast network of often turbulent rivers.

Recruits for the New World

Unmindful of the dangers
awaiting them,
young Europeans set sail
for North America in the hope
of bettering their lot.

*Would they find hardship,
death, or a new life?*

Even before they sailed, those bound for the New World found themselves in an alien environment of which they knew almost nothing and whose inhabitants seemed oblivious to their existence. Many had made their way on their own to St. Malo, St. Nazaire, La Rochelle, or Honfleur to await the day of departure.

Apart from their youth, they seemed to have little in common – poverty perhaps, for many of them had very little baggage. But there was something else. Their eyes and gestures revealed a certain daring, dash, and determination. They obviously had a taste for adventure. And a desire for a new life.

Though France was 85 per cent rural at that time, many of the young men came from cities – and not just from the port cities, but also from Poitiers, Amiens, Angers, Le Mans, and even Paris, the most populous city in the Western world, with half a million people.

The young city dweller was certainly better prepared than the peasant for such an adventure. He was more familiar with the realities of the outside world. A peasant who spoke only a regional dialect was necessarily

confined to his own locale. And he didn't have much of a future – not even on the land where he was born, since the family property, if there was one, was subdivided with each succeeding generation. With almost no resources, the young peasant was a prisoner of his fate. Fear of the unknown held him back. No doubt, he also felt an attachment to the land, his traditions, his religion, and maybe even to his poverty, never having known anything else.

The majority of the French lived in poverty, crowded into uncomfortable and unhealthy hovels. The whole country was at the mercy of poor harvests and the resulting food shortages. There were eleven widespread famines in the seventeenth century and sixteen in the following century.

The story of Tom Thumb (*Le Petit Poucet*) dates from this period and reflects this grim reality. While France, with its twenty million inhabitants, was the wealthiest country in Europe, and while its aristocracy enjoyed numerous, inalienable privileges, the common people lived poor, wretched lives. Those who had been lucky enough to find work in a physically demanding trade, such as stonemason, had their wages cut after age thirty-five because they were no longer as strong and oftentimes maimed. Rarely did men live beyond the age of fifty.

Many of the young men who turned up at the ports in the spring seeking to embark for New

Before leaving for the New World, the men received an advance equal to six months' wages. This enabled the poor emigrants to replace their cotton or linen garments and wooden shoes with woollen clothing and leather footwear more suited to the Canadian climate.

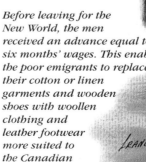

France were orphans. Half the children they had known in their lives had died before the age of twenty; out of their four or five siblings, only one or two, rarely three, were still alive. These young men were survivors. They had the strength to leave despite their fear and the danger.

Tales of the first winters spent in the New World were indeed terrifying. In St. Malo, horror stories were passed down from generation to generation, brought back by the sailors who had survived Cartier's expeditions. In Honfleur, everybody remembered that twenty of the twenty-eight men who had accompanied Samuel de Champlain when he founded Quebec in 1608 had not survived the winter. And everyone knew that more than a third of the emigrants who set sail for New France returned home before the end of their contracts. The winter was too cold, life too harsh, the Indians too bloodthirsty.

Under the reigns of Louis XIII and Louis XIV, the French, despite their abject poverty, were not easily attracted by the land across the sea. Throughout the seventeenth century, the peopling of New France occurred gradually, much more slowly than on the Atlantic seaboard, where the English and the Dutch settled. Part of the reason was that in New France

Travelling chests like this eighteenth-century wooden model with a cover and a lock were often the only furniture the settlers had.

not everyone was welcome. In 1667 the king's intendant, Jean Talon, set age restrictions; no one under sixteen or over forty need apply. There was no place for anyone who would not be productive. Excluding members of religious communities, 90 per cent of immigrants were very young, had no training, and were from the lower classes. More than half were labourers, unskilled workers, or farm workers. Almost 15 per cent were involved in war-related occupations, while commerce and public administration accounted for another 10 per cent. Those who were members of the minor aristocracy and the bourgeoisie could be counted almost on the fingers of one hand. Most of the new arrivals were young bachelors who had few ties, nothing to lose, and their lives ahead of them; their average age was less than twenty-four.

During the first year, the immigrant's wages rarely exceeded thirty livres (compared to, say, two hundred livres for a ship's captain). But a hardworking and resourceful young man could earn fifty to seventy-five livres a year or even more.

Nearly a third of the immigrants could read and write. More than half of them – and almost all of the Parisians (83.6 per cent) – were able to sign their names on their contracts with the Compagnie des Cent-Associés, the Communauté des Habitants, the Jesuits, the Ursulines, the Société de Notre-Dame de Montréal, or one of the traders in Rouen or La Rochelle who were recruiting people for the New World.

All declared themselves Catholics. The king didn't want any foreigners, Huguenots, or Calvinists in his young colony. These heretics might be permitted to work as crew members and even spend the summer in New France; however, if they wanted to settle there, they had to renounce their faith.

In the early decades of the colony, there were still not many women. A few came to join their husbands, sometimes bringing their children. Others were there to help evangelize the Indians or to found a hospital or convent. By the mid-seventeenth century, not counting married women and nuns, there was only one woman for every seven men of marrying age.

It was thus a very strange yet exciting adventure on which these young men were embarking.

JEAN NICOLLET'S STORY

The Winnebago thought Nicollet was a god and called him Manitouiriniou, or "Man of Wonders."

Unlike many young Frenchmen who came into close contact with Aboriginal cultures, Nicollet never became assimilated.

When Jean Nicollet de Belleborne drowned near Sillery in October 1642 it was truly a tragedy, for his knowledge of the fur trade route and Indian customs and languages was almost unrivalled in the young colony of New France.

Like Champlain, and everyone else in those heroic early days, he thought he could find a route to the Western Sea and the fabulous lands described by Marco Polo.

In 1618 Champlain had sent this ambitious and adventurous young Norman to winter on Allumette Island on the Ottawa River, a strategic centre for the fur trade and a gathering place for the nomadic Algonquin. His mission was to consolidate the alliances that Champlain had established a few years earlier.

Nicollet spent two years with the Algonquin, learning their language and customs and gaining their confidence and friendship. Two years later, Champlain entrusted him with a new mission: to establish ties with the Nipissing, an Algonquian tribe further inland. Nicollet stayed with the Nipissing for nine years. While organizing the fur trade, he also kept a journal in which he noted his observations of the people among whom he lived. These papers were unfortunately lost. However, Father Paul Le Jeune, the Superior of the Jesuits in New France, had them in his possession for a while and used them in describing the ways and customs of the Ottawa Indians in the reports he sent back to his superiors in France, the first of what would become the *Jesuit Relations*.

In the early 1630s, Nicollet set off into uncharted territory where no European had gone before. This time his mission was to help make peace between the Algonquin, who were French allies, and the Winnebago, an Indian nation that was largely unknown to the French. It was hoped that Nicollet, a good interpreter and diplomat, would be able to settle the disputes that, if exacerbated, could compromise the fur trade. But Nicollet also had something much more exciting in mind.

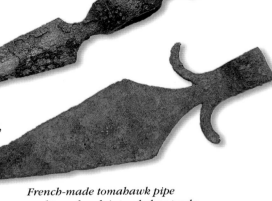

French-made tomahawk pipe and tomahawk intended as trade goods or gifts for the Indians.

The Algonquian word for sea was *ouinipeg*, meaning "foul-smelling water." The Winnebago were so called because they had lived on the shores of a great sea, though their name for themselves was Hochangara, "people of the true word." Nicollet believed that from their territory he would be able to reach the China Sea.

In order to be appropriately attired when he arrived in the Orient, which he had no doubt he would reach, Nicollet had brought with him a long robe of Chinese damask patterned with flowers and birds of various colours.

After crossing Georgian Bay, he followed the north shore of Lake Huron up the spectacular rapids that would later be called Sault Ste. Marie and into Lake Superior. He continued along the north shore of this great lake to the land of the Winnebago, up the river leading to Lake Nipigon.

There he assembled several thousand Indians. He must have been an awesome figure standing before them in his damask robe. Although the Indians found white men rather ugly, they were impressed with their clothing and their technology, which they assumed was magic. They thought Nicollet was a god and called him Manitouiriniou, or "Man of Wonders." They listened to him with great respect. Thus, when he wanted the Algonquin and the Winnebago to make peace, the chiefs of the enemy nations passed around the peace pipe, began talking to each other and buried the hatchet.

Nicollet, however, was preoccupied with thoughts of the sea and was constantly questioning the Indians, especially the elders, as to where it was located and how to get there. He was disappointed to learn that the sea on which the Winnebago used to live lay to the north and thus could not be the hoped-for passage to the Orient. But the Indians spoke of great rivers, just south of Lake Superior, that led to other "foul-smelling waters," which could only be the China Sea.

Nicollet did conduct a number of expeditions in that direction. It is believed that he reached the country of the Fox, the Illinois, and the Mascoutin and that he may have made it as far as the Wisconsin River, which flows into the Mississippi, though no one knows for sure. As he descended into these unknown lands, he would have met other tribes and heard other stories. While he never did discover the China Sea or a westward route, he, more than anyone before him, extended the territory over which France would exercise its influence for more than a century as it monopolized the lucrative fur trade.

On his return, Nicollet settled down in Trois Rivières. For his services to the colony, he was granted 160 acres of uncleared land, which he worked with his brother-in-law Olivier Letardif, who was also very familiar with the Indian peoples and their cultures. The two men subsequently became joint owners of the estate of Belleborne, near Quebec.

In October 1637, Nicollet married Marguerite Couillard, granddaughter of Louis Hébert, New France's first farmer. They had a son and a daughter.

Unlike many young Frenchmen who lived in close contact with the Indians, Nicollet did not become assimilated into their culture. Although he spent many years among them and had a daughter, named Madeleine-Euphrosine, with a Nipissing woman, he never adopted Indian ways and beliefs. He was always the French colony's representative in the fur country. He returned to the St. Lawrence Valley because he missed the comforts of his religion and wanted to make his mark in the young colony, which he had always faithfully served.

During the Kirke brothers' occupation of Quebec from 1629 to 1632, he refused to have anything to do with the English and convinced the Nipissing, with whom he was living, not to have any contact with them either.

In 1642, on a stormy day in late October, Nicollet set out from Quebec for Trois Rivières to rescue a prisoner whom the Huron were about to torture and put to death. However, his boat was capsized by a strong gust of wind, and Nicollet, who didn't know how to swim, drowned in the frigid water.

His death was an enormous loss to the colony. The Jesuit priests described him as a good man who was faithful to his religion and his people. For the Winnebago, he would always be the Man of Wonders.

The Nipissing controlled the fur trade route and were thus valuable trading partners for the French.

IN THE SERVICE OF GOD AND KING

Under the seigneurial system, people lived in fear of famine and, most of all, in fear of God.

The upper classes kept all the wealth for themselves and exercised inordinate control over the common people.

Louis XIII was king of France when the new colony was founded. Under his reign, the common people had no one to speak for them.

The worst thing about life in those days was that there was little hope of improving one's condition. The chances were so slim that almost no one dared dream of it. In seventeenth-century France, a poor young man could at best hope to become a poor old man – and that by the age of fifty – if he survived the famines and epidemics and wasn't killed in one of the wars in which the common people were unwillingly enlisted, with little idea of what they were fighting for.

The poor man's fate was sealed at birth, and there was not much he could do to change it. His was a life of little joy, less freedom, and no choice. Whether peasant or city dweller, he was constrained by church and state, and by the habits and mentalities of his milieu, to lead a life of servitude in a society where inequality was the unchallenged rule.

All the country's natural resources – lands, forests, and waterways – and all the sources of its wealth, knowledge, and power were passed down from generation to generation by an aristocracy who, though they represented less than 2 per cent of the population, were all powerful and servilely respected. Happiness lay in their hands.

Even the making and wearing of clothes, an external sign of one's social condition, was regulated. The poor had to display their poverty and humility, just as others ostentatiously displayed their wealth and nobility. The common man was not allowed to carry a sword, or to fight a duel, or, like the young nobleman, to make a show of his courage and strength. The circulation of firearms was strictly controlled, with peasants most everywhere not being permitted to own them. Hunting, too, was reserved for the aristocrats, who engaged in it for sport, while the people were denied this desperately needed source of subsistence.

Kept in a constant state of physical, intellectual, and psychological subjugation and weakened by famines and chronic malnutrition, the people found it hard to foment any kind of uprising.

Unless he could read and write, which was exceedingly rare, a boy could not hope to join a religious community in any capacity other than that of a lay brother entrusted with only the hardest and most thankless jobs.

A bright and enterprising young man could, if he had good connections and a lot of luck, learn a trade, such as stonemason, carpenter, or toolmaker. But to open his own shop, he first had to become a master in his trade, which required long years of apprenticeship and journeymanship. Only a very small part of the population had the means to acquire the knowledge required of a master tradesman.

What about joining the army? All ranks other than foot soldier and canon fodder were, of course, reserved for the aristocracy. In the military, too, any social ascension was unthinkable, impossible, and entirely against the prevailing culture.

France was constantly at war with anyone who posed a real or potential threat to the frontiers of its still undefined territory. It was also battling certain extremely rich and rebellious nobles who wanted to share or seize power from within.

To wage these wars, the government needed the country's young men and its riches. France's meagre agricultural and industrial output was thus heavily taxed. The Royal Treasury charged its tallage, the seigneur his rent, and the church its tithe.

This immutable order was maintained by the church, which enforced it as the will of God; poor people were thus obliged to respect it whether they wanted to or not. In the seventeenth century, a huge missionary offensive was undertaken in rural France, which was rife with pagan beliefs. The fanatical *Sorciers de Dieu* considered it their mission to re-Christianize the peasants.

Anyone who broke the commandments or rules would suffer terrible and inescapable punishment. Begging was considered shameful and thus was harshly repressed, especially in wealthy areas. Beggars were not allowed to enter Paris on pain of flogging for first-time offenders or, for second-time offenders, the galleys for men and boys, and banishment for women and girls.

Women who dared to think for themselves and speak their minds, thus threatening the power of the church and of the king, God's incontestable representative on Earth, were accused of being witches and burned at the stake. The priests' powers extended to the depths of each person's conscience and soul. Members of the lower classes were little able to oppose all those who sought to

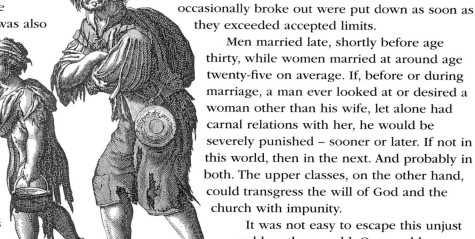

Entire families were reduced to vagrancy and begging, an activity that not only was seen as shameful but was severely punished.

keep them in a state of absolute subjugation from cradle to grave. Any anger they might have felt was never heard and soon abated. The minor revolts that occasionally broke out were put down as soon as they exceeded accepted limits.

Men married late, shortly before age thirty, while women married at around age twenty-five on average. If, before or during marriage, a man ever looked at or desired a woman other than his wife, let alone had carnal relations with her, he would be severely punished – sooner or later. If not in this world, then in the next. And probably in both. The upper classes, on the other hand, could transgress the will of God and the church with impunity.

It was not easy to escape this unjust and heartless world. One could sometimes find relief in brief moments of folly, wild bouts of drunkenness that numbed both body and soul. Or one could indulge in mystical experiences of various sorts. Religious orders appealed to the hopeless, with more-or-less deviant sects offering shortcuts to eternal happiness.

A few brave souls dared to imagine a better world – and began to believe in it. They listened to the lovely fairy tales with which dreamers filled their happy heads, stories in which shepherd girls became princesses and toads were transformed into Prince Charming, in which lovers lived happily ever after and had lots of children, none of whom died in infancy.

Mixed in with these fairy tales were stories of wondrous travels that adventurers had undertaken in a world where everyone had a chance to make a life for himself, where a peasant could become a king if he truly wished.

Somewhere on the other side of the ocean lay this treasure as yet unclaimed by the rich men and nobles of France. Young men could throw off the yoke of oppression and start over. This time it wasn't a fairy tale or a dream; it was real. Now, at last, it was a New World.

French towns were still very rural, with numerous vegetable patches, stables, and animals.

A WORLD OF FREEDOM

Europeans discovered
a world that appeared
infinitely more just,
permissive, and tolerant
than their own.

*Indian girls were mistresses
of their own bodies
and could give themselves
to whomever they wanted.*

In much of the New World, no one – no judge, priest, or captain, not even the greatest leader – could oblige anyone to do anything. For the most part, there were no legal institutions and no police. There were some taboos but no religious interdictions. Unless enslaved by force, each individual – man or woman, young or old – was free to forge his or her own destiny. This wild, untamed world, though it showed its enemies no mercy, generously welcomed all well-meaning strangers, accepting them as its own.

In this world, a man's prestige depended not on his birth or his name, but on the courage he showed in battle and in the face of torture or death. And also on his hunting skills, his story-telling ability, his kindness, tolerance, and consideration, his care for his own people and understanding of others, and his respect for the elderly. He need only be brave, strong, and generous to earn respect, to assert his authority, to be listened to and admired by his peers, and to be raised to the highest honours among them. And, best of all, to win the love of women.

A chief's son, if he was a coward, received no respect. A coward's son, however, if he was brave and good, enjoyed everyone's admiration and friendship; he could rise through the ranks of society and become a chief.

In this world, hell did not exist. Women were mistresses of their own bodies and could give themselves to whomever they wanted, whenever and however they pleased. Sexual play, so severely condemned by French morality, was practised freely. No one, male or female, felt the need to have exclusive possession of another, as in European society. At any rate, this was the impression one had in viewing these Aboriginal societies from the outside. This is what was recounted by all who had penetrated such societies and returned.

Nothing and no one prevented each member of the tribe from enjoying nature's abundance in the New World, be it hunting and fishing, gathering and cultivating, or erecting a dwelling wherever and whenever one wanted. It was truly the land of freedom. All men had the ability, nay the duty, to bear arms to protect their loved ones and defend their honour. This world, clearly better, apparently more just, and infinitely more permissive and tolerant than that of Europe, seemed to be in perfect harmony with nature.

The Indians could be extremely cruel to their enemies but never subjected members of their own tribes to torture and rarely if ever executed them. They could not understand why the Europeans would do such things to their own people simply as retribution for something considered wrong or forbidden. Rather than punishment, the Indians required reparation.

The Indians shared everything: their food, shelter, joys, and sorrows. Anyone who wanted to amass material possessions was viewed with contempt. There was no private property, nor were there any social classes. Community life was based on a culture of sharing, exchanging, and gift-giving. This ensured peace and order and prevented the concentration of wealth since everyone was expected to give back as much as, if not more than, he or she had received. Among the Indians, the truly noble owned nothing. Those who had given everything away were the wisest and most respected members of the tribe.

Accounts circulating on the Atlantic coast of France added to the allure of the New World. La Hontan, for instance, in his famous *Dialogue de M. le baron de La Hontan et d'un sauvage de l'Amérique,*

The inhabitants of the New World had everything they needed to survive. This catlinite tablet was used in conjunction with a bow and drill for starting fires.

had lauded the primitive life, evoking the myth of the noble savage long before Jean-Jacques Rousseau, and had also severely criticized European society and civilization.

According to this line of thought, which soon became widespread, French society was founded on injustice, inequality, and privilege, while Indian society was based entirely on the full equality of individuals, tolerance, and indulgence. The children had to assume their freedom at a very early age. Though it was a hard and demanding life, it was also enriching. Young Europeans, born in a world where the concept of individual liberty did not exist, undoubtedly had the impression that they would be able to lead an ideal life in this marvellous New World.

From their reports, collected as the *Jesuit Relations*, it would appear that even the Jesuits were charmed by the "Savage" societies of America, especially in the early part of the seventeenth century. Father Paul Le Jeune wrote that the Indians "feel no jealousy toward others, they help one another, they share the wealth and food. [...] The women and the men each know what is expected of them and never interfere in the other's work."

Duties and roles were clearly defined according to gender and age, but no single function was deemed more important than another or thought to elevate anyone to a more important stature than that of the others. Prestige was not associated with a particular function; however, prestige acquired through virtue and strength conferred upon an individual the right or the privilege to exercise a function with authority. Among many Indian nations, such as the Iroquois, the women spoke freely and were listened to and respected.

The apparent, and to some extent very real, absence of

Each individual was free to forge his or her own destiny, unless overwhelmed by force and enslaved like this young Blackfoot woman.

coercive institutions created the impression that there was total anarchy among the Indian societies of America – a very exciting impression for young Europeans.

In the seventeenth century, the ocean separating Europe from America was a cultural threshold. Those who crossed it found themselves in a completely different world. A man could leave his past behind and start anew, going from an extremely restrictive society to a very permissive one that put no limits on individual freedom. Listening only to his own heart and using his mind and muscles, a man could live his life as he saw fit, without the commandments, rules, and orders of the church, seigneur, and king.

However, becoming a part of this apparently ideal world was not easy. It is not in everyone's nature to be strong, brave, and generous. The young Europeans who planned to go and live with the Indians were certainly valiant and worthy. But freedom is not within everyone's reach. They had to be incredibly daring and courageous to undertake this terrible adventure that only the strongest could survive.

This contact between the old and new worlds gave rise to serious problems. But from this union of the bravest of the Europeans with the Indian peoples of America would emerge a unique culture founded on tolerance and individual freedom, a frontier culture, a new world such as had never existed before.

In the New World, all men carried weapons for fighting and hunting, both of which were a normal part of everyday life.

The Land of Plenty

More than the beauty and
diversity of the flora and fauna,
it was their profusion
that initially
astounded the Europeans.

*Before they had access to
European technologies, the Indians
altered nature very little.*

First there was the forest – ever-present, lush, and sovereign, hemming in the continent on all sides, as though there had only ever been the forest from sea to sea, covering and weighing down the land with its impenetrable mass. Along the quiet coastal waters of the Florida Peninsula, where manatees swam, mangrove trees presented an inextricable tangle before giving way to giant palm groves and swamps teeming with alligators. Farther north, dense coniferous and deciduous forests came right down to the sea, often in vast homogeneous stands of maple, oak, cedar, or pine or in mixed forests of elm, beech, ash, and larch, or of hemlock and birch, a mix of softwoods and hardwoods. The dark, mysterious forests full of wild animals offered danger and unimaginable riches, an incredible abundance that for centuries awed and astounded the Europeans.

The cod, which Europeans had been coming to catch off the coast for over a century, was the most important marine resource in the history of the world. Like everything else, it seemed inexhaustible. The first explorers to make their way inland boasted that the abundant natural resources they had discovered could feed and clothe everyone till the end of time, no matter how large the population grew. Nature's plenty would keep them warm and provide everything they needed to make tools, weapons, ships, and shelter – indeed, everything required to create a history and legends. Everything, in short, to make a world.

*River otters were found all across
North America and even in the lakes
and rivers of the tundra.*

Before penetrating inland, they sailed around this vast continent. On the other side, they found more forests, palm-fringed beaches, great stands of cacti, and giant pine and fir trees rising 150 metres into the air, many of them hundreds of years old.

In both the East and the West, the rivers, streams, and lakes abounded with sturgeon, pike, trout, walleye, and salmon. The land and the sky also teemed with wildlife, feathered and furred, big and small. As the Europeans entered this new world, they were endlessly amazed at its prodigious wonders.

Trees dominated the landscape, lining the banks of the rivers the Europeans took inland. Occasionally coming upon a natural clearing, they would cautiously advance to the edge of the woods, which they hesitated to enter. They were afraid of the forest, for it was so deep, thick, and luxuriant and inhabited by innumerable wild animals: bear, moose, caribou, deer, elk, beaver, mink, marten, lynx, cougar. On the coasts, they saw sea otters three times the size of those found in Europe. And birds everywhere! Flocks of passenger pigeons blackened the sky, and flights of Canada geese and snow geese passed overhead for days on end.

All summer long, in the gulfs and bays of the Atlantic Coast, they would see colonies of puffins, gannets, tundra swans, and great auks. And herds of seals, porpoises, walruses, and belugas. On the tidal flats, they found oysters, periwinkles, mussels, and lobsters. In the Hudson and Connecticut Valleys and up the Lake Champlain basin as far as the St. Lawrence River were great gobbling flocks of enormous turkeys and chickens.

*The lynx population rose
or declined along with that of its prey,
the snowshoe hare.*

In following the major rivers and their tributaries into the heart of the continent, the Europeans discovered another incredible marvel: the Great Lakes. These freshwater, inland seas, too, were surrounded by vast forests teeming with wildlife.

Venturing further north and west, they reached the "height of land," from which other mighty rivers flowed toward the North Sea across the taiga and tundra, those harsh, barren lands inhabited by wolves, Arctic foxes and hares, migrating herds of caribou hundreds of thousands strong, musk oxen, and polar bears. Even the frigid ocean was home to narwhals, walruses, belugas, and right whales. During the short summer season, the skies swarmed with millions and millions of birds.

As they advanced into the West, they discovered another wonder as amazing as the Great Lakes: the Prairies. Under the great bowl of the sky spread a vast sea of grass, salt meadows, and wild rice. Here and there were oak and walnut groves, oases in this strange desert. The horizon was frequently obscured by herds of buffalo, thousands and thousands of massive, slow-moving, shaggy beasts, and by equal numbers of antelope, moose, and white-tailed deer. They also came upon more great rivers, some rushing down from the formidable Rocky Mountains that blocked the way west. From out of the Southwest blew hot winds off the desert, which the white men explored too, wanting to go everywhere, to see everything: the ochre sands, the badlands, the mesas, and the canyons.

The antelope were as plentiful as the buffalo and inhabited the high plains and Rocky Mountain foothills.

They encountered an infinite variety of landscapes that constantly changed with the light and the seasons. Any ecosystem they had ever seen, in Europe or on their travels, was here too, but on a much larger scale.

It took them over two and a half centuries to explore the North American continent. Everywhere they went, they marvelled at the grandeur and untamed beauty of the land. Seeing the Europeans exclaim over these natural wonders, the Indians thought that they must have come from a very poor, desolate country.

The white men believed, and often stated in their published writings, that everything in this world they had discovered was there for the taking with no effort or toil. The early explorers claimed that the land gave generously, unlike in Europe, where for too long the fruits of the soil had been paid for in sweat and blood. In the New World, one could simply gather whatever one wanted. And everything was pristine, practically untouched. The Indians were few in number and, before they had access to European technologies such as firearms, altered nature very little and never permanently.

At first, these local inhabitants were friendly and unthreatening, offering Cartier's men, the first to make their way slightly inland, "as good a welcome as ever a father gives his child, with a marvellous joy."

However, it wasn't long before they understood that the newcomers saw this land of abundance as a resource to be rashly and ruthlessly plundered.

Herds of caribou hundreds of thousands strong roamed the tundra and taiga.

A Continent of Three Hundred Nations

Nature determined their way
of life, delimited their territory,
and shaped their culture.

*The curved leather hair ornament
worn by this young Apache indicates
that she is still single.*

At the time of contact, the American continent had a larger population than Europe. Over seventy-five million – some authors say as many as a hundred million – Aboriginal people occupied this immense land stretching from the Atlantic to the Pacific and from the Beaufort Sea to Tierra del Fuego. The vast majority lived south of the Rio Grande. In North America, they didn't build great empires like those of the Aztecs, the Mayas, and the Incas. However, there were people everywhere, from the tropical forests to the barren tundra, in the swamps and sierras, in valleys covered with great leafy trees, on windswept prairies, on high plains and the flanks of the steepest mountains, on lake shores and river banks, on every seacoast, and even in the middle of hot, arid deserts and in the frozen wastelands of the North.

All these different environments, with their diverse resources, shaped the people who inhabited them. Thus, although the North American Indians were much more ethnically homogeneous than the Europeans, a great many nations developed, each with a highly distinctive character, language, art, style of clothing and social structure.

The Creek and the Natchez of the Mississippi Valley built fortified villages, while the Hidatsa of the Missouri Valley spent the summer in huts made of rushes and straw matting. In the winter, the Bannock of the Southwest lived in semi-subterranean earth lodges. The Kwakiutl of the Pacific Northwest made large, solidly built, and partitioned cedar houses. The Apache and the Comanche used teepees made of buffalo or antelope skins, while the Montagnais favoured birchbark tents. The Inuit slept in temporary igloos in the winter. In Arizona, the Pueblo Indians built small houses out of adobe bricks. The Iroquois of northern New York gathered in longhouses in phratries consisting of dozens of individuals.

Among these peoples there were rich nations and poor. There were religious nations, warring nations, and industrious nations. Some nations travelled and traded widely, while others were shy and reclusive. Some had a complex social structure, highly sophisticated technology, arts and architecture, and slaves and great wealth. Others lived a wandering, hand-to-mouth existence under constant threat. The opulent Haida of the Pacific Northwest, who carved magnificent totem poles and created a very elaborate oral literature, had little in common with the Naskapi, who hunted caribou on the taiga, except that both had adapted perfectly to their respective environments.

*Ihkas-Kinne, chief of
the Siksika,
one of the three tribes
that formed
the Blackfoot nation.*

The way of life of all these peoples was dominated and determined by nature. It was nature that established the frontiers and that forged the soul and culture of each nation, tribe, and individual. Changing one's environment necessarily meant changing one's culture. Almost all of the tribes – through marriage, slavery, or adoption – took in individuals from other, sometimes very different, cultures. As a result, many men and women understood two or three languages.

With an overall population of only about five million, the Indians of North America spoke close to a thousand languages, averaging fewer than five thousand speakers each. Some 220 of these languages have been identified and grouped into twelve major language families. Except for a few isolated languages, these languages never defined a political unit. For instance, the Huron southeast of Georgian Bay were at war with the Five Nations Iroquois, to whom they were closely related by language and culture. On the other hand, they had friendly relations with the Nipissing, who spoke a very different language, one belonging to the Algonquian family.

When a voyageur from the St. Lawrence Valley travelled up the Great Lakes, Lake Winnipeg, and the North Saskatchewan River toward the Rocky Mountains, all along his route he was sure to meet Indians who spoke a dialect closely resembling that used by the Algonquins who had made his canoe in Trois Rivières or Montreal.

After the continental divide, as the voyageur descended toward Great Slave Lake, the Mackenzie River, and the Beaufort Sea, he would enter the territory of the Athapascan nations. These two cultural and language groups, the Algonquian and the Athapascan, covered the entire area east of the Rockies, north of the Great Plains in the centre of the continent, and south of the land of the Inuit, who had a very homogeneous language and culture from Alaska to Greenland.

Southeast of the Great Lakes were the fierce nations of the Iroquois Confederacy, an invincible island in the vast Algonquian world. West of Iroquois territory lay the Great Plains, home to the numerous and very powerful Sioux.

In the early seventeenth century, some 200,000 Indians of Algonquian, Iroquoian, or Siouan origin lived around the Great Lakes and on the eastern edge of the Prairies, an area that the French called the Pays d'en Haut – the high country or back country.

The Prairies have always exerted an irresistible appeal. Small groups would break off from the Algonquian, Iroquoian, or Athapascan communities and try to move into these open spaces, waging war on or making peace with the local inhabitants. This resulted in an extraordinarily complex and dynamic cultural and linguistic mosaic, an immense melting pot in which a multitude of tribes and clans mixed and merged, sometimes scattering throughout the territory.

The high plains in southwestern North America – present-day Arizona, Colorado, and New Mexico – also attracted the peoples of the North and East. The Pueblo Indians, such as the Hopi and Zuni, who were successful farmers and remarkable craftsmen, had developed an almost urban way of life that was admirable in many respects. Aggressive tribes of nomadic hunters and raiders fought over the surrounding lands. One of these was the Apache, an Athapascan people who had come from the North over a thousand years earlier, not long before the arrival of their Navajo brothers, who became sedentary farmers and herdsmen as well as skilful, prosperous craftspersons.

The introduction of firearms and horses following European contact would greatly accelerate the migration and intermingling of peoples and races, profoundly altering the demographic structure of the continent within two generations.

The largest populations, the most advanced and highly organized societies, and the greatest number of language groups were found on the West Coast. The rich resources of the land and sea and the temperate climate had enabled these nations to become sedentary and to develop a much more elaborate technology, art, architecture, and culture than was possible for nomadic hunters and gatherers or even for the farming peoples who lived in the interior of the continent. However, as soon as these inland nations were better armed, they too would try to control nature in an effort to improve their lives. Great changes were coming that were not governed this time by the natural environment.

CONTINENTAL TRADE

Since resources were not
equally distributed,
a vast trading network
developed among
the Aboriginal nations.

*Traded from tribe to tribe,
rare and useful materials often
travelled considerable distances.*

For reasons of war, diplomacy, or trade, the Aboriginal people travelled widely throughout the continent, by land and by water. Across the endless plains, the barren tundra, the steep mountains, or the semi-desert of the Southwest, they found their way by means of natural landmarks or markers of various sorts erected for that purpose.

In the vast lands of the North and the East, which were inhabited mainly by nomadic or semi-nomadic tribes, trade was limited to the more-or-less fortuitous exchange of small items, raw materials, food, and some clothing and ornamentation.

Those who are constantly on the move cannot burden themselves with too many possessions. They can carry only essential food, clothing, weapons, tools, and the materials needed for making some kind of shelter. The

technology of the North American Indians was characterized by its light weight and adaptability. They made a point of creating things that were easily transported and readily made or repaired with materials that were not difficult to find or carry with them: canoes and tents made of bark or hides and wooden harpoons and arrows with flint or bone tips.

However, since resources were not equally distributed, all nations had to maintain trading relations with their neighbours. Certain goods and

*Iron weapons initially
traded on the Atlantic Coast
followed the trade routes
across the continent.*

foodstuffs as well as useful but rare materials such as meteoritic iron, copper, obsidian, and quartz were frequently traded, sometimes travelling considerable distances before reaching their final owners.

Highly prized for its sharpness, obsidian was used to make knives, arrowheads, and harpoons. It came mainly from igneous outcroppings in the Rocky Mountains and was traded from tribe to tribe across the Great Plains as far as the Great Lakes and down through the Mississippi Valley. Farther east, it was extremely rare and thus very expensive.

Around AD 1000, Vikings who had settled in Greenland obtained quartz in Newfoundland that had originally come from Ramah at the northern tip of Labrador. This quartz later made its way down the East Coast as far as Cape Cod and up the St. Lawrence River to Lake Ontario, where galena from the land of the Illinois, seashells from the Atlantic, and copper native to the Great Lakes could already be found at the time of Jesus Christ.

Copper from this area had been traded since time immemorial in all directions: with the Cree, the Sioux, and the Assiniboin to the south, down through the Mississippi Valley, and along the eastern seaboard from the Bay of Fundy to the head of Chesapeake Bay. The Indians of the Saguenay whom Jacques Cartier met on his first voyage had knives made of copper that had likely come from the Great Lakes. A thousand years before Christ, the Inuit of the Coppermine River were already trading it for amber from northern Ellesmere Island.

*Raw copper used for making this spearhead
and socket harpoon was taken
from a deposit north of Lake Superior.*

Iron, the most useful of all raw materials, was always extremely rare. Nevertheless, it was traded around Bering Strait long before the arrival of the white man, and has been found in abandoned Viking settlements in southwestern Greenland. Meteoritic iron from outcroppings of ferruginous rock in northwestern Greenland was also traded throughout eastern North America as far as the Canadian Prairies.

Aboriginal traders had established agreements and rules of diplomacy among themselves. In the Prairies and along the Mississippi Valley, a peace pipe often served as a guarantor of safe passage, even in enemy territory. The bearer had only to show the peace pipe to be permitted to travel freely. A sacred and venerated object, the pipe was the very embodiment of peace. The Illinois presented one to Father Marquette to protect him among all the nations through which he had to pass on his journey.

Wampum, another sacred object of Indian diplomacy, was used in the same way by the Algonquin of the Atlantic Coast and by the Iroquois.

Venetian trade beads used for making necklaces or decorating clothing followed the traditional trade routes.

Obsidian used by the Mandan of Missouri originated in the vicinity of Yellowstone, Wyoming.

Wampum consisted of an assemblage of shells of great symbolic and metaphorical value. It was also the Indians' main currency and circulated in all the trading networks of the American Northeast.

On the West Coast, there was a very active trade in fish oil from a type of smelt, the eulachon. Also called a candlefish, the eulachon is so oily that, when dried, it may be used as a candle. The traders had developed a network of heavily used trails throughout the Rockies.

Control and ownership of the trade routes, river crossings, portages, passes, and bridges were of prime importance. Business-minded tribes thus established actual toll stations at strategic points along the busiest routes in order to tax traders and exercise rigorous control over the circulation of goods.

The Tlingit, for instance, controlled trade between the Athapascans and the peoples of Alaska. Trade was well organized all along the very populous and highly cosmopolitan West Coast, from Alaska to southern California. Some nations had developed veritable empires. The Pomo of the California coast traded sea salt, among other goods. The Nootka on western Vancouver Island controlled trade in the finest seashells, used throughout the region as currency. The Chinook on the lower Columbia River served as very active middlemen between the coast and the interior.

Just before the arrival of the white man in the late sixteenth century, the Huron south of Georgian Bay exercised almost absolute control over the Great Lakes trade routes.

Clever farmers and shrewd traders, the Huron had developed their territory into the breadbasket of the northeastern tribes, whom they supplied with corn, beans, squash, sunflower seeds, tobacco, and hemp yarn for making fishing nets; in exchange they received furs, meat, and slaves. The nomadic Algonquin, with whom they had developed a strong trading relationship, supplied them with canoes and other goods such as shells, copper, and catlinite for making clay pipes, which they had received in barter during their travels.

Living at the hub of the major trading networks, the Huron played a key political role throughout northeastern North America. Although their territory was much smaller, they had a larger population (30,000) than their great rival, the Five Nations Iroquois Confederacy (20,000), which they threatened by establishing alliances with numerous other nations.

With the arrival of the Europeans, this social and political order would be forever altered.

New power relationships soon developed among the Aboriginal peoples, radically changing their lives.

This catlinite pipe bowl found in Ontario comes from Minnesota, a region rich in red clay.

THE WHITE TIDE

As the Europeans
advanced across
the continent,
their goods and diseases
preceded them.

*The Indians soon disdained
the trinkets offered by the Europeans
and asked for textiles,
guns, and gunpowder instead.*

The Indians initially greeted the white men with fear and respect, believing them to be manitous, sorcerers, or all-powerful spirits. The Plains Sioux whom the Jesuit priest Louis Hennepin encountered in the 1680s approached him with great caution, offering him food at the end of a long stick. Even earlier than that, the Algonquin and the Iroquois had been amazed and astounded by the Europeans, with their technology and power to make things.

The almost divine status that the Indians accorded the Europeans rarely lasted more than one or two seasons, by which time they realized that these greedy, self-serving newcomers wanted only to get their hands on beaver pelts and give as little as possible in return. Among the Aboriginal peoples, all alliances were based on the generosity of the partners. Most of the

Europeans, however, had only one, ill-concealed goal: to exploit the resources of this new land they had discovered. Once the Europeans' mean-spiritedness became evident, their Indian partners could easily, and justifiably, break off the relationship. The white men thus had to at least partially accept the rules of a commerce based on giving and sharing, while the Indians had to adapt to the logic of the market, learning to play on the competition between the European powers.

The handle of this seventeenth-century trade bayonet was made to be inserted into a musket barrel.

As soon as they approached the coast of the New World, the Europeans set off a powerful shock wave that swept across the continent, sometimes dozens of years ahead of them. Hundreds or even thousands of kilometres before their advance, they were preceded by rumours and legends, and by various objects that they had discarded or bartered with the coastal Indians and that had then been traded from tribe to tribe.

When they were seeking the mouth of the Mississippi in the spring of 1673, Louis Jolliet and Father Jacques Marquette encountered Indians who had never met a white man but nevertheless had European-made hatchets and clothing, which they had obtained in trade from tribes living farther east, who in turn had likely received them from the English on the Atlantic Coast. A few years later, at Green Bay on the western shore of Lake Michigan, Nicolas Perrot met Indians who had travelled in the West and seen horses and men who looked like the French, no doubt Spaniards from New Mexico. By the middle of the seventeenth century, all the Aboriginal peoples of North America were aware of the existence of white men – and were expecting them, with wonder and trepidation.

At first, the Indians were attracted to anything that was bright, shiny, or tinkly: mirrors, metal rings, bells, ivory or wooden combs, colourful fabric. On their first expeditions inland, the European traders took along small tin mirrors and glass and porcelain beads. However, such baubles and trinkets soon lost their appeal; by the mid-seventeenth century, they represented only 3 per cent of the value of barter goods used in the fur trade.

French trade axes. The one in the centre is marked with the name Chouinard, likely the blacksmith who made it.

Each year, the European traders had to update their stocks as styles changed. For a while the Indians greatly valued vermilion, a red powder used as a dye; then Brazil tobacco, which was darker and more aromatic than the tobacco grown by the Petun; then scalping knives, which were traded for scalps collected by certain white men.

Some right-minded Europeans were scandalized. Baron de La Hontan wrote that they were swindling the Indians by selling them junk for six or seven times the price charged in Montreal. Actually, the Indians knew what they wanted and were not easily cheated.

The Indians soon became interested in metal utensils and tools for cutting or piercing: knives of various sizes, scissors, arrowheads, blades, axes, and tomahawks. Iron was new to many of them, and they were especially impressed with its strength and ability to hold an edge. And, needless to say, they wanted firearms.

It seems to have been the women who were behind the trade in utilitarian items. They wanted pots and pans, copper kettles, awls for leatherwork, and textiles: things that would make cooking and sewing easier and help in their domestic chores.

The most coveted item long remained the copper kettle, which in the mid-seventeenth century accounted for almost 5 per cent of the total value of trade goods. Within a few years, it radically transformed the Indians' traditional cooking methods, and eventually their diet. Previously, their only means of heating water for cooking had been to place red-hot rocks in birchbark containers or terracotta vessels.

In addition to providing Indian families with these necessities, the Europeans offered other trade goods as well. The most powerful was alcohol, which the traders had in endless supply and which, unlike trinkets or kettles, would never lose its appeal. Quite the contrary.

A Mohawk chief proudly displaying the cloth garments and trade rifle that he had received in trade from the Dutch or the English.

By the end of the seventeenth century, approximately 8,400 litres of alcohol (rum, brandy, and occasionally wine) were being sent to the fur country each year. It was supposedly for the garrisons at the trading posts since trading alcohol with the Indians was strictly forbidden. However, although it never amounted to more than 5 per cent of the total value of goods shipped to the Indians, alcohol did play a major role in the fur trade. It was not used directly for barter but was very helpful for establishing friendly relations with the Indians, ensuring their loyalty, instilling an ever-greater dependence on the white man, and sometimes for outright cheating them.

Small traders, who had little or no credit to acquire trade goods, had only alcohol with which to obtain furs from the Indians. If they were unable to procure it in New France, they could easily get rum from the British or Dutch colonies. After the onslaught of European infectious diseases, it was alcohol that took the greatest toll on Indian society.

The visceral fear felt by the Sioux on seeing Father Hennepin and the interpreters accompanying him turned out to be well founded. The white men unwittingly carried lethal viruses. Like an incredibly powerful tidal wave sweeping across the continent, an invisible army of microbes accompanied the Europeans as they moved inland, decimating the native populations, claiming more victims than all the famines and intertribal wars put together.

At the time of European contact, the American continent had boasted a population of seventy-five to a hundred million inhabitants, more than all the countries of Europe combined. Two hundred years later, by the end of the seventeenth century, the Aboriginal population of North and South America had been reduced to twelve million, a seven or eightfold decline since the white man's arrival.

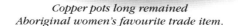

Copper pots long remained Aboriginal women's favourite trade item.

Chapter 2

CHILDREN OF THE COUNTRY

The very situation of the embryonic colony, its dependence on furs, its small population, and the disintegration of political and military power obliged the French to adapt to the type of relations that the Indians entertained among themselves. This model gave birth to a new being, the coureur des bois. The quest for furs, learning the language, and an identification with the Indian lifestyle were all essential traits of this being who grew up in the heart of the Canadian forest. In this generation of coureurs des bois there also appeared other characteristics that would become more pronounced in the ensuing years: an avoidance of social and religious constraints, an attraction to Indian women, and a fascination with independence and adventure.

The difficult voyage over prepared the new arrivals for the particularly harsh environment awaiting them.

To the east, the Laurentian and Appalachian Mountains blocked movement inland.

THE INTERPRETERS

Young men were sent to
live with the Indians
in order to learn
their languages and customs
and to establish useful ties.

*Many interpreters became so
assimilated into the Indian way of
life that they renounced
their country, king, and religion.*

To serve as an interpreter and intermediary between the Indians and the Europeans, one had to be very young, brave, ambitious, and perhaps unaware of what one was getting into. The task required living alone with the Indians in order to learn their languages and customs. Young adventurers who took on this role were the first Europeans to enter the heart of the American continent, learn its true nature, and acquire a respect for the Indians, sometimes to the point of becoming totally and whole-heartedly assimilated into their world, never to return.

Having set sail for the New World only a few months earlier, these young men were perhaps disposed to embark on this more radical adventure, one that would totally change their lives. They were about to leave behind the culture and civilization of their birth to live among the "Savages," knowing that they would lose all contact with their own people for months, possibly years.

Fortunately, the Indians considered hospitality a sacred duty. When a young Frenchman arrived among them, everyone in the tribe treated him as a brother or son. They also did their best to teach him the rudiments and refinements of their language and culture.

Fluency could not be acquired without lengthy immersion among the Indians, whose languages are especially difficult to learn since they use practically no labials; almost all the sounds are made inside the mouth, so the speaker's lips barely move. One had to be able to hear the unfamiliar sounds and intonations without visual cues – and, when speaking, to use mouth muscles not often required by European languages. One had to persevere and be willing to be laughed at. It took patience to learn these new languages.

But the aspiring interpreter had all the time he needed, especially in winter, when the tribe remained inside for days on end and there was nothing to do but sleep, dream, make love – and learn the language.

Mastering the Indians' languages meant learning about all the different aspects of their lives, understanding how they thought, sharing their fears and dreams. The interpreter ended up resembling those with whom he lived, assimilating their idea of happiness and comfort, work and trade, love and war.

There were, however, some daunting obstacles. Indians and Europeans who learned to live together had to overcome their mutual repugnance. The Indians found the white men's beards and hairy bodies disgusting, and the paunches some of them had grotesque. They considered the exaggerated gestures they made while talking ridiculous, and their tendency to keep certain things for themselves and never spontaneously share what they had immoral. The Europeans, for their part, were appalled at the total freedom the Indians allowed their children and at the cruelty with which they treated their enemies. They were put off by the extreme disorder and claustrophobic closeness in which the Indians lived and by their eating habits.

The staple food of the tribes of the St. Lawrence Valley and the Great Lakes region was *sagamité*, an unappetizing gruel into which the Indians threw hunks of red meat, small animals, birds, fish, and frogs, usually tossing them in whole without bothering to skin, pluck, or gut them. The men, women, children, and dogs all slept huddled together, sometimes lying around for days in deadening idleness. The shelter was often filled with thick, eye-stinging smoke. Other discomforts were the cold, heat, and swarms of mosquitoes. Fatigue and hunger were frequent.

*This gunlock, recovered from
the Delaware River, is one of the
few Swiss trade goods
discovered in North America.*

For the sake of politeness and convenience, the interpreter adopted the Indians' hairstyle and way of dressing. In the summer, he would go around half naked, wearing only a leather breechcloth and leggings. He either had moccasins on his feet or went barefoot. In the winter, he would wrap himself in his beaver coat, which he wore day and night.

By learning their languages, the interpreters were able to establish strong trading relationships with the Aboriginal peoples.

He was patient with the children, courteous to the women, always respectful to the elders, deferential but not servile to the young warriors, and ruthless to the enemy. He learned to contain his feelings, since the Indians thought the white men made a ridiculous display of their emotions. He would avoid making expansive gestures while speaking, since only women did that. And he would gradually find his own voice in the war songs and his place in the dances of departure, scalping, sacrifice, and marriage. Eventually, he would develop a taste for *sagamité*, the wandering life, and the close quarters.

Many of the interpreters discovered a welcome freedom and brotherhood among the Indians and adapted very quickly to this new life. The missionaries were shocked at their behaviour. They felt that, far from helping to convert the Indians, these young men were undermining the missionaries' efforts by acting like savages and setting a bad example.

In 1635, a few months before the death of Samuel de Champlain, all the interpreters were recalled, supposedly to save them from the influence of the Indians.

However, nothing and no one could make these young adventurers forget the intoxicating freedom of Indian life. Most of them returned to the woods. But their presence brought a new and unsettling spirit to the young colony. The knowledge they had acquired gave them a power that could not be reined in. Some people viewed them as renegades and others as inspiring role models, whom many of the bravest and best young men would soon follow.

The man negotiating with an Algonquin trader is wearing colourful clothing, trying perhaps, like many interpreters, to impress the Indians with his appearance. The merchant for whom he is working is dressed more soberly, although the silver buttons on his doublet and his high, spurred boots are indications of his rank.

ÉTIENNE BRÛLÉ'S STORY

The young man Champlain had sent to live among the Huron came to regard them as his true brothers.

Brûlé's descriptions helped the French to understand the immensity of the continent they were just beginning to penetrate.

Young Étienne Brûlé was part of that first generation of Europeans who went off alone to live with the Indians. Developing a profound love and respect for them, he became totally assimilated into their way of life.

It was Samuel de Champlain, founder of New France, who in 1609 had sent the nineteen-year-old Frenchman from Champigny sur Marne to live with the Huron. He was to explore their country and learn their language and customs in order to establish trading relationships with them and better organize the fur trade.

The people of the colony were stupefied to see Brûlé return the following spring accompanied by Indian warriors and not only dressed like them, but with his hair like theirs and his face painted too. After greeting Champlain, he left again with his fellow Indians. Champlain was profoundly shocked and grieved to see that the young man he had called his son, and who had suffered through the first horrific winter in Quebec with him, had renounced Christ and king and chosen to live with the "Savages." He had mastered their language, learned their customs, songs, and dances, and slept with their women; he had gone completely "native."

Brûlé nevertheless remained a valuable contact. He served as an intermediary between the French traders and the Huron, with whom he lived for eighteen years, considering himself one of them. And they, in turn, loved him like a brother, a son, and a father.

The Huron were shrewd traders and soon became allies of the French. They had taken control of the fur trade route, which in ascending the Ottawa River to the Great Lakes crossed their territory. Seeing how they were benefiting from their friendship with the French, the other Indian peoples became jealous. The Iroquois nations, particularly the Seneca who lived just south of Huron territory, were threatening to upset things and block the fur trade route.

In 1615 Champlain undertook a voyage of peace through the Pays d'en Haut. He travelled up the Ottawa River and the Mattawa, crossed Lake Nipissing, and then went down

Pipe bowl made by the Ojibwa, a tribe that lives around the Great Lakes near Huron territory.

the French River to Lake Huron. After being wounded in a skirmish with the Iroquois, he spent the winter in Huron territory with his "son" Brûlé.

Brûlé already had a fairly good knowledge of the land and the peoples of the Great Lakes basin from direct experience and from listening to others. He had travelled around Lakes Ontario, Erie, and Huron. From his descriptions, Champlain, a good cartographer, made remarkably accurate maps of the region. Brûlé's descriptions thus helped the French understand the immensity of the continent they were just beginning to penetrate. He helped them learn about a territory that, since Jacques Cartier, had for all intents and purposes been limited to the area around Montreal.

When the Kirke brothers captured Quebec and raised the British flag over Cap Diamant in 1629, Brûlé had no compunction about selling his furs to the British. He had lost his emotional ties to France; his home was now with the Huron.

Like a few other adventurers, such as Jean Riche and Nicolas Marsolet, who were living with the Montagnais and the Algonquin at that time, Brûlé no longer had any interest in European politics and trade. Champlain thought that he had betrayed his king in working for the Kirke brothers. But by 1629 Étienne Brûlé had no king. He was no longer a Frenchman; he had become a Huron warrior and trader. And yet it was the Huron who would execute him a few years later, in 1633.

Brûlé had managed to avoid torture and death when captured by a group of Seneca, the Huron's implacable enemies. How could they have spared him if he were a true Huron?

He told his Huron brothers that a miracle had enabled him to escape from the Seneca. They had started to torture him; young warriors had torn out his nails with their teeth. But just as they were about to kill him, a violent storm had broken out. Brûlé told his captors that the gods had created the storm to show their opposition to his execution. The Seneca immediately freed him and gave a great feast in his honour. He had become their brother, a Seneca too. And, unfortunately, the Huron were sure to find out.

The Huron knew that the Seneca were trying to make friends with the French so that they could trade with them. Like all the Iroquois and Algonquin, they wanted the tools and weapons that had brought prosperity and protection to the Huron. The Huron believed – probably not without reason – that Brûlé had

served as an intermediary between the Seneca and the French and that he had invented the story of the miracle. Actually, the Seneca might well have freed him against his will and without the providential storm. In sparing his life, they had condemned him to almost certain death.

Brûlé, who was very familiar with Indian customs, no doubt knew that he was in an untenable position and, in fact, had confided his fears to the Récollet priest Gabriel Sagard soon

after he was freed. He could easily have sought refuge in Quebec but chose to go home and face Huron justice. Not believing his story, his Huron brothers executed and ate him.

Étienne Brûlé was the prototype of the coureur des bois who became totally assimilated into Indian society – a key figure in the history of the New World.

A Huron couple.
The Huron were the main trading
partners of the French.

AN ABUNDANCE OF FUR-BEARING ANIMALS

Life in the New World initially revolved around the fur trade.

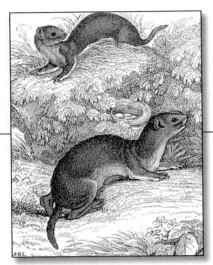

Some European species, such as the ermine, were much more plentiful in America and had richer fur.

In the early seventeenth century, European furriers obtained their raw materials from Scandinavia and Russia. The Germans and Poles bought their pelts in Novgorod, while the English went to Murmansk. Dutch ships sailed around the Scandinavian Peninsula to Arkhangel'sk, on the White Sea, to take delivery of fine Arctic furs, which they distributed at a great profit throughout Europe. French furriers were dependent on these middlemen and had little access to quality pelts.

The French thus turned to the New World for their supplies, and it was not long before France's fur industry surpassed all the rest. Russian and Scandinavian furs, which were more expensive and often of lesser quality, no longer interested European artisans, who were won over by the beauty and great diversity of North American furs.

At first the most sought-after furs were marten, ermine, lynx, mink, and otter – species that were also native to Europe, though never in Europe had they been available in such abundance and quality. The animals' coats grew lush and thick in the cold, damp climate of Acadia and the St. Lawrence Valley, and even more so in the frigid North.

Large animals, such as moose, deer, and elk, which were hunted in southern Ontario and Quebec, and caribou, whose winter migration used to take them as far south as the St. Lawrence Valley, provided very resistant hides that were appreciated by European leather-dressers. Sealskin was used for making various straps and harnesses for use in the colony and for making coats and blankets in Europe.

However, it was beaver pelts, which were used to produce high-quality felt for making hats, that had the greatest impact on the fur industry, revolutionizing European fashion. As early as the 1620s, beaver accounted for 80 per cent of shipments. Trade in beaver pelts, more than any other commodity, created an intensive circulation of goods throughout the New World. It was the quest for beaver that pushed the white men farther and farther inland and that gave the Indians access to goods manufactured using European technology – admittedly a mixed blessing.

The most valuable pelts, considering their small size, remained marten and otter. But beaver pelts, which were five or six times as large, were soon worth as much, if not more. Although a lambskin was twice the size of a beaver pelt, it fetched only a fiftieth of the price on the French fur market.

During the first two decades of the seventeenth century, the French in Acadia and the St. Lawrence Valley shipped as many as 20,000 beaver pelts a year to Europe. In 1624 the Dutch on the East Coast shipped over 7,000 beaver pelts to Amsterdam as well as 850 pelts from otter and other small animals. And the fur trade was just getting started.

A flask for holding castoreum, an oily substance secreted by the beaver's sebaceous glands that was used for baiting traps.

The hunting territory expanded as the traders advanced inland, gaining access to new territories and tribes. By the mid-1690s, the Ottawa, Illinois, and Miami were acting as middlemen, trading with nations living on the edge of the great Prairies in the interior of the continent. The European market was soon flooded, and the price of beaver plummeted. Because the hat-making industry, practically the only outlet for beaver, was strongly concentrated (in Paris and Lyon), it was not really able to absorb surpluses.

The best beaver was called "coat beaver" since it had already been worn and softened by the Indians. In 1660 its going price in Canada was 210 sous per pound; by 1710 it was selling for only 30 sous per pound. Untreated beaver pelts, known as "dry beaver" or "parchment beaver," which had sold for 90 sous per pound in 1660, sometimes fell to less than a third of that price. Nevertheless, the volume of exports continued to rise, sometimes even exceeding 200,000 pounds a year.

As the beaver trade declined in value, the trade in peltries (pelts used for fur) and hides grew stronger, in some years accounting for half to three quarters of the total value of shipments. By the beginning of the eighteenth century, Montreal merchants were paying three livres for a prime marten pelt, two livres and ten sous for otter, and as much as sixteen livres for good-quality lynx, the same price as for a moose hide.

Since furs and leathers were sent to numerous small manufacturers throughout Europe, they were not as vulnerable to market fluctuations as beaver. The French, Italian, and Spanish leather-dressing industries absorbed all the moose, deer, and elk hides shipped from Canada or Louisiana. Any surpluses were usually re-exported through the French ports of La Rochelle, Rouen, or Bordeaux to the former distribution centres of Amsterdam and Moscow. Many important Dutch traders abandoned the Russian market and bought shares in French fur trading businesses, which were now the most prosperous.

Around 1715, buffalo hides began arriving from the West, soon followed by the hides of pronghorn antelope, which were used to make fine leather. The best fur of all also made its appearance, that of the Pacific sea otter, which was already the subject of intense and very lucrative trade with China.

It was not long before certain species were threatened by overhunting. Moose and elk became scarce. Walruses, great auks, and tundra swans were fast disappearing from the Gulf of St. Lawrence. And, with each passing year, the flocks of passenger pigeons grew sparser. To find beaver, one had to go higher and higher up the rivers – and thus deeper into the continent.

Without the beaver and other fur-bearing animals coveted by the European market, colonization of the New World would have been much less likely and much more difficult. Cartier's and Roberval's attempts to establish settlements in the St. Lawrence Valley failed because they did not really have any reason for being there. Quebec, on the other hand, thrived because Samuel de Champlain had founded it for a very specific purpose: to organize and protect the trade in furs on the new continent. Initially, life in New France centred solely on the fur trade.

Although this trade did not require a complex and expensive infrastructure, it did require the active participation of the Indians, who knew where and how to catch the beaver and often brought the pelts to where the white men had set up their trading posts. It was thanks to this mutually advantageous exchange that the French gradually came to know the New World and to live with its peoples.

Even before the mid-seventeenth century, certain species were threatened by overhunting.

A HIGHLY COVETED COMMODITY

By the early
seventeenth century, furs from
the St. Lawrence Valley
had taken over
the European markets.

*The quality and abundance
of furs revolutionized fashion and
resulted in colossal fortunes.*

*Never before had the European fur industry had access to such an
exciting and wide choice of furs and such lush, thick pelts.*

There was no lack of excuses for going off to the woods – exploration, defence of allied tribes, scientific missions, conversion of the Indians – but the vast majority of Frenchmen who went upriver in the spring, to the back country they called the Pays d'en Haut, were there for one reason: to obtain furs. White, blond, red, black, or silver; short haired or long; spotted, striped, or uniformly coloured; glossy or dull – a seemingly endless supply of furs was shipped from the New World each year. European furriers had never had such a wide choice of materials.

In the colony, bearskins made excellent rugs for use on sleds, while the tough hides of large marine mammals were ideal for making harnesses, straps, and soles for boots and shoes. The finest furs and leathers were exported to Europe.

Members of the Mustelidae family have always been prized for their fur. These long-bodied, short-legged carnivores are found from coast to coast in practically all environments, but especially in dense forests and wetlands. The colder the climate, the thicker their coats.

Some mustelids – such as the wolverine, which lives in the boreal forest, and its close cousin the badger, which like the weasel lives in open country, prairie, or cultivated fields – were of less interest to European furriers. Aboriginal peoples on the tundra used wolverine for the hoods or collars of their parkas since the long, stiff guard hairs prevented frost from sticking to the fur, which is a problem with wolf or lynx fur. The badger, whose fur is rather coarse, was used for covering armchairs or making bedside rugs. The fisher, which looks like a large black cat with long, coarse fur, was also not highly valued in Europe, where it was used to make coat collars or everyday cloaks.

The otter, marten, mink, ermine, and long-tailed weasel, considered the most noble members of the Mustelidae family, had the richest pelts. Their fur was in great demand for making collars and cuffs for the finest coats as well as stoles, cloaks, capes, and muffs. Occasionally, they were even used to make entire coats.

The fur of the European marten ranges from light buff to dark brown; since the dark colour was rarer, it was considered more valuable. However the thick coats of marten found in the

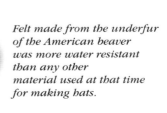

*Felt made from the underfur
of the American beaver
was more water resistant
than any other
material used at that time
for making hats.*

36

coniferous forests of North America were nearly always dark, almost black, even in summer. Its pelt thus quickly became the most sought after and the most expensive of all. In the mid-nineteenth century, the Hudson's Bay Company, which had a monopoly on the fur trade in the area of the "North Sea" and the Rocky Mountains, sold as many as 180,000 marten pelts a year, for $100 each.

The long, slender, and very ferocious ermine, which prefers the boreal forest and tundra, was hunted mainly in winter, when its coat turns pure white. Since the tip of its tail remains black, furriers could arrange it to very striking effect, using it to trim the robes of kings and high-ranking dignitaries.

The sea otter of the Pacific Coast, which is much larger than a river otter and has a softer, thicker, brown underfur, was already the subject of lucrative trade with China in the eighteenth century. It soon outsold all other furs, in terms of both unit price and overall value of shipments.

The red fox was hunted for its winter coat, and the lynx was also much appreciated in Europe for its thick, silver-grey fur. Its close cousin the bobcat, which could adapt to a variety of environments, had a soft, glossy coat that was even more highly valued.

Beaver was not of interest to furriers but became extremely important to hatters. They would scrape the skin side of the pelt to destroy the roots of the guard hairs so that they could be combed out of the fur. Then they would shave off the soft, thick underfur, whose very fine, short fibres would be cleaned, fluffed, and pressed together to make high-quality felt.

The thin underfur of French beavers was not very valuable. Beaver imported from Russia or Scandinavia was of better quality but still not highly prized. At the time that North American furs were introduced to the European market, beaver was only the eighth most important fur species, after sable, marten, lynx, ermine, otter, racoon, and squirrel.

However, beaver rapidly became the most popular species as soon as it was discovered that the American beaver had a very dark, glossy underfur, much thicker than that of its European cousin. Baron de La Hontan called this underfur the most beautiful beaver wool in the world. It produced a very fine felt that was exquisitely soft and easy to work with.

But the most wonderful find was "coat beaver," beaver robes that the Indians wore day and night during the cold season. They were made from half a dozen pelts scraped, rubbed with animal marrow, brains, or grease, and stitched together with moose sinew. The long guard hairs, which were worn turned toward the skin and whose roots had been loosened by the scraping, soon fell off, leaving only the underfur. With the constant effect of the wearer's sweat and grease, the underfur acquired a magnificent sheen and softness. It was far superior to "dry beaver," or "parchment beaver," the untreated pelt that was simply skinned from the animal and dried in the sun. European hatters were willing to pay two to three times as much for coat beaver as they were for dry beaver, which required lengthy processing and never produced as fine an underfur.

Felt made from American beaver was more water resistant than any other hat material at that time. In the seventeenth century, umbrellas were still practically unknown; people wore wide-brimmed hats to protect themselves from the sun and rain. The suppleness of beaver felt made it possible to mould the brims into extravagant shapes. Beaver hats soon became the rage throughout Europe, at almost all levels of society. The king's musketeers wore them, to spectacular effect, and even men of limited means began to sport them.

By the end of the eighteenth century, the Hudson's Bay Company was shipping enough beaver pelts to Europe each year to make over half a million hats. To the Europeans, the beaver was not just a highly coveted commodity; it had developed into a mythical creature and the symbol of the New World.

THE BEAVER

Without the plentiful beaver
and the fortunes
to be made from it,
the French
probably would not
have settled the
St. Lawrence Valley so soon.

*Fascinated by their building skills,
the Europeans believed that beavers
had a social organization
based on the common good.*

The beaver belongs to the order Rodentia. It is one of the world's largest and heaviest rodents, second only to the capybara of South America. The earliest inhabitants of North America would have known its ancestor, which was about the size of a black bear and disappeared almost ten thousand years ago. Nowadays, an adult beaver typically weighs twenty kilograms and rarely exceeds forty-five kilograms.

The beaver has a squat, thickset body, with short legs and almost no neck. Each foot has five toes ending in sharp, curved claws; its delicate forepaws are excellent prehensile tools, while its large, webbed hind feet serve as powerful flippers. Its tail, almost hairless except at the base, has many uses, notably as a rudder when swimming and as a prop to balance the beaver when it is sitting or standing upright. The beaver is very industrious, especially at night. It is a sociable animal and lives in small, hierarchical colonies, whose base unit is the family. Within this unit, each individual has specific duties and responsibilities.

It is the females who decide where the family will live, usually in a lake, stream, or slow-moving river in a dense stand of trees, preferably aspen, willow, or alder. Often they will choose a narrowing in the river, which can be dammed to create a pond that will provide the beavers with a secure environment and safe access to food supplies.

Once they have selected their spot, the entire colony sets to work collecting materials to make the dam. They start by jamming long sticks into the bottom of the river, facing the current. Under these sticks they stuff twigs, rocks, clumps of grass, roots, and mud, which the force of the water then compacts against the interlaced sticks. Beaver dams have been seen that are 50, 75, or even 100 metres long, over 2 metres high, and 3 metres thick at the base. Behind the dam, the pond needs to be 2 to 3 metres deep so that the beavers can swim freely even in the middle of winter, when the ice can be up to a metre thick.

It takes the beavers a good month, in the fall, to build their lodge. In the middle of the pond or near the shore, they construct a foundation of branches, solidly anchored on the riverbed and extending a dozen centimetres above the surface of the water. On this platform they spread a layer of willow bark and small twigs. This base is then covered with a tangled pile of sticks and branches and topped with roots, flat stones, and mud to form a dense mass 3 metres high and sometimes up to 7 metres in

*A beaver pelt on a drying frame (*mishkuatui *in Montagnais) made of cord and black spruce.*

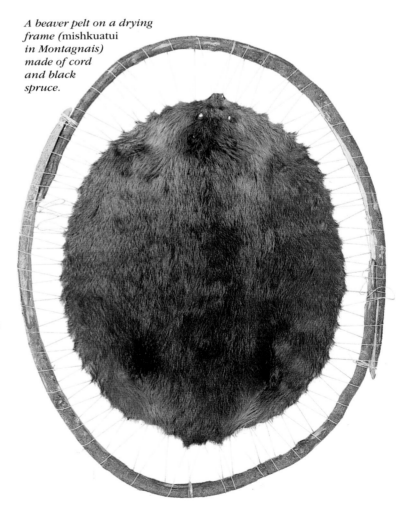

The industrious beaver was perfectly adapted to the New World and was found all across the continent, from the East Coast to the central plains and the western mountains.

diameter. Finally, tunnelling up from below, the beavers hollow out this mass to create a chamber about 2 metres in diameter and 60 centimetres high. Usually there will be two entrances, about a metre under water. The lodge is waterproof and practically impenetrable. Even a black bear using all its weight and force would have a hard time breaking through to the beavers inside.

Near the shore, the beavers build secondary lodges, constructing well protected burrows where they can hide if attacked. Once chased out, they can be formidable adversaries able to fight off all but the most powerful carnivores. Young beavers, however, are sometimes killed by otters, which are able to enter the lodge from under water.

Each beaver fells over two hundred trees a year. If there are no predators in the vicinity, a colony of beavers can clear the woods for up to 150 metres around the pond. With its constantly growing, chisel-like incisors, the beaver makes a notch in the tree trunk, followed by another lower down, then pries out the wood in between, working its way around the tree until the trunk snaps. It then removes the branches and gnaws the tree into transportable lengths. For construction materials, beavers choose fairly large, strong trees.

Beavers mate in the middle of winter, and the young are born in May following a hundred-day gestation period. There are two to five kits to a litter. They are weaned at the age of six weeks but usually live with their parents for two years. If conditions are favourable and there are no epidemics, the colony's population will increase by 20 per cent a year. It is believed that there were at least ten million beavers in the lakes and rivers of North America when the white man arrived and five or six times as many at various periods before that.

The beaver was very generous to the Europeans and the Indians, providing them with meat as well as fur. Its tail, boiled, roasted, smoked, or cooked in a soup, was considered a delicacy by all. The beaver was also a source of castoreum, an oily substance secreted by the sebaceous glands of both sexes. It had been a popular medicine since the time of the ancient Greeks and was used as a stimulant and as an antispasmodic for nervous disorders. The glands that produce castoreum are located in the anal region, along with other glands that secrete an oil the beaver spreads on its fur to waterproof it. All beavers take meticulous care of their coats. They moult in late fall and again in the spring. The colder and longer the winter, the richer and thicker their fur. The colour of the fur varies. Champlain, the first big fur trader, noted that the pelt paled as one went further south, becoming almost fawn or straw coloured by the time one reached the land of the Illinois.

Encouraged and armed by the Europeans, who created new material needs that could only be fulfilled in return for pelts, the Indians began hunting beavers all year round, going so far as to destroy their dams in order to drain the ponds and lakes so that they could capture every last member of the colony.

Eventually, everything came to depend on the beaver. All ties binding nations together and all conflicts opposing them centred on the fur trade. Even the missionaries understood that it was the only means of entering into contact with those they wanted to convert.

For the Indians, the beaver was a source of firearms, axes, knives, kettles, cloth, bread, and alcohol. Beaver pelts procured whatever they needed or wanted. As a result, however, they forgot much of their traditional knowledge and many skills. The fur trade completely disrupted their culture and way of life.

For the French, the beaver was an extraordinary stimulus. Without it, they probably wouldn't have settled the St. Lawrence Valley so soon. Nor ventured into the Pays d'en Haut. And it would have taken them much longer to reach the Prairies and the West Coast.

Indian Hunting and Trapping Techniques

For the Indians, hunting was an art
of observation, an act of
close communion with nature.

*The hunters noiselessly advanced
on their prey, sometimes crawling
and camouflaging themselves
under branches or skins.*

More than any technology they had developed,
it was the Indians' intimate knowledge of the
land and its flora and fauna that enabled
them to survive. Their hunting weapons were
simple and rudimentary, consisting of clubs,
bows and arrows, and spears or harpoons with tips made
of bone, wood, or possibly flint or copper, or even iron.
They also used dead-fall traps, and
snares fashioned from leather or
plant fibre.

However, Indian hunters had
developed a sense of observation
that amazed the Europeans. They
could lie patiently in wait for hours
or days, making their own blind or
decoy, if necessary or imitating
animal calls.

The Indians hunted any animal
they came across, day or night,
whatever the season, alone or in a
group. In fact, they were always
hunting. If they spotted a deer, elk,

*Hidden under animal skins,
the hunters approached from downwind
so as not to alert their prey.*

or moose swimming across a lake, all canoes would
converge on it. As soon as the animal neared land,
they would kill it. If seals, walruses, or great auks
were seen basking on the shore, the Indians
would run up and bludgeon them to death. If a
bear appeared at the edge of the woods, they
would drive it out. If the hunter was alone, even
if his chances of success were minimal, he
would lie in wait or try to approach the prey.
It was unthinkable not to take advantage of
even the smallest chance to make a kill.

Hunting was an art that required observation, patience, and self-control; it was an act
of communion with nature. The Indians were even
able to roust hibernating bears from their dens.
If, on a cold, dry, sunny day, they noticed a wisp of
vapour escaping from a bear's den, they would go
up and bang on the surrounding rocks and trees. As soon
as the bear appeared, dazed by the bright light and the
hunters' cries, it would be killed.

On the Prairies, when buffalo and antelope were
impeded by deep snow, the Sioux, the Blackfoot, and the
Assiniboin were able to approach on snowshoes and kill
them. The Montagnais on the Laurentian Plateau north of
the St. Lawrence River, the Iroquois south of the Great
Lakes, the Neutral, and the Illinois liked nothing better
than a good ice storm or a thaw followed by a freeze-up.
This would produce a crust on top of the snow that was
solid enough to bear the hunters' weight but not that of a
deer, moose, or elk. In trying to flee, the animal would
wear itself out and injure its legs. If the crust was not
strong enough to support the hunters' weight, they would
put on snowshoes and, without too much difficulty, follow
the trail that the exhausted animal had opened through
the snow.

Hunting was not always this easy. Most of the time, the
hunter had to track the game, flush it out, and drive or lure
it into a trap, which sometimes required the help of the
whole community. Men, women, and children would beat
through the forest and with loud shouts drive the moose
or deer toward a lake, where the
hunters were waiting in their
canoes, or toward a clearing, where
they could easily surround it and
move in for the kill.

In the Rocky Mountain foothills
at the western edge of the Prairies,
the Indians organized great drives
to stampede buffalo herds over
cliffs; the animals would either
plunge to their deaths or break
their bones, making them easy to
finish off. Stone cairns were built to
direct them to the right spot. Some
of these buffalo jumps were used

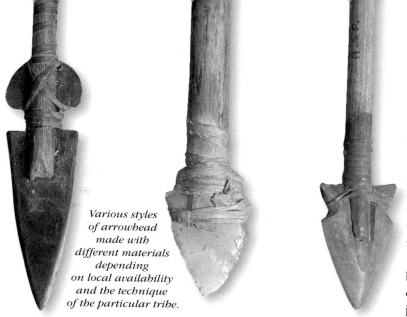

Various styles of arrowhead made with different materials depending on local availability and the technique of the particular tribe.

for thousands of years. In the North, the Inuit built *inukshuit*, piles of rocks in the shape of a human figure, which they would erect on hilltops in converging lines in order to funnel their prey toward the awaiting hunters. The Huron would drive stakes into the ground to make long fences that sometimes extended over two kilometres. Here and there, they would leave openings where the hunters would lie in wait or where they would place snares made of moose or caribou sinew or leather in which the deer and elk would be strangled.

During the mating season, on dark, moonless, windless nights, the Micmac and the Maliseet of the Gaspé Peninsula would attract and kill bull moose by imitating the call of the female.

The Indians would also take advantage of moonless nights in the fall to hunt migrating birds. Hidden in their canoes, they would drift on the current or with the wind into a flock of geese. Suddenly they would light torches made of birchbark dipped in pine gum and then club the startled birds as they fluttered in confusion around the canoes. On bright, moonlit nights, they would sneak up to trees in which wild turkeys were roosting and kill them one by one.

To catch small fur-bearing animals, they used dead-fall traps consisting of a simple support with a precariously balanced weight that, when disturbed, would

fall and crush the animal. A snare attached to the end of a pole was used to catch ptarmigan, ruffled grouse, or squirrel. The Indians also set snares on hare paths. Porcupine, which was appreciated for its tender flesh and for its quills, which the women dyed bright colours and used for decorating clothing, was unquestionably the easiest prey to catch. They simply struck it with a club, threw stones at it, or shot it with an arrow if it had escaped up a tree. To catch passenger pigeons, the Indians would hang large nets made of plant fibre between two tall trees and wait for the birds to fly into them.

The Indians used a variety of techniques to catch beaver. They made traps out of sticks pulled together at one end to form a very long conical basket. They would jam the pointed end into the beaver dam. When the beaver rushed out to plug the hole, it would advance into the bottom of the basket, where its head would get stuck between the sticks, causing it to drown.

But the best time for hunting beaver was in the winter, when the lakes and rivers were covered with ice and the beaver had its thickest coat. The most frequent technique was to trap the beaver above its dam. Before freeze-up, the hunters would locate the beaver lodges and stick a small row of stakes on each side of the underwater entrances and in front of the caches and secondary burrows.

After winter set in, they would break the ice with a trenching tool and spread nets between the stakes to block access to the burrows and to any waterways the beavers might use in trying to escape. The hunters would then smash in the top of the lodge. Wherever the beavers tried to flee, they would get caught in the underwater nets and drown. Otters, which live in the same habitat, were often hunted at the same time and in the same manner as the beaver.

To ensure the success of the hunt, the Indians would appease the spirits and forces of nature. And they always showed great respect when hunting, killing, butchering, and eating their prey.

The hunters would stampede the buffalo over a steep bluff and then finish off the wounded animals.

THE BIRCHBARK CANOE

This ingenious craft,
which was perfectly adapted
to the environment,
opened up the New World to
explorers and fur traders.

*The canoe made it possible
to establish a network of river routes
connecting the different regions
of North America.*

Without canoes, the French would never have managed to penetrate so deeply and quickly into the interior of North America, to enter into contact with so many tribes, and to organize and control the highly lucrative fur trade. Perfectly adapted to the environment, the birchbark canoe was light, easy to handle, and capable of carrying heavy loads – arguably one of the greatest achievements of Indian technology. With a hatchet, a knife, an awl, a few sheets of birchbark, spruce roots, pine or spruce gum, and a little help, a good craftsman could make a canoe in several days. If it was well maintained, the canoe could last many seasons.

Canoe building was usually a group effort overseen by an experienced builder. The Indians made their canoes in early spring, when the sap was running in the birch trees and the bark was thick, strong, and supple.

The men would select a tree with a smooth trunk and no branches for a considerable height. With a flat knife, they would cut a ring around the trunk just above the snow and another ring five to seven metres up, joining them with a vertical slit. They would then peel off the outer bark, or "rind," carefully separating it from the inner bark. A good sheet of birchbark would be at least five millimetres thick. They would immerse it in water to keep it supple. During this time, the women and children would prepare the construction site on a flat piece of

An Abenaki crooked knife used for making birchbark canoes, among other things.

ground near the river or lake. They would carefully clean the site and cover it with a bed of sand banked slightly higher at each end. Wood would be gathered for making the frame: softwood for the gunwales and ribs, and hardwood for the thwarts. The builder in charge of the work would prepare two long, narrow pieces of white cedar or black spruce (at least 5 metres long and no more than 5 centimetres wide) to be used for the gunwales. For the ribs, he needed slats approximately 1.5 metres long, 5 centimetres wide, and just over half a centimetre thick. After soaking the ribs in hot water, he would bend them into the desired shape and set them to dry in the sun or near the fire. Then he would assemble the frame of the canoe, with the thwarts holding the gunwales apart.

The women would already have prepared the *watape*, the long spruce roots used for sewing the canoe. After removing the bark, they would have split each root into two long strands and left them to soak in warm water. They would also have prepared gum for waterproofing the seams. This involved cutting notches in spruce or pine trees, collecting the resin that seeped out, and boiling it to remove impurities.

The Algonquin were great travellers, renowned for their paddling abilities and canoe-making skills.

The builders would place the canoe frame on the building bed and drive in seven or eight pairs of stakes on either side to mark the outline of the canoe. Then they would remove the frame, laying the birchbark in its place with the white side facing in. They would place the frame on top of the birchbark, where it was firmly supported by the stakes. The women would remove any surplus birchbark and with the *watape* sew the bow and stern pieces and lash the birchbark shell securely to the gunwales. The builder in charge would insert the ribs to give the canoe its final shape.

Despite its lightness and fragility, a seven-metre canoe could carry a considerable weight. Loaded to the gunwales with up to two tonnes of merchandise and provisions, in addition to four, six, or even eight paddlers, it required only fifty centimetres of water. It could be easily carried on one man's back for portaging.

Canoes were made of birchbark wherever suitable birch trees (*Betula papyrifera*) were found: throughout the St. Lawrence Valley, the eastern Prairies, and northern Minnesota. Certain Indian peoples, such as the Miami, Fox, Illinois, and Sioux, who lived outside the birch tree's growing zone, had no canoe tradition. Almost all Algonquian tribes, however, were remarkable canoeists and highly acclaimed builders. The Ojibwa northwest of Lake Superior and on the shore south of Rainy Lake were skilful canoe builders. The Algonquin of Trois Rivières were also renowned for their craftsmanship and, for a century, were the main suppliers of canoes for voyageurs travelling to the fur country.

Birchbark is fairly resistant to rot and able to withstand heat and freezing. It may be fragile, but as long as the frame remains intact, the canoe can be easily repaired. Voyageurs always carried along spare pieces of birchbark and supplies of *watape* and pine or spruce gum.

The coureurs des bois soon adopted the birchbark canoe, which was light enough to be portaged by one man.

If the shore was at all rocky, the paddlers had to get into the water and unload the canoe before carrying it to land. As soon as a crack was noticed in the birchbark shell, it would be sealed with pine or spruce gum melted on a hot stick. Since the gum hardened and cracked easily in the cold, bear grease would be added to make it more pliable. In the spring and fall, the canoe brigades had to get under way before dawn. Often, an hour or two after sunrise, as the day warmed up, the bear grease would start to melt. The crew would then have to stop, unload the canoes, and carry them up onto land in order to wipe off the melted grease and re-gum the seams.

South and west of the Great Lakes, where birch was scarcer, as well as in the Rockies, where the shallow, rushing rivers were full of sharp rocks, the Indians often used dugouts, which were much more solid but heavy and hard to manoeuvre and thus not really practical for running rapids. In Iroquois country, especially among the Mohawk, canoes were also made from the bark of elm trees, though these tended to be heavier and slower than birchbark canoes. The tribes along the Mackenzie River and the Interior Salish used the bark of white spruce, which had the serious drawback of remaining sticky and never properly drying.

The birchbark canoe was perfectly suited to the local environment and needs. It enabled the Europeans to explore the entire Great Lakes basin and the land beyond and to exploit the riches of this immense territory. Without it, large-scale organization of the fur trade would have been unthinkable. The canoe was also strategically useful.

The making of an Ojibwa canoe started with choosing good-quality birchbark at the end of winter. Another necessary material was black spruce (or cedar) for the gunwales, ribs, and planking.

In 1686 the Chevalier de Troyes and his men travelled inland by canoe all the way to Hudson Bay, where they destroyed the Hudson's Bay Company forts. The following year, canoe brigades led by Daniel Greysolon Dulhut and Nicolas Perrot successfully fought the Seneca.

An Outpost of Intercontinental Trade

Montreal was to become the centre of the fur market.

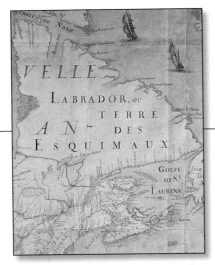

Not only was the young town a trading centre, but it would also become the capital of the French-Indian alliance and the gateway to the Pays d'en Haut.

Each year, in late May or early June, the governor and intendant of New France would leave Quebec and set up headquarters in Montreal. There they would spend most of the summer, receiving delegations of Indians who had come down the St. Lawrence River and its tributaries or from the land of the Iroquois. The Quebec-based traders also made the trip to Montreal to do business with the Indians from the fur country.

Some of these Indians would stop at Lachine. Most, however, ran the rapids and beached their canoes just outside the stockade surrounding the small town of Ville Marie, as Montreal was called by its founders. Men and women alike were flamboyantly painted and feathered for the occasion. They would erect their birchbark huts on the river bank at Pointe à Callière, where the trading took place. Before getting down to business, the Indians presented gifts to the traders, the governor, and the intendant, and passed around the ceremonial pipe.

The traders would set up stalls displaying their goods to the avid gaze of the Indians. To keep things under control, the sale of alcohol was strictly forbidden, though this rule was often disregarded in the interests of encouraging trade.

Montreal at that time was very multiethnic and multicultural. It was a place not only where European and Indian cultures intermingled but also where numerous Indian nations met. In addition to being an important commercial centre, the young town soon became the diplomatic hub for the Indian nations of northeastern North America and the capital of the French-Indian alliance.

In 1535 Jacques Cartier, the first European to set foot on the Montreal archipelago, came upon an Iroquois village called Hochelaga. A century later, when Maisonneuve arrived to found Ville Marie, the village had disappeared. When the French established their colony there, the islands were practically deserted. Some four thousand Algonquin roamed the lands north of the river. To the south, a few days away by canoe or foot, lived the Mohawk, their mortal enemies.

From the outset, the tiny settlement was a centre of attraction for the Indians. In 1643, a year after its founding, the Jesuits baptized no fewer than seventy-six Huron, who did not leave in the fall but remained close to the town.

For almost a quarter century, until 1666, the Indians of the region outnumbered the French. By 1695, however, there were just over seven hundred Indians in the vicinity of Montreal and around three times as many white men huddled in the small colony.

The Huron and Algonquin who came to trade with the white men in Montreal had braved or outwitted the Iroquois, or possibly negotiated treaties or agreements with them. There was no way of really knowing what went on between the Indian tribes; no one knew whether they were still friends or had become enemies again. Moreover, while trading in Montreal, the Indians would cobble together alliances, often unbeknownst to the colonial authorities. Once they had what they wanted, they would leave. Some traders thus started giving the Indians advances to ensure that they would come back the following spring.

Rather than seeing the colony's young men risk their lives and souls in the land of the "Savages," in 1663 the civil and religious authorities began holding an annual fair to which the Indians could come to trade their furs. Young Montrealers were thus exposed to Indian culture and society right on their own doorstep. Each summer, a few dozen of them would leave

Unscrupulous small traders would buy rum from the English and then trade it illegally with the Indians.

with the Indians when they were through trading and paddle back up the Ottawa River with them to the fur country. They wanted to go as high up the rivers as possible and enter into direct contact with nations farther and farther inland. In complicity with the outfitters, these coureurs des bois established a clandestine fur trade network between Montreal and Lake Superior, eliminating the Indian middlemen.

The Montreal merchants became very rich and powerful. They were New France's first home-grown aristocracy. And they owed it all to the fur trade.

In 1681 Minister Colbert decided to legalize the fur trade by instituting a system of "trading leaves," or licences. The holders of these licences (initially limited to twenty-five per year) were authorized to outfit a canoe with goods and three paddlers in order to go and trade in the Indian villages. This system contributed to the decline of the Montreal fur fair. Fewer Indians made the trip down from the Pays d'en Haut since the dealing was done on their home turf.

Nevertheless, Montreal remained the hub of the fur trade and the gateway to the fur country. The Montreal merchants and outfitters had everything necessary: the know-how, the capital, and the materials for making the indispensable birchbark canoes.

Each spring, brigades of canoes would set off from Lachine, upriver from Montreal, stopping at the western tip of the island for the men to pray and leave an offering at St. Anne's Church. This was the last church they would see before arriving at Michilimackinac on the straits between Lake Huron and Lake Michigan, after six or seven weeks of strenuous paddling and portaging. It was a perilous journey. Even after the fall of Huronia, the Iroquois, supported and armed by the Dutch and the English, continued to pose a serious threat.

To protect the fur trade, Governor Frontenac led several military forays against the Iroquois and obliged them to begin negotiating. His successor, Louis de Callière, continued this policy of reconciliation, bringing together in Montreal representatives from some forty Indian nations in the summer of 1701. Over 1,300 Indians, including at least 200 Iroquois, set up camp near Montreal, which at that time had just over 2,000 inhabitants. The diplomatic meetings took place at the residence of Governor Callière, who presented the representatives of the different nations with thirty-one wampum collars he had had made by Indian women. The Great Peace, as it was called, was ratified at a grand assembly on 4 August.

Just before arriving in Montreal to meet with the French plenipotentiaries, the Indian ambassadors from the West had stopped for a day at Kahnawake, where they had concluded trading agreements and alliances among themselves.

Quebec remained the official administrative seat of New France, while Montreal increasingly carved a place for itself as the centre of the fur trade and the link between European and Indian societies. There, more than anywhere else, the two worlds met and merged.

Each spring, brigades of heavily laden Montreal canoes would set off from Lachine before daybreak.

Chapter 3

THE COUREURS DES BOIS

The men are thought not to be very spiritual, which comes from the way they are raised: They are brought up more or less like the Savages, who never reprimand their children and allow them complete freedom. Apparently they take greater care of the girls. It would not be good to imitate the Savages in this regard since, among them, until the girls have chosen a husband, they may have as many lovers as they wish without their parents saying a word, believing as they do that everyone is born free, a prerogative that is jealously guarded. It is this lack of any inhibition and this ease found among the Savages that debauches the Canadians, and leads them to take to the woods with the Savages, and to live like them.

Most of the young Frenchmen who went off to live with the Indians ended up adopting their way of life and taking Indian wives.

The primarily coniferous forests to the north were home to an abundant, though not very diverse, wildlife.

THE DONNÉS

Committing themselves
body and soul to the service
of the Jesuits,
these domestic servants
and labourers
helped the missionaries
in their work.

*A number of donnés, such as René
Goupil, paid with their lives for
associating with the Black Robes,
whom the Indians distrusted.*

T he Indians, both the Huron, who were friends
of the French, and the Iroquois, who were their
worst enemies, distrusted the Black Robes.
These strange, secretive beings did not act like
real men; they never carried weapons, or
waged war, or made love with women. To
enable them to pursue their missionary work,
the Black Robes recruited young men in
France and the colony who had
impeccable morals and were willing to
serve the Jesuits and devote their lives to
saving and converting the Indians. These
"donnés," or voluntary labourers, were
expected to paddle and portage the
canoes and to clear land and construct
buildings. If necessary, they could also
come to the aid of the missionaries with a
musket or knife.

Simply through their association
with the Black Robes, the donnés lived
in danger, much more so than the other
young men who went off to the woods

*Although the voyageurs took
few personal belongings
with them to the
Pays d'en Haut,
they all made sure to
take their rosaries.*

in the early days
of New France.
They had nothing to
gain from the
experience, other than the
salvation of their souls, for they
owned nothing; they had given
everything away before
committing themselves body and
soul to the service of the Jesuits.
Without them, the missionaries
would never have been able to survive in this untamed
world, let alone reach Ste. Marie des Hurons, the mission
they established north of Lake Ontario. Nor would they
have made it to the land of the Iroquois.

It was Father Jérôme Lalemant, Superior of the Jesuits
in New France, who had the idea of creating an auxiliary
body of lay assistants. It was a very old institution. As far
back as the eleventh century, there had been men in
France who renounced marriage and devoted their lives to
serving a religious community. They donated all their
possessions to the community, which in turn took care of
all their worldly needs. Spanish missionaries in Peru also
used lay assistants to whom they entrusted various
manual and spiritual duties.

However, Father Mutius Vitelleschi, the General of the
Jesuits, had forbidden use of their services in the missions
of Canada, fearing their conduct would discredit the
Society of Jesus. How could one control young men, who
were often ill-educated if not illiterate, in the face of the
constant temptations of a heathen world?

Despite the reluctance of their European superiors,
the Jesuits of New France hoped their lay assistants
would commit themselves fully to the mission,
taking vows and signing a civil contract
binding them to the order for life: *"I, the
undersigned, hereby give myself of my own
free will to the Society of Jesus to serve
and to assist with all my might the
Fathers of the said Society who are
working to save and convert the poor
savages and barbarians of New France."*

Theoretically, when he signed this
contract, the donné was using his "own
free will" for the last time in his life.
Thenceforth, his whole being, body and soul,
and all his possessions would belong to
the Society of Jesus, to which he at all
times and in all things owed obedience.
The community undertook in return to

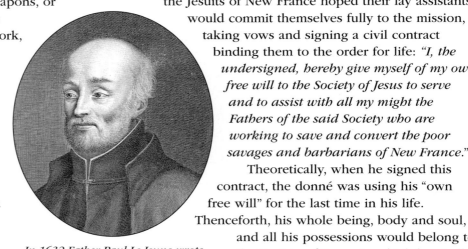

*In 1632 Father Paul Le Jeune wrote
the first of the* Jesuit Relations, *informing
people in France about the work done
by the missionaries in the New World.*

care for his modest needs. In addition to the various duties he would happily fulfil, the donné was expected to practise his religion with devotion and, unlike the interpreters who scandalized and contaminated the Indians, to set an example for all.

In the enthusiasm of the early days, some recruits asked for riders to be added to their contracts and made vows of perpetual poverty, obedience, and chastity. Chastity was a particular challenge for a young man who was going to live in intimate contact with the Indians, who were known for their sexual licence.

In the spring of 1643, a young French physician named François Gendron, travelling on his own, managed to slip through Iroquois territory and reach Ste. Marie des Hurons to inform the missionaries of Father Vitelleschi's decision: Rome was ordering them to liberate the donnés. It was a terrible blow.

Father Lalemant and his supporters begged the General of the Jesuits to reconsider their situation and their great need of having lay assistants to help them in their work. They described the invaluable services provided to the community by the donnés, who were not only useful through the sight of their exemplary lives, but also edifying through their heroic deaths, since a great many of them were unfortunately martyred.

Perhaps touched by these stories, Father Vitelleschi rescinded his decision but on condition that the donnés not practise all the Jesuit rites and not be bound to the Society by religious vows. Instead they would sign a civil contract binding them to serve the missionaries, who in return would provide them with food and shelter and care for them if they fell ill.

The authors of the *Jesuit Relations* spoke often of their perpetual servants – "secular in dress, but religious in their hearts," in the words of Father Charles Garnier – who admirably assisted them in all their duties. Year after year, they transported provisions and trade goods to the mission at Ste. Marie des Hurons. They cleared the land, grew crops, and built a hospital, a church, a hospice, and a convent. They also supported the Jesuit fathers in their missionary work among the Iroquois and Huron, suffering and sometimes dying with them, for the greater glory of Christ.

While there were martyrs among these perpetual servants, there were also defectors. As devout as they were, these young men could not always remain indifferent to the charms and temptations of the Indian world.

Living with the Jesuits, they had received excellent training, many of them learning to read and write. They had also had incredible adventures and experiences that had seasoned and transformed them. They now had everything they needed to become good coureurs des bois. Some could not resist and, like the interpreters, "went native." A few joined the fur trade, which in the mid-seventeenth century was where the most intrepid adventurers sought their fortune.

The donné working on the plane is wearing locally made wooden shoes. Having taken a vow of poverty, he is dressed very simply. The Jesuit missionary talking to him is wearing moccasins, his only concession to local customs.

GUILLAUME COUTURE'S STORY

Although the young man seemed in good shape, he bore visible scars and burns.

Captives were often tortured to make them true members of the tribe.

On 5 July 1644, Kiotsaeton, an Iroquois chief of the Mohawk tribe, appeared in Trois Rivières draped from head to toe in wampum belts and collars. He had brought with him the donné Guillaume Couture, whom he had agreed to free in exchange for Tokhrahenehiaron, a

Tomahawk made from a single piece of wood, with a knot forming the head.

friend of his who had been taken prisoner by the French.

Young Couture seemed in good shape. His captors had obviously cared for his wounds and fed him up before offering to trade him to the French. However, he had clearly been tortured. The Mohawk always "caressed" their prisoners. Couture had burns and scars on his hands, arms, legs, chest, and face. He was missing a finger, likely sawn off with a sharpened shell. His fingernails, which a young warrior had torn out with his teeth, had almost completely grown back.

Although he had obviously suffered unspeakable torture, he did not look broken or scared; quite the contrary. He was on warm and easy terms with his torturers, showing them his strength and good humour. He had survived the horror, withstood incredible suffering, and witnessed the execution of several of his Huron friends and his fellow donné, René Goupil. Despite this, he seemed to like and understand the Mohawk. Everything he had undergone at their hands had given him a new view of Indian society.

Ten days later, when Kiotsaeton and his warriors returned to Iroquois territory, Couture willingly went back with them at the request of Governor Charles Huault de Montmagny in order to help carry the gifts the governor had given them, but also to show that the French trusted the Mohawk. After being a prisoner and a trade item, Couture thus became a diplomat who was well respected by his former torturers.

Guillaume Couture was born in Normandy around 1618. Someone of his social condition who was strong, intelligent, and brave but not well born had no future in France. No doubt that is why he had decided to seek adventure in the New World. Leaving his mother and sister his few belongings, he had bound himself over to the Jesuits as a donné, or perpetual unpaid servant.

New France, and especially the Jesuit missionaries, had great need of courageous young men like him. During the summer of 1641, the Iroquois had stepped up their raids and ambushes. With little knowledge of how to handle a canoe or firearm, Couture went off that year to live among the Huron in the still unstable Ste. Marie mission, headed by thirty-three-year-old Father Isaac Jogues.

The following summer, the two Frenchmen returned to Quebec with several Huron chiefs who wanted to meet with Governor Montmagny, whom they called Onontio, which in the Huron language means "big

The Indians used to string "Jesuit" rings onto necklaces. The rings were associated more with the fur trade than with missionary work.

mountain." This term of respect for Montmagny's great stature was subsequently used for other governors of New France.

The Huron chiefs wanted to secure the support of the French so as to present a common front against the enemy Iroquois, who were conducting deadly raids right up into the St. Lawrence Valley. Father Jogues and young Couture left with the Huron, along with another donné named René Goupil.

Their party consisted of some forty people in twelve canoes. In early August, after a few days' stop in Trois Rivières, they crossed Lake St. Pierre in broad daylight, making for the cluster of low-lying islands at the far end of the lake.

There, they stopped for the night. The low banks did not provide much protection. Everyone was nervous and slept badly. The men took turns standing guard throughout the night. In the morning, they noticed some tracks on the beach and saw that the grass had been trampled. Their apprehension grew. Scarcely had they put the canoes into the river when gunshots rang out. Couture realized that the Iroquois could easily catch up with them on the water and therefore suggested they return to shore as quickly as possible. They dragged the canoes into the reeds and tried to hide in the adjacent woods.

Goupil, who was deaf, unfamiliar with the country, and not really used to the woods, was easily captured. Father Jogues made it safely out of reach. However, unwilling to simply abandon Goupil to his fate, he revealed himself to the Iroquois and was taken prisoner too. He spoke their language better than Goupil

and hoped he could convince them that the Black Robes did not mean them any harm.

Couture was armed and had managed to flee into the woods. In making his escape, he had shot an Iroquois warrior. He had seen him grab his chest and fall to the ground. Couture was very familiar with the country and was sure he could get

away; he need only wait until nightfall. The Iroquois were not on their home ground and knew they were in danger. They would no doubt eventually leave with their prisoners, if they had not already killed them. And then, with a little luck, he would find one of the canoes and return to Trois Rivières. If worse came to worse, he could make his way back on foot, following the shore of the St. Lawrence River.

But he had his duty and the vows he had made as a donné. He wanted to discover what had happened to the others. So he went back to the beach, where he found pools of blood and the scalped corpses of some of their Huron travelling companions. Suddenly, the howling, jeering Iroquois were upon him. They grabbed him and bore him away. He saw that they had tortured Jogues and Goupil and some of the Huron.

They had a special treatment in store for him; the man he had killed was a chief. Couture was in for a lengthy "caress." He knew full well that the only way to escape with his life was to withstand this test with courage and dignity. He therefore hid his fear and refused to scream or beg for mercy, thus winning his torturers' respect. And so, as one of the very few people who were accepted in both European and Indian society in those difficult early days, he became an invaluable intermediary for the French colony.

Although the Jesuits had come to the New World in order to convert the Indians, they also engaged in the fur trade with them.

The Walking Dead

A prisoner's fate depended
on his attitude,
the mood or whim
of his captors,
and the needs of the tribe.

*Prisoners who were unable to adapt
to their new tribe were killed
or treated as slaves. Only the most
valiant were tortured.*

*An Iroquois
scalping knife. Its sheath
is made of dressed and
smoked hide, decorated
with birchbark
and porcupine quills.*

The Indians regarded any prisoners they took as spoils of war and thus theirs to do with as they pleased. Some tribes, such as the Illinois, were avid kidnappers and sold their captives as slaves. Other Aboriginal peoples had very close, complex, and ambiguous relationships with their prisoners. Some they executed, often after lengthy torture; others they adopted, expecting them to replace lost family members or to fulfil various functions within the tribe. They preferred to adopt children, especially girls, who were thought to be easier to acculturate and more likely to increase the fertility of the tribe. But, among bellicose nations like the Iroquois, there was often a shortage of able-bodied males to serve as husbands, progenitors, and warriors. So they would go to war to capture young men.

However, before being accepted as full members of the tribe, the captives had to prove themselves. All were subjected to excruciating torture. Until their fate was decided, they were considered the walking dead.

If they endured these horrific ordeals with dignity and courage, some of the captives would be assimilated into the community. For a young Frenchman, this trial was the most terrible and definitive way of entering Indian society, becoming one with their culture, adopting their world view. He would have an Indian wife and brothers; his very heart and soul would be Indian.

The prisoners' fates depended on their attitudes, the moods or whims of their captors, and the needs of the tribe. On the way back to the village after a raid, those who couldn't keep up – the elderly, pregnant women, young children – were eliminated. The survivors would later be exchanged for ransom, kept as potential slaves, condemned to torture and death, or adopted. Depending on the fate awaiting them, their faces were painted either red or black. They were between life and death, the walking dead.

As they approached the village, a messenger would run ahead to tell the others how the war party had fared. Armed with sticks, thorns, and rocks, the women and children would be waiting in a double row through which the prisoners, their heads shaved, had to pass. The prisoners were hit, jabbed, stoned, and jeered at. In this way, the whole village, women and men, young and old, would participate in the humiliation, defeat, and appropriation of the enemy, the first step in their adoption.

Those unable to bear this ordeal without complaint were swiftly and simply put to death by a woman or child, and their bodies thrown to the dogs. Only the strong were entitled to the honour of ritual torture and execution.

The village council would distribute the prisoners to families who had lost a relative. If the clan mother refused to adopt the prisoner offered to her, he would be taken away for torture and death or kept as a slave.

If he was to replace a son or a husband, he eventually had to show true affection for his adoptive parents or the woman who had chosen him as her mate. He would then be given the same privileges and responsibilities as any other member of the tribe and

*This tomahawk was used
by the Indians of the Prairies.
Its bronze blade made it a formidable
weapon in hand-to-hand combat.*

would end up assuming its customs and attitudes, loves and hates. Until the walking dead man's identity shift was complete, his status remained precarious. He was only a slave and kept just strong enough to work. Considered socially dead, he was no more than a commodity.

A prisoner who merited the farewell feast, however, in some regards entered into the intimacy of the tribe and was treated with respect. He was an active participant in the great ceremony of his own execution.

The torture usually lasted an entire night. If the victim was strong, his captors might even "caress" him for several nights. He would be revived if necessary, given food and water, and allowed to rest or sleep if he were able.

First his nails would be torn out, his fingers crushed, chewed, or cut off, and the stumps cauterized in a burning pipe. His feet and hands would be pierced with a hot iron, his wrists sawn with the string of a bow, his scalp ripped from his head, and boiling water or melted pine gum poured onto his bloody skull. Children would poke burning embers into his crotch, armpits, and ears.

In the morning, before the final moment, a collar of red-hot tomahawks would be hung around his neck and burning coals stuck in his eyes. He would sing his war song one last time. A truly courageous man would insult and curse his torturers. Or he would declare that he had no fear of torture and death, encouraging them to do their worst. He would remind them that he himself had tortured and killed members of their family. His torturers would tear out his teeth and tongue and cut off his lips.

Then they would untie him and, if he still had the strength, let him stumble around the village, blind, burnt, and mutilated – but also admired and adulated. His dead body would be lovingly devoured.

Torture and cannibalism were marks of respect. They gave the victim a chance to demonstrate his dignity, courage, and strength. In drinking his blood and eating his flesh, the others assimilated these qualities. The macabre ceremony of torture was a sacred ritual reserved for the most highly respected prisoners.

Cannibalism, like adoption, was a means of social integration. In eating their enemy, or in adopting and assimilating him into their society, the community took him into itself, thus strengthening itself, possessing the enemy's soul, and dissipating its fears.

53

PIERRE-ESPRIT RADISSON'S STORY

He understood the main issues at stake in the New World and was determined to play a key role in them.

To impress their enemies, the Iroquois stuck human heads on the stockades surrounding their villages.

Taken prisoner by the blood-chillingly ferocious Iroquois, bitter enemies of the French, seventeen-year-old Pierre-Esprit Radisson kept telling himself, "Be like them. Bear it the way they do."

Torture is an initiation, a rite of passage and belonging. It is intended to alter the person's identity. Radisson endured the torture so well, did such a good job of "being like them," that he actually became one of them. He learned their language. He learned, like them, to remain indifferent to pain, hunger, thirst, and fear, to live like them, and to kill like them. He also understood the importance of the spoken word and a sense of theatre for surviving among them, for winning the recognition and respect of the community. He had his death song and his war song. He lived happily with the Iroquois for a summer, the following winter, and another summer. But then he wanted to see his family and friends in Trois Rivières again.

Killing three of his adoptive brothers with a tomahawk, he managed to escape along with an Algonquin prisoner but was recaptured before he reached Trois Rivières and tortured again. And, once again, he was spared by his adoptive family because he was able to endure and to make brave speeches and sing. Once again he succeeded in escaping his beloved captors and made it to Fort Orange. From there he eventually embarked on a Dutch ship heading to Holland and then made his way to France. It was not long before he found another ship that would take him back to Canada. At twenty years of age, Radisson had a taste for adventure.

Born in Avignon, and raised and educated in Paris, he was always moving between societies and cultures, changing his clan and way of life, living with the Algonquin on the north shore of the St. Lawrence River, with the Huron, the Ottawa, the Ojibwa, and other tribes around the Great Lakes, and with the Mohawk. He took part in military expeditions to the Mediterranean and the Caribbean. He associated with New England adventurers, British aristocrats, and upper-class French traders.

In 1657 he returned a third time to Iroquois country, this time of his own free will. For a year, he accompanied the Jesuit missionaries, serving as their guide and interpreter

Tumplines for portaging loads were often used for attaching prisoners and taking them back to the village

and also studying with them.

He came to understand the main issues at stake in the New World and was determined to play a key role in them. With his brother-in-law Médard Chouart des Groseilliers, eighteen years his senior, he made several journeys to the Pays d'en Haut.

During their first major expedition, the brothers-in-law probably made it to Lake Superior, or possibly as far as Lake Winnipeg, in the company of the Ojibwa and Cree. They would then have encountered

An Onondaga warrior with his prisoner, who is singing a ritual song to show he has no fear of death.

the highly organized society of the Sioux, passing between cultures with remarkable ease.

Radisson liked exploring new country and was endlessly awed by what he saw. "Lake Michigan is the most delightful lake in the world," he wrote in his memoirs. "I can assure you that I have never loved any land as much as this."

When the fall of Huronia cut the French off from the network of alliances with Indian nations that had supplied them with furs, Radisson managed to build a new network. If only for that, he felt he deserved France's recognition.

An intelligent observer in a world that was almost unknown to other Europeans, he accumulated an enormous store of geographical, ethnographic, and anthropological knowledge that was perhaps even more valuable than the bales of furs he brought back from the Pays d'en Haut.

Radisson was fascinated with the different cultures he discovered but always kept his distance. He made fun of the Parisian bourgeoisie, with their carriages and elaborately coiffed hair, as well as of the Indians, with their feathers and superstitions. When Jesuit missionaries accompanying him and Groseilliers on an expedition were unable to bear the hardship and had to turn back, he called them cowards and weaklings, saying that they often were more concerned with gathering furs than souls. He was generally contemptuous of the faint-hearted

After destroying a village and massacring its inhabitants, the Iroquois would leave their calling card: a tomahawk marked with the number of warriors who had participated in the raid.

colonists of New France, who claimed to dominate the Iroquois but lived in fear. He also accused the governor of getting rich at his expense.

In the spring of 1660, he was returning from a long journey with Groseilliers. They arrived at Long Sault, just up the Ottawa River from the Lake of Two Mountains, a few days after Dollard des Ormeaux and his companions had been massacred by the Iroquois. They found the small fort burnt to the ground and the inhabitants scalped or decapitated.

They were leading a brigade of sixty canoes carrying the equivalent of 300,000 livres worth of furs. This treasure, amassed at the risk of their lives, was confiscated by Governor d'Argenson on the grounds that they had traded without a licence and infringed on the monopoly held by the Company of New France.

Radisson wrote the governor a scathing letter, reminding him that Groseilliers and he were discoverers, that they had saved the country through their generosity and daring, and that no one else had ever had the courage to do what they had done.

On returning from their next expedition, Radisson and Groseilliers therefore decided to sell their furs to the English. It was also to the English that they revealed the routes to the untold riches of Hudson Bay and with whom they founded the powerful Hudson's Bay Company that would shape the history of North America.

Radisson wasn't being hypocritical or opportunistic. He felt that, through his courage and the knowledge he had acquired, he had earned his independence; he owed nothing to anyone, least of all to the French, who had failed to understand the importance of his explorations.

On retiring from the fur trade, he married a highborn English woman and spent a comfortable old age in London. "What greater pleasure," he wrote, "than good conversation, especially when you can see the smoke rising from your own chimney, and kiss your wife or your neighbour's wife with ease and enjoyment." He died at the age of seventy-four.

Throughout his life, he went back and forth between cultures, always keeping his distance and his ironic view of people, whom he found essentially all alike. At the end, he was no longer a Frenchman, or an Englishman, or an Indian, but a new combination of all three – a true inhabitant of the New World.

THE IROQUOIS WIFE

In Iroquois society,
the children's clan identity
was conferred by the women,
some of whom
had enormous power.

*Clan mothers often gave male
prisoners to young widows who had
lost their husbands in battle.*

Many Indian societies were matriarchal. Among the Iroquois, for example, women played a role that was valued as much as, if not more than, that of hunters and warriors. The Jesuit missionary Joseph-François Lafitau, a keen observer of Iroquois society, wrote that it constituted "an empire of women." In producing children, the women ensured the survival of the clan. For peoples living under constant threat, there was no more essential and respected function.

Adopting a prisoner of war into the tribe was in some ways akin to giving birth. It was thus to the clan mothers that the Iroquois warriors entrusted their captives, usually after harrowing torture. The women had absolute power of life and death over these prisoners. Only they were capable, if they deemed the prisoners worthy, of giving them a place within the tribe. They would comfort these "newborns" who had come to them after a traumatic ordeal. They would feed them and

bind their wounds, tenderly caring for them until they became devoted sons and developed a deep love for their adoptive tribe.

Through adoption, a woman past child-bearing age could still add new members to the clan and continue to fulfil her noblest duty. The clan mothers were women past the age of menopause who were respected for their knowledge and wisdom. According to Marie de l'Incarnation, founder of the Ursulines convent in Quebec, they were "female leaders, women of worth who had a right to participate and vote in council discussions." They had the power to choose the chiefs, to advise them, and sometimes to impose their will on them – and, if necessary, to depose them.

A young woman who had lost her husband in battle could find a replacement among the captives adopted by the clan mothers. Combining duty with pleasure, she could again experience the joys of love and motherhood.

In addition to producing offspring and strengthening the race, the adopted husbands would become warriors and, with their intimate knowledge of another language, territory, and people, facilitate alliances with other tribes.

Once adopted into the tribe, the young man would join hunting, trading, and war parties and help to fell trees, clear land, build homes, and make fortifications – all the duties expected of any male tribe member. Like most of the other men, he would not live with his wife but in the longhouse of his adoptive mother's clan.

According to Iroquois custom, a young man and woman who formed a couple did not leave their respective homes to found a new family. Each continued to live within the clan in which he or she had been raised. Children born of their union, both boys and girls, lived with the mother's family and were raised by her with the help of their grandmother and maternal aunts and uncles, who constituted their one true family. The longhouse where their biological father lived was as unknown to them as any other house in the village.

The couple was therefore not the basic unit of Iroquois society. Duties and responsibilities were not shared between spouses but between the women and the men, who fulfilled their respective duties as a group.

The women were in charge of farming; they sowed the crops in the spring and looked after the cornfields and vegetable gardens. They also gathered birds' eggs, wild fruit, and berries and dug up edible roots. In addition to hunting small game, they skinned and butchered large game caught

*Iroquois women used clay pots like this one
for cooking a sort of gruel made of ground corn.
They grew the corn in communal
fields just outside the fortified village.*

by the men; scaled, gutted, and dried or smoked fish; and ground corn in a stone or wooden mortar. Women were responsible for all food preparation and cooking, including fetching drinking water, keeping the cooking fire going, and collecting firewood for heating. It was up to them to maintain the longhouse and the clan's burial grounds. They sewed and mended clothing and, of course, took care of the children. Those who were able interpreted dreams. The eldest women chose the chiefs and shamans. Everything having to do with birth, death, health, marriage, or child-rearing was the women's exclusive domain.

Female prisoners brought back to the village, like these Huron women, were never raped since they could become adoptive sisters.

All Aboriginal peoples loved children. They gave them absolute freedom and never bullied, rejected, or reprimanded them in any way, for children were the life and future of the tribe. While the Europeans were amazed at the tolerance and infinite patience with which the Indians treated their cherished offspring, the Indians were horrified at how the white men slapped, whipped, and punished their own children. They couldn't understand why there were so few white women, why they apparently played no role in their society, and why, unlike Iroquois women, they did not in any way participate in the men's affairs or accompany them on their travels.

Among the Huron, women were so valued that the murder of a woman often required greater reparation than that of a man. It was considered that a woman's death deprived the tribe of the children she would have had or, if she were old, of her wisdom and advice. The birth of a daughter was always a happy event, often more welcome than the birth of a son. Within warring tribes, there

were often not enough men to go round. The clan mothers therefore encouraged the war chiefs to organize raids in order to capture prisoners with which to rebuild the tribe. In adopting young prisoners and turning them into devoted and loving sons and daughters, the clan mother ensured the future of her own clan and extended her power over its members.

The women, who instilled a clan identity in the children, were also in charge of acculturating prisoners. The adopted son, brother, or husband enjoyed the same rights as all other men born into the tribe and also had the same duties and responsibilities. For a European, this was the most definitive way of becoming a part of the Indian world.

This newly adopted prisoner has tattoos on his face depicting thunderbirds, the totem of his Iroquois wife's clan. His hair is done in the Iroquois manner, and he is wearing a leather breechcloth and leggings like the warriors of his new tribe, although leather clothing would soon be replaced by cloth.

FRANCIS BACK

The Coureurs des Bois

Seeking furs and fortune,
they moved farther
and farther inland,
discovering new territories
and unknown tribes.

*No threat, law, or decree could
keep the young men
from going off to the woods.*

One could not fail to hear the call of the woods. The forest was everywhere, beckoning at the end of every trail and waterway, offering its mysteries, charms, and inexhaustible but forbidden riches. A licence was required in order to leave the colony and go off to the woods. For some, the temptation was just too great. A few young men in Quebec, Trois Rivières, and Montreal sometimes heeded the call and went off to the woods – usually without a licence – to seek their fortune and adventure, something other than the limited and predictable life of working the land.

There were not that many at first. In the 1630s, for each man like Étienne Brûlé, who went off to live and die with the Huron, or Jean Nicollet, who travelled as far as the land of the Winnebago trying to find a passage to the China Sea, there were a score of colonists who never ventured beyond the Lachine Rapids. By mid-century, only a few dozen Frenchmen were making regular trips to Huron country.

However, furs would change everything, transforming what had initially been the adventure of a few wild renegades into a large-scale movement. By 1672 there were 300 to 400 illegal "wood runners," and within the next eight years, twice that number.

The illegal fur trade was not only profitable but had become necessary following the tragic events of 1650, when the Huron, the main suppliers of furs, had been practically wiped out by the Iroquois. To meet the demand of the European fur markets, the French had no choice but to go to the source of the beaver, to the Indian trappers in the Pays d'en Haut. It was in this context, at a time when the woods were more hostile and dangerous than ever, that the coureurs des bois emerged. However, the very real risks involved in going off to the woods were largely outweighed by the considerable profits to be made.

Some coureurs des bois came back to the colony with a veritable fortune: twenty, thirty, or even fifty canoes laden with furs worth hundreds of thousands of livres (equivalent to millions of dollars today).

*The Indians liked
bayonets, which they
used as knives,
spearheads,
or tomahawks.*

People on the Island of Montreal lived in closer contact with the Indians than did those in Trois Rivières or Quebec. It was thus young Montrealers who went off sooner and in greater numbers to the fur country. Farmers' sons, labourers, and demobilized soldiers were bored stiff in the colony, where in 1660 there was still only one woman for every seven men of marrying age.

But not everyone had what it took to become a coureur des bois. Paddling a canoe full of trade goods for thousands of kilometres was no easy task. Entering into contact with more or less hostile tribes and bartering hardware, pots and pans, weapons, or alcohol for furs also took incredible skill. A coureur des bois had to have great tact, daring, and imagination – and to be in excellent physical shape.

The coureurs des bois were generally young men in their prime. Baron de La Hontan, who himself had led an adventurous life in the wilderness, called them "coureurs de risques" – risk takers. Indeed, the coureurs des bois

*A tumpline, a leather strap
worn across the forehead to help support
heavy loads on portages.*

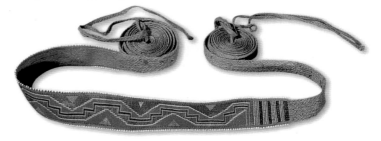

were risking a great deal; they could easily drown or be injured during a portage or might well be tortured and killed if they ever fell into the hands of the Iroquois. But they also risked fines or a flogging, possibly even the galleys, if they engaged in the fur trade without a licence or, worse still, dared to sell their furs on the black market instead of through the trading companies.

However, no threat, law, or decree could halt the young men's rush to the fur country, where in any case they were beyond the reach of the authorities. Some lived in easy familiarity with Indian tribes whose names the governor barely knew and whose territories he would have had a hard time locating. The country was too vast and too sparsely populated. It would never be possible to control the fur trade so completely as to prevent young men from taking advantage of the riches and adventure it offered.

A coureur des bois made more money than any other young man his age back in the colony. But he had to work extremely hard. After making contact with tribes who were not very used to the presence of white men, he had to reassure and convince them, find interpreters and guides, encourage the hunters and trappers, bargain for furs, obtain canoes, and organize brigades of Indians to transport the pelts back to Montreal. The coureurs des bois thus acted as traders, merchants, and outfitters, soon developing a taste for independence that could not subsequently be curbed.

In 1681 the intendant of the colony, Jacques Duchesneau, informed Minister Colbert that 500 to 800 young men were slipping off to the woods each year. Most of them paddled up the Ottawa River to the Great Lakes. Once they reached the back country, nothing was easier than to disperse into the woods. They would seek out the Indians, perhaps shoot some hares themselves, and obtain canoes full of furs in exchange for a few battered pots and pans. Some might also sell guns to the Sioux, traditional enemies of France's Indian allies. Or, for a jug of alcohol that cost four livres in Montreal, a not too conscientious coureur des bois could acquire a hundred livres worth of furs around the Great Lakes. Sooner or later, the Indians would realize they had been cheated and would for a time become enemies of France.

Some coureurs des bois became assimilated into Indian society, adopting Indian manners and customs. In winter they would wear a cape or coat made of moose or caribou hide; in warmer weather, their outfit often consisted of a fringed tunic with a sash, a breechcloth, deerskin leggings, and moccasins. The coureurs des bois never complained of fatigue or hunger and seemed indifferent to the cold of winter and to the heat, mosquitoes, and blackflies of summer. The Indians liked the coureurs des bois because they cheerfully endured the worst hardships, made them laugh, and shared everything they had.

Together the white men and the Indians created new societies whose customs were neither those of the colonies nor those of the Indian tribes, but something altogether different that would soon give birth to a new civilization.

NICOLAS PERROT'S STORY

Taken prisoner several times, he always managed to survive thanks to his great familiarity with Indian culture.

Nicolas Perrot did business with the Iroquois and sometimes fought against them. Their way of life held no secrets for him.

In the spring of 1685, Nicolas Perrot set off for the Pays d'en Haut. Although he had been trading furs there for the past twenty-five years, this time he was going to settle a dispute between the Ojibwa and the Fox that was threatening to seriously disrupt the fur trade.

Perrot first went to the Sault Ste. Marie area to hear the Ojibwa's version of the conflict. The previous year, they had killed one of the Fox chiefs; in revenge, the Fox had kidnapped the daughter of an Ojibwa chief and were planning to torture and burn her.

Taking a party of some twenty Ojibwa, Perrot went to talk with the Fox, who lived farther south, near Green Bay on the western shore of Lake Michigan. He was able to convince the Fox to return the young captive to him, and the two tribes made peace.

During his long career, Nicolas Perrot successfully carried out many such diplomatic missions, though ironically his own business ventures invariably ended in failure. For close to forty years, he was one of the key artisans of the Pax Gallica, the peace that the French had imposed on the Indian nations and that they needed to maintain in order to protect the highly lucrative fur trade. This required constant renegotiation since the Indian world was undergoing profound changes at that time.

In 1660, when Perrot first entered the woods at barely sixteen years of age, the St. Lawrence and Ottawa Valleys, the entire Ontario Peninsula, and the whole region east of the Great Lakes were a vast wasteland whose populations had been devastated by epidemics and the Iroquois wars. The population of Huronia had plummeted from 30,000 in 1600 to a mere 9,000 in 1640. By the end of the century, when Perrot retired to his seigneury at Bécancour, there remained only a few small, scattered Indian communities. Michilimackinac and Chagouamigon on Green Bay, for instance, had become cosmopolitan havens for the defeated and decimated tribes.

The centre of power and influence among the Indian nations had shifted to west of the Great Lakes, the edge of the Prairies, and the upper Mississippi. It was there, in the richest and farthest reaches of New France, that Perrot spent most of his life, from 1665 to 1699. An intrepid coureur des bois, unlucky businessman and trader, incomparable guide and interpreter, and military commander of the most remote outposts, he was entrusted with important and often very delicate diplomatic missions with Indian tribes that he may have been the only European to have met. Usually he needed to convince these tribes to

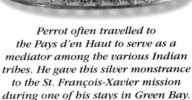

Perrot often travelled to the Pays d'en Haut to serve as a mediator among the various Indian tribes. He gave this silver monstrance to the St. François-Xavier mission during one of his stays in Green Bay.

accept the French as their true allies and to fight the enemy Iroquois, either on their own or alongside the French.

Born in Burgundy around 1644, Nicolas Perrot came to North America as a donné with the Jesuits. After serving for five years in their missions throughout the Pays d'en Haut, he worked as a servant for a widow in Montreal and then for the Sulpicians, but only for a short spell; he longed to be travelling again. Throughout his life, despite his business failures and his responsibilities as a husband and father, he would keep going back to the woods.

What was it that attracted him? The hope of making his fortune, of course, but also a passion for the unknown, for the shifting, unpredictable, often dangerous world of the Indians. He had been taken prisoner on a number of occasions and sometimes even condemned to death, but he had always managed to extricate himself, seeing through the ruses and threats of the different chiefs and playing his influence and friendship with one tribe against another.

In 1671 he achieved the remarkable feat of assembling representatives of fourteen nations at Sault Ste. Marie so that François Daumont de Saint-Lusson could inform them that they

would henceforth be subjects of the king of France. After returning to the St. Lawrence Valley that fall, Perrot married Marie-Madeleine Raclos and settled in Champlain on the north shore of the St. Lawrence River. Six years later, having been granted the seigneury of Bécancour, he moved across the river with his family. He was thirty-seven years old and had six children, five horned animals, two rifles, and eighteen hectares of land, which his wife had to manage almost completely on her own since Perrot was usually off in the woods. He had no choice; since his fur trading expeditions were always financial disasters, he had to keep starting over. He also accepted any diplomatic mission entrusted to him by the governor.

In 1684 he was asked to convince the nations southwest of the Great

Some coureurs des bois carried out delicate diplomatic missions with different Indian tribes.

Lakes to join the war against the Iroquois. He raised an Indian army, which he led to Niagara, where the French forces were encamped. By the time he arrived, however, the governor had already made peace with the Iroquois. The disappointed western Indians had to go back home with no booty or prisoners. That made it much harder for Perrot when the new governor, Brisay de Denonville, asked him the following year to again convince his Illinois, Winnebago, Fox, and

Ojibwa friends to go to war against the Seneca.

The fur trade had been very good that year, and Perrot had collected 40,000 livres worth of pelts – a fortune. Before setting off with his army of Indians, he had stored his furs at the Jesuit mission of St. François-Xavier in Green Bay. When he returned at the end of the summer, after laying waste to five Seneca villages, all that was left of the mission were blackened ruins. A fire had destroyed everything. Once again, Nicolas Perrot was a ruined man.

Undaunted, he went back to Quebec to obtain trade goods for the next season, explaining that he was unable to pay his creditors because he had been busy serving his country. This time he returned to the Pays d'en Haut with the title and powers of commander in chief of Green Bay and the surrounding region.

Perrot continued to act as a mediator between the French and the Iroquois. He was known and respected by all the peoples of the Pays d'en Haut and was also appreciated by the authorities in Quebec. At the signing of the Great Peace in Montreal in 1701, he served as an interpreter for the distant tribes.

Hounded by his numerous creditors, he made the mistake of taking some of the powerful Montreal traders to court. He not only lost, but was also sentenced to pay costs. The administrators, from whom he had claimed back wages and repayment of advances he had made to the king's soldiers, managed to get him a small pension so he could survive.

In 1710 Perrot was made captain of La Côte de Bécancour and commander of the local militia. He died on 13 August 1717, totally impoverished. He had started writing his memoirs but did not have enough paper to finish them.

LIBERTINES AND DEBAUCHEES

The coureurs des bois made their own law in the Pays d'en Haut. They had no respect for authority and would even threaten the governor's and king's emissaries.

The Indian girls were so well got up that, in the eyes of the coureurs des bois, they looked like nymphs.

It must be admitted that when they returned from the Pays d'en Haut, some coureurs des bois presented a very unedifying spectacle. They flaunted their Indian garb and tattoos just for the pleasure of provoking others and squandered their money on women, alcohol, and gambling. They took themselves for aristocrats, while behaving like raucous and carousing savages. Some people said they exemplified the worst of both worlds. Like the aristocrats, they refused to work the land or to do any manual labour; they assumed the right to hunt, carried weapons, and were not afraid to speak their minds.

But their greatest crime was to thumb their noses at authority. From their behaviour, it was clear that there was no king, nor even God, where they came from; they were free men who didn't have to answer to anyone. They had broken with the established order and hierarchy, transgressing all laws and taboos.

Governor Frontenac, who was no angel himself, angrily compared the coureurs des bois to the bandits of Naples and the buccaneers of Santo Domingo. Marie de l'Incarnation, head of the Ursulines convent in Quebec, complained that it was "easier to turn Frenchmen into savages than to achieve the reverse." According to the Jesuit historian François-Xavier de Charlevoix, who wrote *Histoire et description générale de la Nouvelle-France* after visiting the St. Lawrence Valley, Great Lakes, and Mississippi, these young men were good for nothing and incapable of the least restraint. Intendant Champigny felt that these delinquents could only lead to the destruction of the country.

The civil and religious authorities seemed obsessed with the coureurs des bois, as if they were bad thoughts that wouldn't go away. In letters to their superiors, the colonial administrators described them as unreliable, improvident, irresponsible, lawless, depraved, and unfit for civilized society, calling them deserters and men of no faith, who were seduced by a life of wandering, easy gain, and licentiousness. The woods were considered a place of perdition, where the young men risked losing not only their lives, but also their souls. This boundless, uncontrollable country could only be evil.

By remaining unmarried, the coureurs des bois were said to lower the birth rate. Apart from not helping to cultivate the land and colonize New France, through their behaviour they compromised the conversion of the Indians. For those who dreamed of establishing a community founded on religion, order, and authority – that is, on European values – they represented an obstacle and a mortal danger. But, in truth, what the authorities could not tolerate was that the coureurs des bois were the first to exploit the riches of the new land for themselves.

Many coureurs des bois took Indian wives, marrying them in the country manner even though they already had wives back home.

Trade silver, which was very popular with Indian women, was crafted by local silversmiths, such as Pierre Huguet dit Latour and Ignace Duval of Montreal.

If any attempts were made to arrest the coureurs des bois, they simply slipped away into the forest. The vast wilderness gave them a feeling of freedom and impunity. In 1700 Governor Callière sent Henri de Tonti to the Pays d'en Haut to lure them back with a promise of clemency, an offer that most refused. For every dozen or so coureurs des bois who agreed to return, no doubt tired and homesick, at least another eighty went farther into Indian country, across the highlands, and toward the Wisconsin and Mississippi Rivers.

The citizens did not always share the authorities' apparent contempt for the coureurs des bois. On the contrary, the coureurs were admired and envied by the young men of the colony, who feared that a man who had not done his time in the fur country would be seen as cowardly and lazy. The illegal fur trade was said to occupy the most vigorous part of the population. Almost every family had a son in the woods, whom they protected and for whom they prayed each evening.

The young men's participation in the illegal fur trade did not constitute a loss for the colony. They may not have been cultivating the land but nevertheless made a significant contribution to the economic survival of the colony, as they alone ensured French sovereignty over the areas they travelled. Year after year, paddling the rivers and establishing and maintaining alliances with the Indians, they extended the frontiers of France's North American empire.

The coureurs des bois lived their adventurous lives, paying no heed to what was said about them. Indeed, the criticisms levelled against them reveal more about the speakers than about those who were criticized. There seems to be an undercurrent of envy running through the reproaches, a great deal of hypocrisy, and deep contradictions. Those who combatted the illegal fur trade were involved in the trade themselves. While loudly condemning the coureurs des bois, the governor, the intendant, and the commanders of the outposts supported and protected them and invested in their ventures.

Many Indian families wanted one of their daughters to marry a coureur des bois in order to establish ties with the whites.

Soldiers and men working for the fur trading companies frequently deserted and became coureurs des bois. Even the missionaries dabbled in the fur trade. In 1703, under the pretext of supplying their missions, the Jesuits shipped sixteen thousand livres worth of trade goods to the Pays d'en Haut.

The colony could not do without these men – for its defence if for nothing else. It needed these renegades, whom it regarded with both scorn and fascination. Having long prevented the Hudson's Bay Company from moving inland and having kept the Dutch and Anglo-Americans from advancing from the Atlantic seaboard, the coureurs des bois had enormous political clout. Libertines and debauchees they may have been, but they definitely did France more good than harm.

Many of the coureurs des bois gave up the wandering life by the age of thirty or thirty-five. Some had amassed enough money from the fur trade to settle down and make a good life in the colony. Others completely adopted the Indians' ways and customs, choosing to remain part of their world forever.

François Gros Louis,
posing here with his rifle
and his steel traps,
spent his lifetime trapping in
the northern wilderness.

Part Two

ODYSSEY TO THE PAYS D'EN HAUT

He hadn't noticed the landscape change, nor the time pass. Suddenly, he realized that the current had lessened, that the sky had darkened, and that the shoreline, at times low and covered with rushes, was now bare and rocky and unattractive. The river was rushing between towering cliffs.

Apparently, such an experience was not uncommon. His father and his uncles, who no longer travelled, had often spoken of these moments. "There are times when you're simply not there, you don't notice anything, and suddenly the countryside has changed."

Often, this was because the trip was so monotonous. One was plunged into thought by the sheer dreariness of the endlessly repeated movements, unaware of the time that had passed.

They always left early in the morning, at first light. The air was soft and fresh. The trees had started to bud. All day long they would travel up the river, the easy-going, gentle Ottawa River, repeating the same movements without ever stopping. Like automatons, they would dip their paddles rhythmically into the shimmering water. Occasionally, time stood still, became fixed, frozen, immutable. Time needed to be broken

up, marked with bumps and landmarks. The men would sing to grind down the hours, shrink them, and help to make them pass – *À la claire fontaine ... En roulant ma boule ...* or *C'est l'aviron nous qui mène.* They would sing these paddling songs for hours on end.

Every two hours, they would stop for a pipe break, often without beaching the canoe to avoid damaging the bottom on the stony shores. They would simply pull out of the current, drifting while smoking. The tobacco would inflame their spirits, heat up their veins. It felt good. And while they smoked, the older ones would speak of their amorous conquests, the Indian women they had seduced, those they hoped to see on Lake Nipissing, or on the French River, or on arrival at Michilimackinac.

Sometimes, nature disrupted the boredom by putting in their way something to charm or move them. They saw many wild animals, mothers with their young. And they were always happy when they arrived at a waterfall or rapids. At first, they would hear a murmur, the current would slow down, a bit of foam would catch on the sides of the canoe. Sometimes, they would see crosses erected on the banks, just

Cree women sported a distinctive tattoo consisting of three lines running from lip to chin.

65

below the rapids, and those who had come this way before would stop and remove their hats. It was time to portage the canoe. And this is how it would be until they reached Lake Nipissing in two days unless they remained stuck in the gorge they had just entered that day.

The Ottawa River is called *La Creuse* a little beyond Culbute Portage. Was it because the cliffs seemed to strangle the sky and absorb all the light that the men fell silent? You could hear only the rhythmic dip of their paddle strokes hitting the water and their ragged breath amplified by the walls of pink granite, which were hung with dark bunches of cedar, mountain laurel in bloom, a few ferns. Seated in the middle of the canoe, he couldn't see the bow or the stern very well. He thought about how easy it would be for the Indians to set up an ambush at this spot, how they could drop large stones from the top of the cliffs that would knock out the paddlers and smash their canoes, how they would all be carried away by the current.

The first brigades to come up in the spring on their way to the Pays d'en Haut were always at risk. These gorges were dangerous, almost as much so as the portages. The men, heavily

*After a twelve- to fourteen-hour day
of paddling and portaging, voyageurs had to
tend to the canoe, cook their meal,
and prepare their shelter for the night.*

loaded, were often short of breath. The Indians could crop up virtually anywhere. The men, even the more experienced ones, were well aware of the danger. No one spoke; everyone was hard at work, pulling together. He enjoyed these moments of silence best, even more than when they all sang together.

He looked at the calm waters of Allumette Lake. He was impatient. He thought of the trip that lay ahead. He hungered for that day. Soon, he too would travel farther north; he would go to where the waters divide and would joyfully receive his second baptism. One day he too would feel the spray from those northern waters. Between Montreal and Mattawa, where they would arrive in two days, there remained about five hundred kilometres, twenty portages.

The old-timers said that the easy part was behind them. It's true that between the falls and the rapids, the Ottawa River is well behaved. But, they said, referring to the difficult Grand Calumet Portage they had walked two days earlier – more than two thousands steps – why, that was nothing. Twice he had carried two bundles totalling eighty kilograms each times. He was proud of himself. He pretended not to be impressed by their stories. He wanted to be like the Indians, who his father had told him never showed their emotions.

He was tempted to tell the older ones that one day he too would be like them. He understood that a voyageur is never afraid, that he has always

seen something bigger. You had to take life one day at a time.

And then the wall-like cliffs opened up. And the canoes entered Allumette Lake one behind the other. There was a small sandbank to the right, just at the entrance. And that is where it happened.

Still silent, the men carefully pulled their canoes up onto the sand. The older ones always treated their canoes with great gentleness, constantly pampering and caressing them as though they were women.

Then the older ones – the steersmen and the bowsmen – had the young ones go down on their knees, those who were on their first journey to the Pays d'en Haut. They had fashioned birchbark containers that they filled with water. And they baptized the young ones. Then they sprinkled them with cedar boughs that they had dipped into the river.

And he received this water joyfully, seriously. His first baptism, upon his birth seventeen years ago, had heralded his entrance into the Christian world. Today's ceremony announced his leave-taking of his old life, possibly forever. He was throwing caution to the winds. And that explained the seriousness of the men, even if this ceremony was more like a farce or religious travesty. They were entering

Indian women liked the comfort of European textiles.

a new world. The landscape had changed again, and so had he. His soul had changed. He had become a voyageur.

And then the old-timers gave each of them a swig of rum and a pipeful of tobacco. It tasted good. The weather was mild. That afternoon, they crossed the lake. On the other side, they would stop over with the Indians. There would be girls.

The men repaired the canoes. They spoke of what lay ahead of them. And when one of them recalled how he had gone up the Mattawa River – fifty kilometres long – in two short days, another one said that he had done it in one day, in the springtime, and that the river was in flood and so rough that they hadn't even stopped to eat or smoke a pipe. So the first one recounted how he had crossed Lake Nipissing at night, with the wind against him, and luckily there had been a moon that night.

Knowing that the young ones were listening, they related how the French River, which they would go down in a few days, was haunted, and how sometimes you could see the sharp rocks that were sticking up from the bottom move. And from time to time, they would stop, as if to say, "Don't worry. We know the way."

At the mouth of the French River, they reached the inland sea, the Great Lakes. There was a place there called La Prairie because of the rushes. It had been Huron country before the Huron were decimated by the Iroquois. If everything went well, they would stop there for a couple of days. Before launching into the Great Lakes, they would tend to their canoes. Those who had beards would shave. They would unpack and dry out the goods and provisions, and sleep in the grass under the canoes. The rest of the trip would unfold to a different beat, in a different setting.

He was anxious to be on the way, to see everything. He thought of his mother, who worried about him, and of his two young brothers, who had enviously watched him leave. He felt strong. He felt that nothing could happen to him. He had finally become a voyageur, a real one.

Chapter 4

THE PORK EATERS

There are two types of coureurs des bois. The first go to the source of the beaver in the Savage nations of the Assiniboin, Sioux, Miami, Illinois, and so on; these ones can make the journey only every two or three years. The second type, who are not so numerous, go only to meet the Savages and the French-men who descend to Long Sault, Petite Nation, and sometimes Michilimackinac, so as to ensure that only they profit from their peltries, for which they bring them merchandise, most often nothing but alcohol with which they get them drunk and ruin them; these ones can make the journey in about five or six months or even less.

For the coureur des bois, an Indian wife was a valuable helpmate and a key to his survival in a hostile land.

The northern part of the continent contains over two million lakes, including the Great Lakes, the largest fresh surface-water system on Earth.

THE VOYAGEURS

Any man who would lead
the voyageurs
had to be one of them;
he had to be able to
handle a canoe and had to
possess their daring,
endurance, and panache.

Always on the move, voyageurs had few possessions; their most valuable assets were their courage, strength, and good judgment.

In instituting the leave system in 1681, the authorities of New France offered an amnesty to the coureurs des bois involved in the illegal fur trade. This was their chance to return to the colony without fear of fine or imprisonment. While many preferred to stay with the Indians, some did decide to go back and sign on with a Montreal outfitter who had an official trading licence. Thus was born the first typically North American profession: voyageur.

While the coureur des bois was a renegade and an outlaw, the voyageur would be a professional. He had signed (usually with an *X*) a legally binding contract in which he agreed to go to the Pays d'en Haut on behalf of a trader. He would set off in the spring in a canoe laden with trade goods and supplies for the distant trading posts and return either that fall or the following fall with bales of furs.

These tireless workers put in long, hard hours every day of the week, in good weather and bad. Gone was the carefree life of a coureur des bois. The voyageurs had specific responsibilities and a firm date on which they were expected to arrive at Michilimackinac or Grand Portage.

The profession gradually became organized and structured, with a strict hierarchy. Each brigade of canoes was overseen by a gentleman, or *bourgeois* as he was called by his men. He was in charge of the clerks, who kept the ledgers in the trading posts; the guides and interpreters; the voyageurs, who sometimes held shares in the company; and the canoemen. Each had his own job, with its associated pay.

A voyageur was typically fairly small, agile, and inured to cold, hunger, backbreaking work, and boredom. Some were able to paddle for almost twenty-four hours straight and to cover over a hundred kilometres a day.

Although they were often wet and usually slept in the open air, the men were rarely ill. Leaving early each spring, they avoided the epidemics that broke out following the arrival of the ships from France.

Their diet, too, was healthy, though monotonous, consisting primarily of wheat or buckwheat flour, salt pork, dried peas, small game, fish, and berries. They did a little hunting if the opportunity presented itself but did not have time for stalking or lying in wait for game. They would shoot birds, rabbits, and the occasional beaver and do a little fishing. They would also gather eggs on the way out in the spring and berries on the way back in the fall. They might barter for food with the Indians. If worse came to worse, they would eat rock tripe, a type of lichen that was fairly nourishing when boiled into a soup, though it was gluey and unappetizing and tended to act as a purgative.

The voyageurs did not wear clothing made of animal hides. Wet leather becomes very heavy and shrinks and stiffens as it dries. And the voyageurs spent much of their day wet – from sweat and rain, but also from

The seated man is a "pork eater," someone who is just starting out as a voyageur, as can be seen from his cloth trousers. His companion, on the other hand, is wearing the typical garb of the veteran: printed cotton shirt with frills and cuffs, colourful sash, leggings, embroidered moccasins, and a kerchief to keep sweat from running into his eyes while he paddles.

towing the canoe through the rapids, unloading it, carrying it to shore, or putting it in the water. They thus preferred quick-drying fabrics such as cotton, linen, and wool.

Each voyageur had one or two long-sleeved linen or cotton shirts; a pair of leggings to protect him from insects, branches, and brambles; a wool tuque, usually red; moccasins; a worsted sash; and a *capot*, or hooded cape, which he would wrap around himself on chilly nights. He also carried a watertight powder horn and, of course, his plaster or clay pipe and tobacco pouch. Almost all the voyageurs wore their hair long and adopted the Indians' practice of smearing their arms, faces, and necks with bear grease to ward off the ravenous swarms of insects.

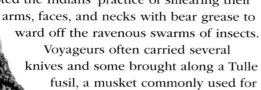

Powder horn with a shoulder strap woven with the same arrowhead motif as the typical voyageur sash.

Voyageurs often carried several knives and some brought along a Tulle fusil, a musket commonly used for hunting or militia duty. Each had his own paddle, usually made of strong, flexible wood such as northern white cedar or basswood. Since basswood is susceptible to rot and worm damage, it was given a good coat of varnish or paint. Each man marked his paddle with his colours or number. If there was an accident and a voyageur drowned, his paddle could be recovered and stuck in the shore along with a small wooden cross to mark where he had died. Drowning was not the only hazard faced by the voyageurs. On the arduous portages, they could easily suffer a heart attack, stroke, hernia, or serious back injury.

The voyageurs generally maintained a cadence of forty paddle strokes a minute, achieving an average speed of six to ten kilometres per hour. To set the pace, they sang repetitive songs, occasionally varying the words. A good singer who could motivate his fellow paddlers would receive extra pay. Every couple of hours they would stop for a short rest, called a "pipe" since they would all take this opportunity to smoke.

Though most voyageurs were illiterate, they had a facility with words. Their speech was often picturesque, extravagant, and boastful. They would spin tales about strong, brave, free men and their canoes, horses, dogs, and women. Sometimes they spoke of their families back home, other voyageurs they had known, and the ever-present danger of their lives. They still retained some vague religious feelings, which would resurface when they were in danger, taking the form of heartfelt vows in return for their safety.

The people in the colony would scoff that voyageurs had never seen small wolves. The rapids they rode were always the fastest and highest, the storms the worst ever experienced, and they could paddle twenty hours a day for ten days straight.

A voyageur could earn 300, 500, or even 1,000 livres a year – three times as much as a surgeon and ten times as much as a soldier. They were paid, in beaver pelts, upon their return. They were also fed and sometimes clothed by the outfitter for whom they worked.

Priding themselves on their stamina and endurance, the voyageurs never complained openly about the harsh working conditions. As true spiritual sons of the coureurs des bois, they were fiercely individualistic. Over time, however, a strong solidarity developed among the voyageurs. In 1794, when Joseph Léveillé was sentenced to the pillory for not fulfilling his contract, all the voyageurs in Montreal went on strike until he was pardoned.

The voyageurs formed a society distinct from that of the coureurs des bois, the *bourgeois*, their families back in the St. Lawrence Valley, and the Aboriginal peoples they encountered inland. They were part of a unique, frontier culture forged by the meeting and melding of radically different ways of life.

A drinking cup attached to a cord with a floater on the end, which the voyageur would slip under his sash along with his tobacco pouch and sometimes a scalping knife.

Jean-Baptiste Charbonneau's Story

As a runner for the Hudson's Bay Company, he travelled throughout the Pays d'en Haut, carrying mail between the trading posts.

Almost all voyageurs wore their hair long, like the Indians, to protect their necks from mosquitoes.

Jean-Baptiste Charbonneau was a man of many trades: stonemason, soldier, farmer, guide, interpreter, and buffalo hunter. During the fierce war between the North West Company and the Hudson's Bay Company (HBC), he served as a runner for the HBC, endlessly travelling between trading posts, carrying messages, orders, parcels, and personal letters, often at the risk of his life. Though he was a rather scrawny young fellow living and working in a very violent world, he got along just fine.

He was born into a farming family in Boucherville on Christmas Day 1795. His ten brothers and sisters all remained on the land. Jean-Baptiste, however, apprenticed to a Montreal stonemason at the age of twelve, but found the work too boring for his adventurous spirit.

In 1812, when the Americans tried to invade Canada, he traded in his trowel for a rifle and volunteered for the detachment holding down Fort Chambly, on the Richelieu River. He then took part in the legendary Battle of Chateauguay, in which 300 Canadian soldiers routed the 7,000-strong American army, thus helping to keep Canada for the British Crown.

Three years later, at age nineteen, Jean-Baptiste Charbonneau hired on with the Hudson's Bay Company and left for the Pays d'en Haut. He was part of the famous brigade of canoemen and voyageurs led by Colin Robertson, whom Lord Selkirk, head of the HBC, had charged with establishing fur trading posts beyond

The crooked knives used by the voyageurs had different shapes depending on the materials available.

Lake Athabaska in order to break the almost exclusive monopoly of the North West Company.

Lord Selkirk also had a plan to establish a Scottish colony in the Red River Valley, which triggered outright war between the fur trading companies and angered the local Métis. Charbonneau arrived at the height of this conflict.

Initially stationed at Fort Douglas, at the junction of the Red River and the Assiniboine, Charbonneau was sent to Lake Winnipeg to build trading posts. He started off with one Métis and two Canadians but halfway there his travelling companions left him – with no weapon, food, or shelter – while they visited an Indian encampment a day away by canoe. The young man waited in vain for their return; they were never seen again. Charbonneau was finally picked up by a Hudson's Bay Company canoe seven days later.

From Lake Winnipeg, he continued on alone to York Factory, on Hudson Bay. Impressed with his skills and resourcefulness, the HBC officers made him a runner. He was based at Fort Île à la Crosse, midway between Lake Winnipeg and Great Slave Lake and between Hudson Bay and the Rocky Mountains, almost at the geometric centre of the immense wilderness known as the Northwest Territories.

Winter and summer alike, Charbonneau carried from one trading post to another packages and letters, which most of the recipients were unable to read. He also delivered verbal messages such as "Your father is dead," "Your older sister is getting married," or "Fort Qu'Appelle has burned down."

He would inform HBC officers of any of the rival company's activities he had heard about or been able to observe first hand. Messengers who carried mail were often intercepted, relieved of the papers and letters they were delivering, and savagely beaten. To keep important information from falling into the hands of the enemy, Charbonneau would therefore memorize certain messages.

The voyageur's cup was often made from the hollowed-out knot of a tree branch.

One day on his return to Île à la Crosse, he found the fort occupied by ruffians working for the North West Company. They took him prisoner and deported him, along with all the clerks and traders in the fort, leaving them stranded on an island in the middle of a lake some 150 kilometres away.

With a few axes and some fishing line, they managed to survive. Two weeks later, a truce was concluded between the two fur companies, and canoes were sent to pick them up. Charbonneau resumed his messenger duties.

He lived at Fort Île à la Crosse until 1830 and regularly travelled around Lake Athabaska and Great Slave Lake, sometimes ranging as far as the Mackenzie River.

At age thirty-five, Charbonneau moved south to Fort Garry, on the Red River, where many voyageurs who had been too long gone to return to the St. Lawrence Valley ended their days. He found a piece of land near the St. Boniface mission and started building

himself a farm, as his father had done in the St. Lawrence Valley.

Two years later, he went back to his initial trade, working as a stonemason for Monsignor Joseph Provencher, the first bishop of St. Boniface, who was overseeing work on the first stone cathedral in western Canada. However, the sedentary life didn't really agree with the former adventurer, and he had become rather short tempered. One day he climbed down from his scaffolding and challenged the bishop to a fight. He had never had a boss on his back before and didn't ever intend to.

Charbonneau shared his Métis friends' dislike of farming and so, like many retired voyageurs, became a buffalo hunter. He moved a little farther south, to Minnesota, where he lived until 1860, never staying long in the same place. He made friends with

Many Indian women were attracted to white men. Charbonneau's close ties with the Sioux also extended to the women.

the powerful Sioux, whose lifestyle he had practically adopted.

In 1862 he watched helplessly as the Sioux massacred a German settlement at Redwood on the St. Peter's River. He was taken prisoner and led away to the Indians' encampment at Lac qui Parle, at the head of the Red River. Fortunately, the grand chief recognized him and spared his life.

Charbonneau subsequently returned to St. Boniface, where he had not set foot for twenty-two years. He was not able to hunt any more; after repeated bouts of snow blindness, he could no longer see.

He died peacefully in 1883 at the age of eighty-eight.

THE VOYAGEUR'S WHITE WIFE

Having to take care
of all the chores during
her husband's absence
made the voyageur's wife
very independent.

*Women in the New World
wore clothes modelled
on the latest French fashions.*

A girl who married a voyageur had to have a strong character and an ability to endure solitude and to turn a deaf ear to gossip. She certainly knew what type of man she was taking up with. The parish priest and her parents would have drummed into her the fact that her husband was no angel. She would often have to take care of the house, garden, poultry, and livestock on her own. She would have to bake bread, smoke hams, salt pork, and bring in the hay. She would be alone during pregnancy and labour; giving birth would be painful and dangerous. She would have no news of her husband for months or even years. During this time, he would be exposed to temptations he might not be able to resist. She had been told that too: Everyone said that Indian women would sleep with any man who wanted them. The white wife of a voyageur thus had to be uncommonly strong. In her own way, she too was an adventurer.

Professional voyageurs married just like other young men their age who had chosen to remain on the farm – slightly before the age of twenty-two on average. And they had just as many children with their wives, not counting the offspring many of them had with Indian women in the fur country. The *engagés*, those men hired to paddle and portage the canoes, were no doubt less resourceful and daring than the voyageurs and usually married a little later and had fewer children.

Because the lifestyle they chose required a certain independence of spirit, voyageurs were likely more determined than others and more sure of what they wanted at a younger age. Their contacts with Indian women may also have given them an earlier and easier experience with the

*An iron dating from
the late eighteenth century.*

opposite sex. If they married in the colony, it was because they eventually intended to settle down. Once they had made their fortune, they would buy a good plot of land, build a large house, and raise a family. That was the hope of a girl who became engaged to a voyageur. She was marrying a capable man who had plans for a good life.

Since her husband was often absent, all the work that was normally shared between a husband and wife would be her responsibility alone. Entrusted with duties and rights she would not normally have had if her husband had been home, she would become much more self-reliant and independent.

According to the Custom of Paris, the legal system governing New France, a woman was considered legally incompetent. For instance, she had no power to manage her own inheritance, sign a contract, borrow money, or make a will. Theoretically the man was the uncontested head of the family.

If a voyageur was going to be away for a long time, he needed to sign a notarized power of attorney authorizing his wife to act in his stead, to make a will in his name, to dispose of the family assets. On his return, he found a woman who was more emancipated and competent in

*A wooden washtub
and washboard.*

Carved from a hollowed-out block of wood, women's wooden shoes existed in a variety of shapes.

these matters than was a farmer's wife.

In the early eighteenth century, over 80 per cent of the women who married voyageurs lived in Pointe Claire or in parishes on the eastern part of the Island of Montreal, where young men who wanted to leave the colony tended to live.

It was a rough life, and hygiene and cleanliness were rather rudimentary. Although Pehr Kalm, the Swedish naturalist who visited Canada in the mid-eighteenth century, was absolutely charmed by the beauty and stylishness of the Canadian women, whom he found much more free-spoken than the American colonists' wives he had met, he was appalled at the dirt and disorder he witnessed in rural homes.

Nevertheless, the women of New France were apparently in better health than those in France; they were more likely to survive their first pregnancies, less likely to die in childbirth, and lived longer. The colony occasionally experienced food shortages as a result of bad harvests but never great famines as in Europe since hunting and fishing could always be relied on to supplement their diet.

Being accustomed to solitude and hard work, a voyageur's wife was relatively well equipped to survive on her own if something happened to her husband. The wives of traders who went off to the woods would manage the business in their absence. Louis Fornel, a bourgeois trader in Quebec, delegated to his wife, Marie-Anne, née Barbel, full authority over his affairs when he left for the Labrador coast. On the death of her husband in 1745, Marie-Anne took over his business and built it up even further. She enlarged and diversified his trading network and obtained a fur trading licence. She put together brigades of voyageurs, outfitted canoes, and continued to exploit her husband's concessions on the north shore of the St. Lawrence. However, the British Conquest ruined her financially; the houses she owned in lower-town Quebec were destroyed in the shelling. Ever resourceful, she managed

The voyageur's wife dressed very simply: a modest headdress, grey homespun mantle, rather short skirt (for reasons of economy as much as for style), knitted stockings, and wooden shoes. A silver cross was her only adornment. This mother is helping her toddler to walk by holding him up by two straps sewn under the sleeves of his dress, a garment that he would wear until about the age of seven.

to rebuild a number of them before she died in 1777 at the age of eighty-nine.

Many of the voyageurs retired young. Some stopped going off to the woods by the age of thirty, as soon as they had acquired a certain self-sufficiency and had saved enough to buy a good piece of land or to establish a trading and outfitting business. But few forgot the Pays d'en Haut. Many of them returned year after year, despite their promises, their children at home, and their wife's remonstrations.

In the wilderness, the voyageur would think about his wife waiting back home. He would speak of her to his fellow voyageurs. She was his comfort, warmth, and tenderness, his purpose and his dream.

Later on, when the voyageurs' wives accompanied them to the Pays d'en Haut, they would bring a new order, a form of authority that inevitably led to changes – and to the end of the voyageur's free and unfettered way of life.

75

THE VOYAGEUR'S COUNTRY WIFE

Indian women were more able than the men to establish ties with the newcomers.

It was considered desirable for an Indian woman to have a white lover.

The nature of the voyageur's work kept him constantly on the move. It was thus difficult, not to say almost impossible, for him to enter into relationships with Indian women. He was paddling from dawn till dusk, day in and day out, Sundays included. While he regularly encountered Indian men between Montreal and the head of the Great Lakes, he had few opportunities for contact with the women, unless the canoes were temporarily halted, by bad weather or a serious problem of some sort, near an Indian encampment or they happened to run into a group of nomads. Any chance encounter a voyageur might have with an Indian woman would be brief, though relatively simple and straightforward. If she were interested in having sex with him, no formalities or lengthy preliminaries would be required.

An Iroquois cradleboard, or nagane, *made of wood and painted with a turtle and other typical Iroquois motifs.*

The Indians had no taboo against sexual relations outside of marriage. They felt that sex was a basic human need and one of the most legitimate pleasures of life. With this great sexual freedom, there was little repression, and consequently rape was almost unheard of. The women were generally very free with their bodies. Apparently, Indian women initially felt a certain revulsion at being approached by white men, whose hairy bodies and beards they found ungainly and ugly. However, they soon discovered that these pale foreigners were more attentive

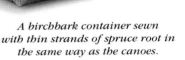

A birchbark container sewn with thin strands of spruce root in the same way as the canoes.

than their own men, paying them compliments and showering them with gifts. While the interpreters and the first coureurs des bois had needed to use their charms to win the Indian women, the voyageurs benefited from their predecessors' reputation as good lovers and were thus welcomed with open arms.

When the voyageurs arrived at their destination, be it the trading post at Michilimackinac, Detroit, Sault Ste. Marie, or Grand Portage, they would stay for a while to rest up, deliver the supplies and trade goods to the person in charge of the post, make any necessary repairs to their canoes, and then load them with furs. It was during such layovers that the voyageurs were able to establish longer liaisons with the Indian women, often lasting several days or weeks.

These romances always took place during the warm summer months. In order to get back to Montreal before winter set in, the voyageurs had to leave the trading posts by mid-August or early September at the latest. The "wives" they had had at the trading post were really only sexual partners. While the women had introduced them to aspects of Indian culture that they otherwise would have had no knowledge of, the couple did not really share domestic duties; they had merely had a good time together.

Some voyageurs would go back to the same Indian woman each summer and spend an enjoyable interlude with her. It was only a matter of time before the voyageur would find his country wife waiting for him with a fair-haired, blue-eyed baby in her arms. The young woman and her children would continue to live with her tribe. The Indians had no concept of illegitimate birth. Although the voyageurs' children constituted a very visible minority within Indian society, they were neither rejected nor adulated; they were treated in exactly the same way as the other children.

It was seen as a good thing for an Indian woman to have a white lover. The Indians were very accepting in this regard. They were curious about other races, and it was much easier for the women than it was for the men to establish fairly satisfactory intimate relationships with them.

An Indian woman might be able to convince her voyageur to stay in the Pays d'en Haut with her. And even if she couldn't, he would come back. Each summer, he would return bearing gifts, pretty clothes, and jewellery, and he and his country wife would resume their idyllic, on-and-off relationship.

Despite being interrupted for varying intervals, many of these relationships were long-lasting, though not necessarily exclusive. The voyageurs often had other wives in other places they visited. And the Indian women could also have more than one husband.

Taking advantage of these free and easy manners, some of the voyageurs acted like sexual predators, which sometimes resulted in serious conflicts. The missionaries tried to curb this freedom by imposing a European morality and lifestyle on the "Savages." Not really

understanding Indian society, they wanted to encourage couples to stay together, doing their best to break up any relationship that was clearly temporary. They tried to teach Indian women to be faithful and submissive to their husbands. Most of all, they tried to stop women from being used in commercial exchanges.

In many tribes, women were offered to the voyageurs as a sign of friendship and hospitality. These gifts were made in accordance with certain conventions whose nuances the white men often failed to grasp. Although they took full advantage of the women offered to them, the Europeans did not really understand their commercial role and tended to consider those who willingly participated in such trades as loose women. In their own communities, however, the women were not looked down on for trading their caresses for gifts or money. They were simply using the white men's desire for them as a source of power – and also as a source of pleasure since there were often not enough Indian men to go around, especially in the warring tribes.

An Indian woman would sometimes travel with her voyageur for several days. However, she would rarely venture far from her home and would never accompany him to his home.

When the canoes arrived in Montreal in the fall, there were always a few voyageurs missing. Some of them were never seen again. Their paddles would be found floating at the foot of the last rapid they had attempted to ride. A cross would be erected on the river bank and the voyageurs would think of their lost comrades and say a prayer for them whenever they passed that spot.

Other voyageurs, however, had simply decided to stay in the back country for a few years – or for the rest of their lives. Pretty and possessive Indian women had gotten hold of them, changing their lives and transforming the itinerant voyageurs into "winterers": North men who lived far removed from white society, almost becoming Indians themselves.

It was customary for an Indian girl who married a voyageur to be fitted out in a "Canadian" outfit. She was also given brooches, earrings, and other silver jewellery, and ribbons to decorate her clothing. It was often observed that voyageurs would willingly go into debt to dress their Indian wives in style.

Marie-Anne Gaboury's Story

On leaving her village for the Pays d'en Haut, she knew that she might never return.

Women in the West endured many hardships, including hunger, and had to make do with the most primitive of dwellings.

Few lives have been as exciting and adventurous as Marie-Anne Gaboury's. Born in Maskinongé on 6 November 1780, she was a hardworking and dutiful daughter who had never left her village until she was twenty-four. The people of the parish probably thought that she would settle gently into spinsterhood and lead a quiet, secluded life in the presbytery, where she had worked for eleven years as a maid. But one day, Jean-Baptiste Lagimodière, who had gone off to the Pays d'en Haut a few years earlier, came back to the village and into Marie-Anne's life. They married in the spring of 1807. Soon after, Jean-Baptiste announced that he was leaving again.

Marie-Anne's biographer, Abbé Georges Dugas, believed that she had known nothing of her husband's plans and did her best to convince him to stay. But Jean-Baptiste was determined. On the advice of the curate and her parents, and from a sense of duty, Marie-Anne decided to accompany him, thus becoming the first white woman in the Pays d'en Haut.

Dugas says that Marie-Anne was worried about being without the comforts of her religion in that barbarous land. She was strongly attached to her faith. Till the end of her life, she kept the scapular and rosary she was wearing on that May morning in Lachine when she climbed into the canoe that would take her to the head of Lake Superior. While one can never know her true motivations, it is possible that she actually wanted to leave behind the small, comfortable world she found too confining. Perhaps one of the reasons she was attracted to Jean-Baptiste was that he offered a possibility of escape and adventure.

The young couple initially lived on the Pembina River, where the Hudson's Bay Company and the rival North West Company had their respective trading posts. That is where their first child, Reine, was born. In the spring, Jean-Baptiste, Marie-Anne, and their baby left for the upper Saskatchewan River Valley, where they would stay for the next four years, living the nomadic life of the Indians in the summer and moving inside Fort des Prairies in the winter. The fort belonged to the Hudson's Bay Company and was an important trading centre and meeting place for numerous Indian bands.

In August 1808, when she was seven months pregnant, they were out hunting on the prairie and her horse bolted after a herd of bison with Marie-Anne hanging on for dear life. A few hours later, she gave birth to her second child, whom they named Laprairie. The blond-haired, blue-eyed infant was an object of wonder and envy to the local Indians. An Assiniboin chief

Not many white women were willing to follow their husbands to the Pays d'en Haut, and then to accompany them on hunting trips undertaken on foot, on horseback, or in a canoe, even when pregnant or nursing.

The swaddled baby was held on the cradleboard by rawhide strips threaded through holes along the sides.

even offered to trade his two best horses for Laprairie. When the young mother refused, he said he would include one of his own children in the bargain. It was only when he saw Marie-Anne's eyes fill with tears that he finally relented.

In the spring of 1811, Jean-Baptiste and Marie-Anne, who was then expecting her fourth child, decided to join the colony that Thomas Douglas Selkirk, the majority shareholder in the Hudson's Bay Company, wanted to establish in the Red River Valley to help his fellow Scotsmen.

However, Lord Selkirk's settling of the area triggered a fierce war between the two fur trading companies. Sure that the colony would hurt their business, the Nor'Westers, with the support of most of the Métis and many Sioux bands, waged a campaign of terror against the settlers in an attempt to drive them out.

Jean-Baptiste volunteered to go to Montreal to ask Lord Selkirk for help. Marie-Anne and her children moved into Fort Douglas, the Hudson's Bay Company fort at the junction of the Red and Assiniboine Rivers, across from Fort Gibraltar. She had no news

of her husband for over a year. He had set off alone, in the middle of winter, taking only his rifle, a hatchet, and a blanket. He travelled almost three thousand kilometres on horseback and on foot, making his way through Nor'Wester-controlled territory at night.

On his way back, he was captured by Indians working for the North West Company and was imprisoned in Fort William. A few weeks later, the inhabitants of Fort Douglas heard that he was dead. At age thirty-four, Marie-Anne found herself a widow with six children. In June the Métis and Sioux who had been prowling around Fort Douglas all winter finally attacked and destroyed the fort, massacring almost everyone in it.

In August Lord Selkirk and a small army of eighty men captured Fort William, freeing Jean-Baptiste, who had not been killed after all. Learning of the destruction of Fort Douglas, Jean-Baptiste believed he had lost his entire family.

Luckily, however, Marie-Anne and her children had taken refuge with a Cree family. They stayed with the Indians that summer and moved into an abandoned cabin near Fort Gibraltar when the weather turned cold. Her husband

was overjoyed to discover her there safe and sound just before Christmas.

For his services to the colony, Jean-Baptiste was given a piece of land on the east bank of the Red River near Fort Douglas. There he built a solid log house, adding onto it several times since Marie-Anne gave birth to five more children, one of whom – Julie, born in 1822 – would become the mother of Louis Riel.

Priests finally arrived in the colony in the summer of 1818. One Sunday in July, they baptized all children under five years of age. As the only Christian woman there, Marie-Anne stood as godmother. For many years, she was called "Godmother" by almost all the children in the Red River colony.

She saw the Red River Métis colony grow, survive famines, floods, and droughts, and develop into a vibrant community. Jean-Baptiste died in 1855. Marie-Anne outlasted her husband by almost twenty years, dying in 1874, at the age of ninety-four, without ever again hearing from her family or seeing the land of her birth.

On the Prairies, some babies slept in spindle cradles, though their mothers often preferred to use the Aboriginal nagane, *or cradleboard.*

THE MONTREAL CANOE

By the mid-seventeenth century,
the birchbark canoe
had to be adapted
to meet the needs of the
expanding fur trade.

*Each evening, the canoe would
be checked for leaks and repaired
if necessary. It then
served as shelter for the night.*

The fur trade territory was constantly expanding, requiring faster and longer transportation of increasingly large loads. While the Indians' small, swift birchbark canoe was perfect for running rapids and navigating the rivers of the Canadian Shield, it was not suited to the open waters of the Great Lakes and the St. Lawrence and Ottawa Rivers. By the mid-seventeenth century, the birchbark canoe had to be adapted to meet these new needs. Thus was born the "Montreal canoe," the product of North American Indian ingenuity and the ambitions of the French fur industry.

Each year, this freight canoe grew longer (reaching ten or twelve metres) and wider (up to two metres across the beam). By the end of the seventeenth century, some Montreal canoes could carry a four-tonne load along with eight to twelve men. The best ones were made by Louis Maître, a boat builder in Trois Rivières, hence the name *canot de Maître*, as they were sometimes called. The canoe was usually painted, decorated, and named for the trader who owned it, or for his wife, or perhaps for the patron saint of his home village. The shell was always made of birchbark, but the structural components were stronger. For instance, ten-centimetre-wide wooden ribs were laid on the bottom of the canoe, making it very solid so that the weight of the merchandise and crew could be evenly distributed.

When the ice broke up in the spring, the canoes would set out from Lachine loaded with twenty or so forty-kilogram bales of provisions and trade goods. Unlike the North men, who spent their lives in the woods, the crews of the Montreal canoes rarely hunted or traded with the Indians and thus had to carry most of their food with them. Along their route, they would occasionally have caches of supplies, which they would arrange for

*Most crew
members carried
several knives;
some brought along
a Tulle fusil and, of course,
a tightly sealed powder horn.*

the Indians to maintain, though they could never be sure that this would be done.

It took five or six weeks to reach Michilimackinac, Detroit, Grand Portage, or the citadel of Fort William at the mouth of the Kaministiquia River, where it flows into Lake Superior. This was as far as the Montreal canoes would go.

These freight canoes were too wide and heavy to be used on the shallow, rocky rivers rushing down to the Great Lakes from the high country. Because of the many portages required, the North men used a smaller craft, known as the *canot du nord*, or North canoe, which could carry only a tonne and a half of merchandise but could go wherever there was thirty centimetres of water. The North canoe could be portaged by one man, whereas the Montreal canoe weighed 275 to 350 kilograms when wet and had to be carried by at least four men. To prevent it from

*The canoes were
decorated and given
a name, often that
of the patron saint of the
outfitter's home village.*

being damaged or scraped on the rocky shore, it also had to be unloaded and turned over before being taken out of the water.

Each voyageur in the Montreal canoe was allowed to bring only eighteen kilograms of personal belongings. On the return trip, the furs were formed into compact bales by means of a screw or lever press, carefully wrapped in waxed canvas, and covered with an oilcloth tarp. Gunpowder and valuable items were placed in small, waterproof barrels. There was also a cask of rum or brandy, which the *bourgeois* would dole out in the evening or when the crew had run a rapid or completed a particularly dangerous crossing.

The Montreal canoe also carried a sail for use on the Great Lakes, along with halyards and a mast that would be attached to the gunwale when not in use. Other essential items included setting poles, towing lines, a sponge for bailing, a kettle, a frying pan, one or two pots, a hatchet, a canoe awl, about five kilograms of pine or spruce gum, spare pieces of birchbark, and several bundles of *watape*.

It took a good following wind to sail a Montreal canoe. Since a canoe has no keel, it tends to slip sideways in a crosswind. Very long, powerful waves would sometimes form on the Great Lakes. Whether they came from the bow or the stern, each wave had to be taken at an angle so that the canoe would cut across it diagonally. If it wasn't supported by water along its entire length, the canoe would break apart and sink.

Even in midsummer, the waters of Lake Superior barely reach ten degrees Celsius. Warm winds from the Prairies often create a thick fog that suddenly descends on the lake in the middle of the day, making navigation

It took four men to portage a Montreal canoe.

extremely dangerous. The north shore is lined with rocky cliffs rising straight out of the water. Approaching them in poor visibility was pure folly; the canoes had to land before the fog set in.

The canoes would thus get under way long before dawn and stop when the wind came up in the early afternoon. They would also often travel at night, when there was less wind on the Great Lakes. The voyageurs called the wind *La Vieille*, the Old Woman. They would talk to her: "Okay, *La Vieille*, we understand. Now go back to sleep; we've had enough of you."

They feared the Old Woman. On the Great Lakes, she would whip up terrible storms, with powerful waves that would roll from one end of Lake Superior to the other, a distance of over six hundred kilometres.

So, whenever possible, the crews avoided skirting the shore, but not just because of the rocks; they couldn't afford to waste time following the indentations of the shoreline. At Thunder Bay, Michipicoten, or Green Bay, for instance, or on Lake Winnipeg, rather than entering the bay, they would cut across its mouth. Nobody liked these dangerous *traverses*, or crossings. The men would pray, commend their souls to God, and make vows in return for their safety.

There was a great esprit de corps aboard the Montreal canoes. With their twelve, fourteen, or even sixteen men, the crews were small societies unto themselves, with a "population" that often outnumbered that of the trading posts they visited. It was largely aboard the Montreal canoes that the mentality and culture of the Pays d'en Haut first took shape.

THE CREW MEMBERS

There was a strict hierarchy
aboard the Montreal canoe.
The men had to get
along and work together like
a well-oiled machine.

*Everyone had specific duties
to perform when
the canoes landed for the night.*

*In addition to his weapons and perhaps
a change of clothing, the voyageur often carried a covered pot.*

If a young man wanted to become a voyageur, it was best that he not be too tall, ideally not more than 1.65 metres. He could not be too heavily built either. What was needed was strength and endurance – and a good dose of courage. A cheerful temperament didn't hurt either. The Montreal outfitters who put together the canoe brigades in the spring had to be able to size up their crews – both physically and psychologically. The men would have to live together day and night for months at a time. They had to be able to get along, to work together like a well-oiled machine. The youngest ones were not quite twenty years of age, the oldest around thirty-five.

There was a strict hierarchy aboard the Montreal canoe. First there were the two "ends" – the steersman and bowsman. Under them were six, eight, or ten paddlers, known as middlemen. The ends were better paid than the middlemen since they had more responsibility. Guides and interpreters were also well paid. Some crew members had more than one job and thus earned additional pay.

The man responsible for maintaining the canoes – sewing on birchbark patches and caulking the seams – also received a good wage. A number of other duties such as preparing meals, leading the canoe songs, and doing a bit of hunting to supplement the meagre rations enabled the men to earn a little extra money.

In 1754 the authorities decreed that, for a three-month trip, each end would receive 250 livres and each middle-man 200 livres – plus about seventy kilograms of provisions per person. The voyageurs were paid on their return, sometimes in cash but more often in furs.

The normal workday was twelve to fourteen hours of paddling and portaging, after which the men had to tend to the canoe and prepare the meal and shelter for the night. They always left before daylight. Near the summer solstice this meant getting under way by three o'clock in the morning. The men would break camp and load the canoe. When the sun came up, they were already on the water.

The hardest part wasn't the paddling. It was the forced immobility, a real torture for the new recruits. Once they were seated in the canoe, they could move only their arms wielding the paddles. To set the

pace, they would sing, usually call-and-response songs or endless, hypnotic rounds. The man in charge of the repertory had to choose a song suited to the desired canoe speed. There were slow chants for a heavily laden canoe, paddling songs for the swifter North canoe, songs for a canoe running empty. All the men knew them by heart.

In the evening, they would carry the canoe to shore, where they would inspect it and caulk any leaks. They would set the pot on the fire. The men slept under the upturned canoe, sometimes with an oilskin thrown over it to protect them from the rain and dew, though not from the mosquitoes, which many considered the worst torment of all.

Going upstream required strength and endurance; travelling downstream called for daring and skill. The bowsman and steersman always had a lot to do, but their most important task was to find and guide the canoe into the safest channel through the rapids.

Another utensil frequently taken along on the voyage: a long-handled frying pan, which enabled the user to keep a comfortable distance from the campfire.

The middlemen provided the power and speed. Going downstream, the canoe had to move as fast as, or a little faster than, the current. Only then could it be properly controlled. If the canoe went too slow, it would be at the mercy of the current; if it went too fast, it was hard to steer.

Going upstream, if the rapids were not too steep, the men would propel the canoe up them using iron-tipped setting poles four or five metres long. If the current was too strong, they would have to completely or partially unload the goods and provisions, then track the canoe, that is tow it with a line, preferably from shore, though often they had to wade through the frigid, waist-high water. The steersman would stay in the canoe to guide it.

The middlemen also had to portage the goods. They would generally use a tumpline, a leather strap that went across the forehead and supported the initial bundle, or *pièce*, they hoisted onto their backs. To this would be added a second or third bundle. Some men were even known to carry four bundles – over 150 kilograms – up the rough, steep trails. When they were loaded up, the men would stagger off, stooping under the weight. At long portages, such as the gruelling Grand Portage with its fourteen kilometres of precipitous trails, they would pause every six or seven hundred metres.

When the men were heavily loaded, the slightest fall could result in broken bones or in a sprained ankle, hernia, or strained back. The portages were perilous for other reasons too. The trails often passed through thick woods that provided excellent cover for ambush. Out of breath and with the enormous weight on their backs, they were very vulnerable to attack by the Indians.

On the homeward run, they could decide to shoot the rapids with the loaded or partially loaded canoe. Although it was risky, it saved time. And time was the big obsession of the *bourgeois* and of the outfitters waiting in Montreal. The men got caught up in the challenge. In the fall, when the canoes were returning from the Great Lakes loaded with bales of furs, they would sometimes race each other. All that sweat and suffering wasn't for the job or the money; it was for honour, for fun, for the pure exhilaration of living dangerously.

This Montreal canoe carried a crew of eight and up to four tonnes of merchandise. Its bow is decorated with a picture of a sturgeon. The sail attached along the gunwale would be raised whenever there was a favourable wind. There were two "ends," the steersman in the stern and the bowsman, who guided the canoe. The six middlemen sat on wooden planks that could be repositioned depending on whether they were paddling upriver or down. The men would sit on their capes and could take along a maximum of eighteen kilograms of personal belongings.

THE OUTFITTERS

After retiring at around the age of thirty-five, some coureurs des bois set themselves up as merchants, outfitting canoe brigades for the fur trade.

The Montreal outfitters were the young colony's first aristocracy, a status reflected in this ex-voto of Pierre Le Moyne d'Iberville.

It took daring, imagination, a certain amount of business experience, and some capital to set oneself up as a fur trader and outfitter. Even more important were the relations one had established back in Europe, in the colony's burgeoning business community, and with the Indians. Many of the outfitters who dominated the fur trade in the seventeenth century started out at the bottom as traders' agents or clerks in town. Having worked as guides or interpreters for missionaries or traders in their adolescence, and then as coureurs des bois when they were a bit older, they had picked up one or more Indian dialects. With this experience, they developed the typically Montreal profession of outfitting brigades of canoes for the fur trade and selling the pelts brought back from the Pays d'en Haut.

The outfitter first had to obtain a licence from the authorities, then purchase or lease good canoes, hire reliable men, and acquire trade goods and provisions for the trading posts and for the crews en route. By about age thirty, the most enterprising and fortunate of these outfitters had become rich, powerful merchants.

The first generation of these outfitters, men like Jacques Le Ber, François Hazeur, Charles Aubert de La Chesnaye, Antoine Pascaud, and Charles Le Moyne, who organized and rationalized the fur trade, were born in France. Sons of traders, innkeepers, low-level bureaucrats, and petits bourgeois, they had well-organized family networks in Quebec and Montreal. Newcomers who wanted to become involved in the fur trade could count on the help of relatives already settled in the colony and on those they had just left behind in the old country. Until the emergence of the large fur trading companies, the business was run primarily by these families.

Luc de Lacorne de Saint-Luc took advantage of his military career to engage in the fur trade.

Between 1660 and 1670, the Montreal fur trade was dominated by Charles Le Moyne and Jacques Le Ber, who were brothers-in-law as well as partners. Together they imported goods, traded with the Indians, and outfitted voyageurs.

In the early 1680s, there were almost three dozen merchants involved in the fur trade in Montreal. The business was extremely profitable and attracted a great many adventurers. It cost approximately 1,600 livres to purchase a licence and buy trade goods; wages amounted to another 1,400 livres. If all went well, the canoes would return laden with furs worth up to 8,000 livres. The merchant could thus make a tidy profit of 5,000 livres – but not without risk.

By the turn of the century, almost all of the most prominent merchants had been born in Canada. Some, like Jean-Baptiste Le Comte Dupré, had been voyageurs in their youth before taking over the family business started by their parents. Charles Nolan Lamarque had led three expeditions to Fort Pontchartrain (present-day Detroit)

Ignace Gamelin started out as an outfitter and became a major investor in an important foundry known as the Forges de Saint-Maurice.

before getting into the business of hiring and outfitting voyageurs around 1720.

At that time, there were some seventy outfitters in Montreal and almost ten times as many voyageurs either working for an outfitter or on their own as independent traders. In all, some seven hundred men were engaged in the fur trade.

Shrewd and daring businessmen, the merchants lived well. They sent their sons to school until at least the age of fourteen, then placed them for several months at a trading post in the back country or with a trader in Montreal, Quebec, or France.

The merchants lived in large stone houses clustered around the marketplace. On the ground floor was the store, containing wholesale and retail trade goods and household items. The living quarters were furnished with solid, locally made furniture, a good wardrobe, comfortable beds and bedding, sometimes silverware, a mirror, a few paintings of religious subjects, family portraits, and one or two armchairs. Books were rare, except in the home of Charles de Couagne, who was rather unusual in that he liked to read (especially history) and had adorned his room with maps of Paris, France, and the world. In the main room, some had a cast-iron stove, a luxury enjoyed only by the wealthy.

The merchants were prominent citizens with a certain authority in the parish. They were serious, respectable men who took part in public affairs and charitable works but were not very involved in politics – though their names do appear on petitions to the authorities. Some particularly successful merchants were richer and had more power and prestige than the seigneurs, who were the owners of large estates that had been granted them by the king.

The prosperous merchants gradually began permitting themselves certain luxuries. They had silverware and candelabras on their imported mahogany tables, and landscape paintings on their walls. Some, such as Jacques Le Ber and Dominique Godet, an illiterate but well-to-do fur trader who was cousin to the highly cultivated René de Couagne, had black and Indian slaves.

Pierre de Rastel de Rocheblave, who had made his fortune in the fur trade, had the means to commission this portrait of himself in 1806.

During the period before the British Conquest, Pierre-Alexis Lemoine Monière was by far the most important merchant in Montreal. In 1747 he married the daughter of René de Couagne, son of Charles de Couagne, one of the richest of the Montreal merchants. Jean Léchelle, the second most important merchant of that period (with 130 men working for him), married René de Couagne's niece. He had amassed a large enough fortune that after the Conquest he simply liquidated his holdings and went back to live out his days in France. Many wealthy merchants, such as Toussaint Baudry and Louis Charly dit Saint-Ange, followed his example.

Others, like the very affluent Jean Orillat, continued to do business in Canada. Starting in 1765, he signed on numerous men, sending them to Michilimackinac and Green Bay. He ordered his trade goods from British traders who had recently settled in the colony. These traders, such as Brook Watson and Gregory Olive, in turn sold his furs on the London market.

But times had changed. Large fur trading companies, principally the Hudson's Bay Company and the North West Company, would soon take over the fur trade and wage bitter battles for control of the continent. The fur trade would no longer be a family business.

While their husbands were away, the outfitters' wives managed the business and kept the books, which they would store in desks like this.

Capital of the Fur Country

The hub of the fur trade, Michilimackinac served all the trading posts in the Pays d'en Haut.

The site was a highly cosmopolitan meeting place for numerous Aboriginal tribes long before the arrival of the Europeans.

Long before the arrival of the Europeans, Michilimackinac, at the junction of major land and water routes into the heart of the North American continent, was already a highly cosmopolitan centre where diverse Indian cultures met and mingled. Throughout the year, passing bands of Illinois, Ojibwa, Sioux, Assiniboin, Cree, Ottawa, and other tribes would stop to talk, trade, forge alliances, and prepare for war.

In 1676 the Montreal fur merchants decided to establish a depot at this site to serve all the trading posts in the back country. As the hub of the fur trade, Michilimackinac became an important source of information on western tribes and a gateway by which European influences entered Indian society. It was also a diplomatic centre to which the colony's bureaucrats, like Nicolas Perrot, would come in order to forge alliances with the Indians of the West.

The journey from Montreal took a month under good conditions. The voyageurs had to paddle some fifteen hundred kilometres and make thirty-six portages. They would ascend the Ottawa, Mattawa, and French Rivers, then slip between the large islands at the top of Lake Huron and into the straits leading to Lake Michigan. On the shore south of this narrow channel, at the tip of the peninsula, was a deep bay sheltered by a large humpbacked island, which the Ojibwa called Michilimackinac because it resembled a turtle.

At the end of the seventeenth century, a small fort, trading post, storehouse, and some sixty houses were built at this strategic location. The Jesuits also built their residence there, as well as a small church at the St. Ignace mission near the Huron village. A half-hour's walk away was an Ottawa village and the St. François Borgia mission, which was practically deserted in winter. There were also a few scattered voyageur cabins and birchbark tents built by visiting Indians.

Found in Wisconsin, this French-made tomahawk pipe, decorated with a man smoking a pipe, likely arrived by way of Michilimackinac.

Some years, Michilimackinac had close to six hundred permanent inhabitants. It was a very heterogeneous world of traders, missionaries, soldiers, and Indians from various nations. From spring until fall, the population swelled with people passing through and with adventurers of all sorts.

There was no colonization or farming at Michilimackinac, not because the land was infertile but because the post was first and foremost a commercial centre focused on trade and exploration, a place to exchange information on the latest discoveries and the mood of the Indian tribes.

Michilimackinac naturally attracted explorers, like Louis Jolliet and Father Jacques Marquette, who before setting off on their great journey came to question the Indians and coureurs des bois who had already ventured into the lands they wanted to learn more about.

By 1696 the fur market had been saturated, so the French authorities recalled all the coureurs des bois, closing the western trading posts one after the other. Michilimackinac, then commanded by Captain Antoine Laumet, also known as De La Mothe Cadillac, was

Copper kettles were popular trade items not only for cooking but also as material for making a variety of adornments.

An Ojibwa hood made of stroud, a British-made cloth that competed with the French-made écarlatine.

officially abandoned. A few years later, in 1701, Cadillac founded Detroit, which would become the new geopolitical and diplomatic centre of the fur country. Nevertheless, the Indians and coureurs des bois did not stop frequenting Michilimackinac, which, owing to its incomparable location, was a logical stopping place. It was no longer the geometric centre of the fur territory, which had been continuously expanding over the past century, but it was still at the junction of the major trade routes.

A more comfortable and better protected and equipped fort was built, along with a larger house for the commander, and gunsmith and blacksmith shops. And the wives came too. Michilimackinac was the first place in the Pays d'en Haut where white women set up permanent residence. The settlement gradually became home to families such as the Langlades, Chaboillezes, Blondeaus, and Montours. Jean-Baptiste and Marie-Françoise Chevalier raised a large family at Michilimackinac. At least twelve of their children grew up there and helped run the family business. The Chevalier children knew how to read and write, a rare accomplishment in Michilimackinac. Some of the sons married Indian girls, while the daughters married boys from important families in the back country and often accompanied their husbands on their fur trading expeditions, staying with them in the remote trading posts. These families made Michilimackinac a real community, which eventually grew into a small town, the first real town between Montreal and the interior of the continent.

Experts who kept abreast of the changing wants and needs of Indian consumers decided what the canoes should carry to Michilimackinac.

The Conquest of New France and the colony's incorporation into the British Empire did not change life in Michilimackinac. The men and women who lived there already formed a fairly autonomous society, with fewer and fewer ties to the St. Lawrence Valley. When Canada became British in 1763, some 120 permanent settlers and their families resided in Michilimackinac. They made a living from fur trading, hunting, and fishing; some also kept small vegetable gardens.

During the War of 1812, the Corps of Canadian Voyageurs defended Michilimackinac, which was always a coveted prize because of its strategic position on the western and northwestern trade routes. If the Americans had taken control of Michilimackinac, most of the furs from the Pays d'en Haut would have been intercepted, the western Indians would have become allies of the Americans, and the Montreal traders would have been ruined.

The voyageurs and Michilimackinac traders who formed this temporary unit were individualists who rejected all discipline. Witnesses agreed that the men were completely insubordinate, arriving on parade with their pipes in their mouths and their bread and pork rations skewered on their bayonets. But they were valiant fighters, for Michilimackinac was their capital, their home, and for many, their birthplace. From these beginnings, Michilimackinac would grow into a vibrant, frontier town that was neither white nor Indian but a melding of both cultures.

A voyageur who returned to the colony after making his fortune in the fur trade would belong to the emerging bourgeois class.

Part Three

ODYSSEY TO THE COLD COUNTRY

This Mandan woman is wearing a beautifully decorated buffalo robe to protect herself from the cold.

The bright light of winter had forced him to walk all morning with his head down and wrapped in a scarf and a hood. He could only see the tips of his snowshoes and his moccasins, his feet swishing along in front of him, alternating in his narrow field of vision. Now and then, without stopping, he would raise his head to look around. The scenery never changed. Pine, spruce, and birch trees stood out, dark and stunted, in the harsh light.

The sun was already high when the pain returned. He felt bracelets of fire bind his ankles, rings of fire bind his big toes. "I've been waiting for you," he said out loud, with all the irony he could muster. "You're having trouble keeping up with me."

Since Michilimackinac, it had often accompanied him, especially in the past two days. He could shake it off momentarily by walking faster until he was hot. Then it would leave him for a while, and he could walk in peace. But if he chased it away, it would undermine his strength. And if he wanted to be at the Detroit trading post before nightfall tomorrow, and drink a little rum with his friends, and sleep with an Indian girl, soft and laughing, he had to save his breath and his strength.

For a long time between two tobacco breaks, he carried on as if the pain weren't there. He stopped talking to it, or even thinking about it. He sang all the songs that he knew, not too loud so that he wouldn't get winded, but loud enough to show the pain that it wasn't bothering him.

Le premier jour de mai
Je donnerai à m'amie
Une perdrix, oh ! là ! volante dans les bois …

Nobody escapes the pain caused by snow blindness and snowshoes – except for people who are sedentary, who spend the winter at the trading post, twiddling their thumbs, being fed by the Indians, or people like the pork eaters, who return to Canada every autumn and sit by the fire, with their wives, their feet resting on the ledge of the wood stove, waiting for the good weather to return.

Not for all the money in the world would he want that kind of a life. He feels that those who choose the soft life envy him, are jealous, and would like to live like him, if only they had the strength and the courage. He notices it every

89

time he arrives at Grand Portage or Michilimackinac or at the Detroit trading post, whether alone or with others, and he also noticed it when he returned to Montreal last summer. They gathered around him, offering him rum and tobacco. They listened eagerly to him, drinking in his words when he told them of his adventures. And the girls would look at him, and smile, and were ready to fall into his arms.

Later, as the fatigue started to set in, he wondered if he had become a voyageur and a winterer for those very reasons, so that those who stayed behind, who didn't travel, who remained in their homes by the shores of the great river, would say: "How strong and brave he is!" At one point he even wondered whether the pleasure he felt at being admired and envied wasn't exacting too high a price. There was something else, of course, a stronger pleasure that he didn't quite know how to define, the pleasure of having gone to the limits of his strength, of having crossed rivers, forests, during the icy nights, alone, without anyone's help. He knows that joy always comes after pain. And he tells himself that the greater the pain, the greater the joy when he arrives at the Detroit trading post, especially when he holds that girl in his arms.

He thinks of how it will be when he is old, around thirty-five or forty. He will leave behind this life of misery and suffering. He will live at La Prairie, like many before him,

who, after crossing rivers and forests, like himself, and enduring all this pain, are finally enjoying the good life. And he will hunt buffalo. They say that it's an exciting life, and easy. It seems the men out there have no government, no police, no priests; they are free. Nobody ever tells them what to do or where to go. One day, maybe in ten or twelve years, he will live like that. He too will be a free man. And then he will remember the pain, the suffering. Some days he might even miss it.

Le deuxième jour de mai
Je donnerai à m'amie
Deux tourterelles
Une perdrix, oh ! là ! …

For a long, very long time, he walked in pain, rooted in his pain, until he almost grew to love it. A few times it wrested cries from him, but he quickly regained control of himself. He presented his apologies. He talked to his pain softly, kindly, he thanked it for the good it was doing him. "You bind my ankles and my toes in velvet," he said. And for a moment, it did what he had said; he felt light and strong.

Le troisième jour de mai
Je donnerai à m'amie
Trois rats des bois
Deux tourterelles …

When the noonday sun started to dip behind him, he and his pain shared a few good moments together.

The open countryside had started to soften. From here to Detroit, he would be walking on terrain that was mostly flat, not heavily wooded, and the snow was still light and dry. He had seen deer and a few elk. Several times he had startled partridge that were hiding in the light snow. And he continued walking, walking, always walking.

And then the pain would hit again, brutal, sharper than ever.

He spoke to it, like the Indians do to all their aches and pains, to their fears, to their sorrow. He imitated them, he insulted the pain in a loud voice, he called it a dirty dog, he said it was weak and useless, that it had no power over him, that it couldn't really make him suffer, that it could never stop him from walking. And he shouted as he said these words. And as proof that it was powerless, he walked until nightfall, maintaining the same step, the same rhythm, without stopping either to eat or to smoke.

The coureurs des bois adapted the toboggan and sled to their needs, just as they had adapted the canoe, using their more sophisticated tools to craft much more robust conveyances.

To provide better insulation, the Indians often wore their garments with the fur turned in next to their bare skin.

He could see his shadow lengthen in front of him, long and thin, until it blurred and vanished in the golden dust of twilight. He knew he could keep his promise because of the slow burn inside him, pushing him. But also because the full moon would already have risen as the sun set behind him. And he could continue walking in its opalescent light.

… Dix veaux bien gras
Neuf chevaux avec leurs selles
Huit moutons avec leur laine
Sept vaches à lait …

He stopped a short half-hour before the moon set, just long enough to make himself a bed of branches. A wolf was howling in the distance, probably the same one he had heard the night before. He didn't even bother making a fire. The wind had fallen, and the night was mild. He ate a few slices of pemmican with a little molasses. And he wrapped himself in his blanket.

He dreamed that he was on Lake Superior in a canoe pushed by a warm light wind towards Sault Ste. Marie. He didn't even have to paddle. Only the steersman and the bowsman were busy. The middlemen were stretched out on piles of skins and were passing around a jug of rum while watching the clouds go by. The low shore was covered with flowering trees that rang with the songs of brightly coloured birds.

Suddenly, a thick fog enveloped the men. They could see nothing, neither the shore nor the clouds. And he thought, "I should have known, joy should never come before sorrow." That is what awoke him, this uneasiness, the feeling that he had made a mistake. So he rose quickly and started off again.

When the pain returned, when it slapped its bracelets and rings of fire around his feet, he smiled. He thought that he would be in Detroit before sunset, and he sang.

Le premier jour de mai
Je donnerai à m'amie
Une perdrix, oh ! là ! volante dans les bois …

Chapter 5

THE NORTH MEN

In following my traveller on his long, difficult treks, so often accompanied by privations and dangers, the reader will wonder: What was the origin of the attraction almost all our coureurs des bois felt for this type of life? What charms tied them to this country where they had to endure such hardship? How is it that most of them forgot their native soil and no longer dreamed of seeing Canada again? More than once I have asked myself this question on seeing these savage lands that, especially then, were far from offering the enchanting aspect of the banks of the St. Lawrence. The only possible explanation for this strange taste that made them so gayly abandon civilization for life in the wild was a love of unfettered freedom.

The North men answered to no man and recognized no law or higher authority.

The Rocky Mountains, rising to over five thousand metres, formed an almost impenetrable barrier to the west.

THE WINTERERS

In the fall, some of the men
would remain
in the Pays d'en Haut,
moving deeper
into unknown lands
and adopting
the Indians' way of life.

*Instead of returning to the colony,
a third of the voyageurs would
spend several years as
North men in the back country.*

Most of the voyageurs who went up the rivers in the spring would return to spend the winter in the safety and comfort of the colony. Some, however, wintered in the harsh world of the Pays d'en Haut with the Indians. These were the North men, also known as the *hivernants*, or winterers, in opposition to the *mangeurs de lard*, or pork eaters, who didn't go beyond the head of the Great Lakes. The winterers wouldn't return to the low country until the following fall, if ever. Many of them had signed contracts for three or five years, long enough for them to forget the faces and landscapes of their youth and to forge new relationships among the Indians.

The fur country exerted a powerful attraction on the young men of the St. Lawrence Valley, and each year more and more of them would heed the call. The longer one was gone and the farther one penetrated into the unknown heart of the continent, the more of a man one was. A North man had to have courage, experience, and endurance; he had to be able to tolerate solitude, brave untold dangers, and live like the Indians.

Each summer, the pork eaters, with trade goods and provisions from the colony, and the winterers, with pelts from the Pays d'en Haut, would rendezvous at Grand Portage or Fort William, at the head of Lake Superior. There they would set up camp, the pork eaters on one side of the trading post and the North men on the other. The pork eaters' camp would be slipshod and slovenly, whereas the North men's camp was always neat and clean, as befits experienced woodsmen. Moreover, before arriving at the post, they would have spruced themselves up, shaving or trimming their beards, donning clean shirts, and adorning their hats with colourful ribbons and feathers. They would also have polished their weapons and fixed up their canoes. They were fresh and relaxed; clearly they had never been tired, never known fear.

The winterers would treat the pork eaters with studied contempt, talking in front of them about all the amazing places they had been, places a pork eater had never set eyes on.

The winterers turned up their noses at pork and poultry and other overfed,

*These Montagnais snowshoes
are made of babiche,
or rawhide webbing, on a birch frame.
The crosspieces are spruce.*

Lake Winnipeg, an obligatory part of the journey for anyone heading into the Northwest via the North Saskatchewan River. The men would eat the pemmican raw or sliced up, dredged in flour, fried, and topped with sugar or molasses. It could also be boiled to make a tasty soup called rubaboo.

Being a North man did not merely require courage and endurance. The winterers had to have better survival skills than the pork eaters. They had to be able to live off the land, obtaining the bulk of their food through their own efforts. They had to build and furnish their camps, maintain their canoes, weapons, tools, fishing gear, and traps, and do a little blacksmithing when necessary. If they weren't lucky enough to have an Indian wife with them or nearby, they also had to mend their own clothing and snowshoes. In addition, they had to establish and maintain good ties with the Indians, encouraging them to trap and hunt, and providing them with the means to do so – but without giving them too much gear lest they fail to return. They might also sell the Indians alcohol, but again not too much lest they not continue to hunt.

Needless to say, the winterers earned more than the pork eaters. The farther one was from Montreal, the more one was paid. Some of the North men would send their earnings back to their families. Many, however, would eventually forget or only occasionally think of their old lives back home. These men ended up staying in the Pays d'en Haut for good. Some had no choice; they had become too indebted to the fur trading company, or they couldn't bear to leave the Indian women who had borne their children.

When the North men were ready to retire, at around the age of thirty-five, not that many of them went back to finish their days in the St. Lawrence Valley. Most of them preferred to remain in the country they had come to know, attempting to settle around Lake Superior or to homestead on the edge of the Prairies. Few, however, managed to stay put; they were too used to a life of action, adventure, and constant movement. For them, hunting held infinitely more appeal than farming.

It was well known that the best hunting was in the Red River Valley, the land of the Assiniboin and Dakota. This soon became a very popular place for North men to retire. Many of those who lost their jobs when the Hudson's Bay and North West Companies merged in 1821 settled in that area. With their Indian wives and mixed-blood children, they would give birth to a new nation, the nation of free men.

A dressed and decorated otter pelt that was used as a tobacco pouch by winterers in the Pays d'en Haut.

domestic livestock. They preferred wild game, eating it practically raw, often without salt. But their staple food was pemmican, which they obtained from the Indians of the Red River and Assiniboine River Valleys. Pemmican consisted of buffalo meat (sometimes moose) cut into fine strips, dried in the sun or over a fire, then pulverized and mixed with melted fat. Sometimes it also included saskatoon berries, which grew in profusion on the Prairies and provided a rich source of vitamin C.

This mixture was pressed into forty-kilogram blocks and sewn into *tauraux,* large buffalo-hide sacks sealed with tallow. Each year, the Indians sold tonnes of pemmican to the North men, usually on their way through

Joseph La France's Story

Harassed by the French authorities, he became one of the English traders' most valuable collaborators.

The coureurs des bois were extremely knowledgeable about the fur country and its inhabitants.

Joseph d'Aragon dit La France was born in Michilimackinac around 1707. He was the son of a North man who, like many coureurs des bois, had married an Ojibwa woman. Although his father had spent the best part of his life among the Indians, he still had a certain nostalgia for the culture, language, and values of the St. Lawrence Valley and wanted his son to become familiar with them. When his wife died, he therefore sent five-year-old Joseph to spend the winter in Quebec in order to learn to read, write, and speak French correctly.

To the young boy, Quebec, the capital of New France, was a foreign and rather hostile world, to which he never really became reconciled. Remaining deeply attached to his late mother's Indian culture, he lived his life as a North man and spent only brief periods in the St. Lawrence Valley.

At age sixteen, he led his first brigade of fur-laden canoes from Michilimackinac to Montreal. In the following years, he hunted, trapped, and traded furs in the region around Green Bay, several times descending the Mississippi River as far as its junction with the Missouri and exploring the eastern edge of the Prairies. By age twenty-five, he had developed an extensive knowledge of the Pays d'en Haut and its riches.

In 1736 he returned to Montreal with two Indians and a huge cargo of furs. He met Charles Beauharnois de la Boische, governor of New France, and made him a substantial gift of furs in addition to paying a great deal of money for a fur trading licence for the next season. In the spring, however, Governor Beauharnois did not grant him his licence and refused to return his money on the grounds that he had given brandy to the Indians.

The following year, La France was again relieved of his hard-earned goods, this time by the governor's brother-in-law, whom he happened to encounter on the Nipissing River. The latter took La France prisoner and confiscated his furs, canoes, and two Indian slaves who were travelling with him. That night La France escaped. Skirting the north shore of Lake Huron, he made his way to Sault Ste. Marie on foot. The 400-kilometre

A shuttle like that used by the Woodland Cree for making nets.

journey took him six weeks. He had managed to take his rifle with him but had only five rounds of powder.

During his long, solitary trek, he decided to trade with the English instead of the French. He had already done business with them and their Iroquois allies at Oswego on the south shore of Lake Ontario and had experienced no problems.

As they advanced up the valleys of Appalachia and as they tried to establish trading posts at the mouths of the rivers flowing into Hudson Bay, the English realized that they needed experienced men who were familiar with the land and its inhabitants. The Hudson's Bay Company officers knew that the French were way ahead of them in this regard and dreamed of training their own winterers. North men like La France understood that their knowledge of the country was invaluable to the English.

Deprived of his rights and privileges by the French in Quebec, Joseph La France would become one of the English fur traders' most valuable collaborators. He had excellent relations with the Indians, was able to organize and lead canoe brigades, and knew the routes to the richest hunting and trapping grounds in the Northwest.

In April 1740 he began to organize his expedition, first going to Rainy

Lake, where he built the necessary birchbark canoes with his Ojibwa friends. He then crossed Lake of the Woods, descended the Winnipeg River to Lake Winnipeg, and spent the winter with the Cree.

The following spring, he and his men made several dozen small canoes since the rivers they were about to descend to Hudson Bay were very rocky and shallow. There would be only two men per canoe, with never more than a hundred beaver pelts, weighing barely seventy kilograms.

La France led his brigade down the Nelson River to York Factory, on Hudson Bay, arriving at the trading post in early summer accompanied by his country wife and a large band of Indians.

At that time, the London committeemen did not allow the Hudson's Bay Company posts to give shelter to French coureurs des bois. However, La France had not only arrived with a precious cargo of some 20,000 beaver pelts, saying that another 50,000 pelts were on the way, but he could also provide a wealth of information about a region the English dearly coveted.

Thomas White, the officer in charge of York Factory, decided to help him get to England to share this information. La France told the English merchants and bureaucrats that it would be far more efficient if a trading post were established on the Nelson River at a place called La Fourche (present-day Split Lake) since ships could sail up the river that far. It didn't make sense to wait on the bay for the Indians to bring their furs down in small canoes.

In London, where he apparently spent the rest of his life, La France recounted his travels and adventures to a man named Arthur Dobbs, who published them in 1744 in a book entitled *An Account of the Countries Adjoining to Hudson's Bay in the North-West Part of America*.

Dobbs provided numerous details on the places La France had travelled, describing the routes, rivers, portages, and shortcuts as well as the French trading posts and the number of soldiers garrisoned at each. He also indicated where La France had seen copper, lead, and, most importantly, beaver. He spoke of the Indian tribes and their customs. La France's story as told by Dobbs was an amazing source of information about a world that was almost entirely unknown to the English.

In order to appeal to his audience, La France may have deliberately painted the French administration as worse than it really was. And Dobbs, who was openly antagonistic to the Hudson's Bay Company, was no doubt using La France's revelations to discredit "the darling monopoly."

The British Parliament launched an inquiry, but La France died before the hearings were completed. Nevertheless, it was thanks to his accounts that the English decided to expand inland and started building trading posts in the interior of the continent.

Joseph La France, along with a few other French adventurers such as Pierre-Esprit Radisson, thus affected the course of history in North America. In helping to promote the growth of the mighty Hudson's Bay Company, he can be said to have played a part in precipitating the inevitable decline of the French empire in the New World.

Before the advent of the Red River cart, the Prairie Indians used travois for transporting their children and possessions.

The Dogsled

It was the Inuit who
invented the "snow canoe"
mounted on runners
and first trained
good sled dogs to pull it.

*Before there were sleds,
the women had to carry
the firewood, while the men kept
an eye out for danger.*

When the cry "Mush!" rang through the icy air, the dogs would prick up their ears, get to their feet, and stretch. "Mush! Mush!" and the sled would glide over the hard-packed snow. This command familiar to all northern dogs comes from the Chinook jargon word *mahsh* (go), derived from the French word *marche* (walk). From the verb "mush" comes the noun "musher," which refers to a good sled dog; it was also a derisive term for a poor dogless man reduced to pulling his sled himself, as the Indians did more often than not.

Before the introduction of firearms, an Aboriginal family could generally not support more than one or two dogs. Often malnourished, the

The Europeans crossbred the native siwash *with other dogs imported from Europe, selected for their strength and stamina.*

dogs were rarely able to pack more than about fifteen kilograms on their backs or to pull a sled carrying over forty kilograms, even for short distances. In times of famine, they were soon sacrificed.

Most loads were thus transported by humans, usually the women, since the men were busy hunting or breaking trail. Improvised sleds consisting of a few thick pieces of birchbark lashed together with raw sinew would be used to carry household goods, any game they killed, the children, or anyone who was injured and unable to walk.

These crude conveyances evolved into the more elaborate toboggan, a flat-bottomed sled made of birch planks curved up at the front, which would float over snow that had been tamped down by the puller's snowshoes. Where the snow was hard and well packed by the wind – that is, everywhere throughout the tundra and taiga – the Aboriginal people would use a sled mounted on runners and pulled by dogs. Farther south, dog teams would run along the frozen rivers, following much the same routes as the canoes in summer. Sled drivers tried to avoid hilly terrain and forests, where the going was much more difficult.

It was the Inuit who invented this "snow canoe" and who first trained good sled dogs. Over time, they developed a very distinctive type of dog, known to modern breeders as the spitz family but popularly called huskies. Within this family there came to be recognized breeds such as the blue-eyed Siberian husky, the white Samoyed, the powerful Alaskan malamute, the *qimmiq* or Canadian Inuit dog, and the Greenland dog. Sled dogs were already in common use throughout the Northwest when the fur traders arrived in the region. They took to calling this native dog *siwash*, Chinook jargon derived from the French word *sauvage* (savage or wild).

All these dogs have compact, muscular bodies, wedge-shaped heads, erect ears, and bushy tails curled over their backs. Although they do not mate with wolves, there is a strong resemblance; the two clearly have a distant ancestor in common. They are endowed with amazing endurance, are indifferent to cold, and can go without eating for four or five days at a stretch. However, they are

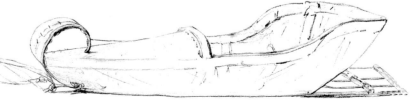

Montagnais-style toboggan used for carrying food, firewood, traps, animal carcasses, and pelts.

not very affectionate. While rarely aggressive with humans, they fight frequently among themselves. The males typically weigh thirty-five to forty kilograms, while the females tend to be much smaller. The pups are precocious and reach sexual maturity earlier than most other dogs. The *siwash* does not bark like its civilized cousin; it howls like a wolf.

The white trappers gradually crossbred this native dog with other dogs imported from Europe, which they selected for their strength and stamina. They also adapted the toboggan and sled to their needs, just as they had done with the canoe, using their more sophisticated tools to craft much more robust conveyances.

They also popularized the use of larger teams, hitching four, five, six, or even more dogs to pull heavily laden sleds. The sleds were up to three metres in length but very narrow (barely fifty centimetres across), so they could easily slip between trees in the woods. They were made of narrow slats of tamarack connected by crossbars. This platform was mounted on hardwood runners that were slightly tapered and curved up at the front.

In favourable conditions, on firm, well-packed snow, a good sled dog could pull a load of 150 or even 175 kilograms for several kilometres. A team of four strong, well-fed dogs could pull 225 to 275 kilograms for 65 to 80 kilometres. Some teams have even been known to do up to 100 kilometres in a single day.

South of Hudson Bay, they used a collar with two necklines that were brought together over the dog's back and attached to a tugline secured directly to the toboggan. There was a separate tugline for each dog.

The trappers learned to hitch their dogs one behind the other so that they could proceed in single file through the trees. They fashioned harnesses to fit the individual dogs in order to avoid injuring them and, in extremely

The sled driver often had to break trail for his dogs by walking ahead of them on snowshoes.

cold weather, dressed them in colourfully embroidered felt coats hung with little bells. If the trail was hard and icy, they would protect the dogs' paws with leather booties.

Even when travelling by dogsled, the North men always brought along snowshoes since it was often necessary to walk in front of their teams to break trail through the deep snow. Different types of oval or round snowshoes – beavertail, swallowtail, beaverpaw, or bearpaw – were used depending on snow conditions. Most were nearly a metre long by about thirty centimetres across at their widest point, often ending in a long tail at the back. They consisted of a birch frame with deerhide or moosehide webbing, known as *babiche*, stretched over it. The wearer had to walk with his feet pointed slightly in to keep the backs of the snowshoes from knocking together.

Pressure on the foot frequently caused *mal de raquettes*, an extremely painful inflammation of the tendon of the big toe, which could shoot up the foot and into the ankle. Often, in the vast, empty expanses of the frozen North, it was impossible to stop. Unless they could find a safe shelter and had something to eat, the men and dogs had no choice but to keep on going, despite the pain, hunger and cold.

It was important to make camp before nightfall, if possible in a place that provided shelter from the wind and where some kind of firewood could be found. The driver would unhitch and feed the dogs, hang all other food out of their reach, then go and gather firewood. In the mountains, where the snow lay incredibly deep, he would cut green wood to make a bed for the fire, often using the tops of trees since the lower trunks were buried under the snow. When the snow melted in the spring, one would see stumps four or five metres high. The North men would tell the pork eaters that this country was inhabited by giants. Which, in some ways, was true.

TRADE GOODS

Furs were not bought
but were received as gifts.
The trader had to merit
this gift and to reciprocate by
presenting the Indians
with something
they wanted or needed.

*Menominee Chief Kitchie-Ogie-Maw
wearing a blanket
and other trade goods.*

Owing to their complementary needs and their circumstances, the white men and Indians were equal partners in the fur trade, something that was very rare in relations between so-called primitive and civilized societies. The French traders tried neither to enslave the Indians nor to conquer their land or souls, but merely to engage in mutually profitable exchanges with them.

In embarking on the fur trade, the white men had to accept entirely unfamiliar business practices based on barter and the Indians' tradition of trading and gift-giving. One did not pay for goods; one honoured the giver by giving something in return. Champlain was the first to understand this. He also understood that to receive furs from the Indians, one had to have merited this gift in some way and had to reciprocate by presenting the Indians with something they wanted or needed. The

trader's art was knowing what to give to whom and when to give it.

The Indians were not naïve consumers. They quickly developed a critical eye, becoming tough customers who sometimes took malicious pleasure in refusing what the white traders had expended considerable effort in bringing them from the St. Lawrence Valley. They knew how to play on their alliances and how to take advantage of rivalries among the French, Dutch, and English traders or among representatives of the different fur trading companies.

At first, it was hardware, tools, utensils, and copper pots the Indians wanted. Once the tribes were well equipped with these items, their interest turned to textiles and clothing. The traders initially brought them a great deal of rough, unbleached linen and hemp fabric, though they later had to offer them good-quality clothing, beaver hats, red tuques, capes, cotton shirts, blankets, and sometimes even luxury items or apparel. By the mid-seventeenth century, mirrors, imitation gold or silver buttons, and gold-braided coats started to be included in the cargoes destined for the fur country.

*Scalping knife
with a brass
handle inlaid with
tortoiseshell,
along with
a scabbard made
of tanned
and smoked
leather decorated
with porcupine
quills.*

A trader who turned up with a few novelties would be assured of success. As in all markets, he needed to pique his customers' interest in order to create a demand. Some years, for instance, bells and plumes for decorating hats or swords were very popular. However, it was textiles that long constituted the bulk of trade goods.

By 1680 the French colony was even making shirts, capes, and stockings specially for the fur trade, with several different sizes for men and women and one size for children. Clothing, blankets, and fabric accounted for

*An important trade item,
tobacco was spun
into a rope and coiled
around a stick to make
it easier to transport.*

as much as two-thirds of the value of goods taken to the Pays d'en Haut.

On an ordinary trading expedition in the seventeenth century, a canoe might carry 275 to 300 kilograms of gunpowder in twenty-kilogram barrels. But the French were reluctant to provide the Indians with firearms and ammunition and thus only gave these items to nations whose loyalty was assured. Arming allied nations was a duty and a necessity; arming enemy nations was a crime.

The Indians considered trade guns primarily a status symbol, using them more for war than for hunting, for which they continued to prefer their traditional weapons. Muskets and rifles were thus important trade goods, serving to impress the Indians and cement alliances. Later, medals and insignia played a similar role. Alcohol, too, helped to facilitate contacts and seal bargains.

Year after year, the traders' inventories became more varied and refined as they added items like buttons, cords, combs, and sewing supplies such as needles, thread, thimbles, and scissors. In 1782 the Detroit post alone traded 18,600 pieces of trade silver. At that time, a large silver cross was worth an average-sized beaver pelt or deerskin. A pound of gunpowder traded for a small beaver pelt. And a reel of the best gartering would fetch two doeskins or six racoon pelts.

The Europeans were never interested in transferring knowledge and technologies to the Indians. Although it would have been relatively easy to teach them how to weave cloth and to make lead bullets and musket balls, they wanted to continue to trade these items in return for furs.

In the mid-eighteenth century, fabric accounted for nearly half (45%) of all trade goods, whereas prior to 1664 it had represented only 10%. If one includes blankets (8%) and clothing (14%), textiles made up over two-thirds (67%) of the value of trade goods. Guns, gunpowder, musket balls, and shot accounted for 15%. The

The French had to accept Indian trading practices based on barter, exchange, and gift-giving.

previously popular copper cooking kettles had fallen to 3%, as had mirrors, porcelain, bells, and rings, which had once accounted for up to 20% of goods traded. Tools also declined to about 5%.

The French canoes were loaded with strong, heavy cloth but also with lighter fabrics such as flannel, serge, and calico. The Indians came to prefer wearing European blankets to their traditional fur robes, which took longer to dry.

The Indians were very fond of stroud, a wool fabric made for the fur trade in the English town of Stroud, since it was thicker and better dyed than *écarlatine*, the scarlet wool fabric produced by the French. In 1765 a blanket made of two metres of stroud traded for two large beaver pelts or three tanned deerskins; it was thus worth as much as a man's gold-braided coat, twice as much as a tin pot, and almost as much as a three-gallon barrel of rum.

Nevertheless, some French towns did produce good-quality cloth. For instance, towns in the province of Languedoc shipped 100,000 blankets to Canada in a single year. The French also had better contacts than the British. Even after the Conquest of New France, it was mainly the French who continued the trade with the Indians in the Pays d'en Haut and on the Prairies.

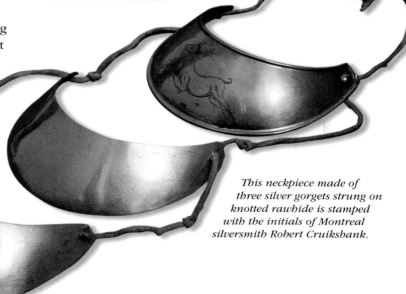

This neckpiece made of three silver gorgets strung on knotted rawhide is stamped with the initials of Montreal silversmith Robert Cruikshank.

THE TRADING COMPANIES

The powerful trading companies established alliances with the Indians and waged merciless wars for control of the rich fur territory.

Fur merchant Isaac Todd, one of James McGill's associates in the North West Company.

I n later years, the fur trade was controlled by big companies belonging to the French, the English, the Dutch, and eventually the Americans. Each claimed, over an often poorly identified territory, a vaguely defined monopoly, which it exercised avidly and defended fiercely. For over two centuries, these companies maintained a climate and culture of extreme violence throughout the back country. They acted like nation states, waging merciless wars and seeking to establish alliances with the Indians, among whom they either fomented or quelled uprisings according to their commercial interests.

Although their knowledge of the territory was initially very limited, the English nevertheless established a highly structured enterprise that would, after many difficulties, turn out to be formidably effective – the legendary Hudson's Bay Company (HBC). Established in 1670 at the instigation of two French adventurers, Pierre-Espirit Radisson and Médard Chouart des Groseilliers, the HBC obtained a royal charter granting it control of the fur trade and minerals throughout what came to be called Rupert's Land, a territory much larger than anyone in Europe at that time suspected. Comprising over 2.5 million square kilometres, it was almost twenty times the size of England.

The Hudson's Bay Company required its employees to live an excessively austere existence. They were badly housed, often ill-fed, and poorly paid. The officer in charge of the trading post, the factor, had absolute power over the men and often abused it. Defections, suicides, murders, and mutinies were not uncommon.

In 1682 the HBC's overseas governor demanded country lads who were industrious and not too hard-drinking. He was sent men from the Orkney Islands in the north of Scotland. Inured to harsh conditions, thrifty, and surprisingly sober, they formed a strong clan within the company. Nevertheless, it remained a feudal and paternalistic organization that was arrogant and contemptuous with its own employees and in its dealings with the Indians.

The wages of the HBC's employees were nothing like those of the Canadian voyageurs. An HBC servant received less than £10 a year and sometimes as little as £6, while the Canadian canoemen received 600 livres (£25), the

Although the bosses of the trading companies were Scottish or English, most of the voyageurs were French.

steersmen up to 800 livres (£33), and the guides and interpreters 1,000 livres (£41).

With the British Conquest of New France in 1763, the Hudson's Bay Company thought that the competition had been eliminated. But Scottish merchants in Montreal, working in conjunction with the outfitters and using Canadian voyageurs, reorganized the fur trade, eventually forming the North West Company in 1783. Twenty years later, while the venerable HBC (some wags claimed that the initials meant "Here Before Christ") still had only three hundred badly trained and poorly paid employees, the North West Company employed over a thousand experienced voyageurs, some fifty clerks, a score of competent guides, and seventy interpreters. All the directors were partners in the company and had spent at least one full season in the fur country. The governors and committeemen who ran the Hudson's Bay Company, on the other hand, never set foot in their territory. Even by 1850 only 4 of its 232 shareholders lived in Canada.

The Nor'Westers continued the inland advance begun by the coureurs des bois and voyageurs, who had already explored a good part of the territory for the French outfitters. Each summer, the *bourgeois*, officers, and men would gather, usually at Grand Portage or Fort William, where the North men and pork eaters met up. There they would report on the results of their activities and plan and prepare for the upcoming year. It was an occasion for eating, drinking, and wild revelry. The officers of the North West Company considered this a necessary and sacred tradition that enabled them to maintain the confidence and loyalty of the men in the field.

The genius of these Highland Scots was their creation of a solid esprit de corps among the men. Almost all the officers, clerks, voyageurs, guides, interpreters, and canoemen were devoted to the company and were willing to suffer, fight, and kill for it if need be.

Each trading company had to begin by establishing an efficient supply system in its territory. In 1770 Thomas Frobisher had built a fort on the Red River, where the Indian and Métis women prepared the pemmican that was shipped to Lake Winnipeg for the North men who were setting out across the bleak Canadian Shield. Other provision posts were scattered throughout the territory so that the brigades of Montreal canoes and North

The two great rivals, the Hudson's Bay Company and the North West Company, merged in 1821.

canoes could find provisions wherever they went. Not having to waste time hunting or fishing, they could keep to very precise schedules.

Although the Hudson's Bay Company lost numerous battles in the war to control the fur trade, it eventually emerged the victor. With the amalgamation of the two companies in 1821, it added the North West Company's ninety-seven trading posts to the seventy-six it already had. Finally run by people with a better grasp of the realities of the trade, the Hudson's Bay Company evolved into a modern, capitalist enterprise with a vision and business strategy. It even adopted its rival's methods, recruiting Highland Scots and hiring the Canadian voyageurs, without whom success in the fur trade would have been impossible.

The HBC's governors and London-based committeemen had often suspended payment of dividends when the company was short of funds. The partners in the North West Company, however, would never have thought of giving up their dividends. In depriving the company of its operating capital, their greed had contributed to its downfall. This turn of events left the Hudson's Bay Company free to penetrate inland, thus enabling the expansion of its empire west to the Pacific Ocean – although it ran up against the American fur trading companies in Montana and Oregon.

Unlike the Hudson's Bay Company, which had almost no French-speaking officers, the American companies were usually headed by Canadians who, along with the old French Creole aristocracy, controlled the fur trade in the Mississippi and Missouri Valleys at the beginning of the nineteenth century. Most of the American entrepreneurs were associated with the French in Montreal or St. Louis, establishing trading companies with names such as J. Picotte & Co.; Clark, Primeau & Co.; and Larpenteur, Lemon & Co. Until the mid-nineteenth century, all these companies used the language of the St. Lawrence Valley voyageurs.

In bringing together the great English capitalist tradition with the feistiness of the Highland Scots and the American frontier mentality, the fur trading companies would give birth to a new spirit that, combined with the practical know-how of the Canadian voyageurs, would inspire the world of the fur trade and profoundly mark the history of North America.

The rival companies often built forts facing each other, like these two on the Red River.

The Trading Posts

First the colonial authorities, and then the trading companies, established posts in an effort to control the territory.

A new society emerged in these posts, which gave birth to towns such as Fort Laramie, Wyoming.

Another popular entertainment was checkers. This checkerboard was discovered in a former trading post.

I n the mid-seventeenth century, the voyageurs and French soldiers began building a network of trading posts. Later, the fur trading companies also established posts in their respective territories. These posts were like islands in the endless wilderness, oases where the inhabitants often lived lives of unrelenting boredom.

Often associated with a fort and a mission, the trading posts enabled the French to exercise a certain control over the territory and effectively organize the fur trade. They served as depots for provisions, trade goods, and furs. Whether simple relays or large trading posts, they were generally surrounded by a rough wooden stockade and a rudimentary moat, sometimes flanked by bastions at the corners. At first, this square enclosure would be no more than twelve metres on each side, but as time went on some ambitious commanders built much larger forts. The one in Detroit, erected in 1701 by La Mothe Cadillac, had an inside area of four thousand square metres.

The trading posts tended to have a very diverse, fluctuating population of ten to twenty individuals, almost exclusively young men. These included the commander, one or two missionaries, a few soldiers, the occasional voyageur passing through, one or two interpreters, and the clerk in charge of the storehouse where the furs were kept. The furs would be packaged in buffalo skins, sometimes after preliminary processing, then weighed and put away safe and dry to await the arrival of the canoes. Some of the larger posts also had skilled tradesmen, such as a gunsmith, a blacksmith who repaired weapons and traps and made bullets, a carpenter, a baker, and perhaps a surgeon. Sometimes the same person fulfilled two or three of these functions.

The more-or-less illegal fur traders known as coureurs des bois gravitated around the trading posts though they didn't really live there. Indians also gathered nearby and served as guides, hunters, porters, and outfitters for the fur traders. Over time, they developed a mutual dependence and friendship. More than anywhere else, the French in these isolated trading posts lived together with the Indians, sharing work, food, women, and leisure activities. These outposts scattered across the North American continent thus gave rise to a very open and multicultural society, which grew increasingly distinct and autonomous.

The organization of the trading posts was quite simple and crude, especially in the difficult early days. Inside the stockade were the commander's residence, the missionary's residence, the men's quarters, and a few cabins for visiting voyageurs. The walls of the buildings were made of upright or horizontal logs covered with sheets of bark plastered with mud or, like the roof, protected by rough-hewn shingles. The chimney was made of stone. Oiled deerskin stretched over openings in the walls served as windows. The inhabitants might also put up a flagpole so that they could fly their colours to impress the Indians and show the other traders they had taken possession of the area.

The commander was expected to establish ties with the various

French playing cards dating from the 1750s. Games helped to while away the long winter months.

A resourceful and unscrupulous commander could easily make ten times his salary. The sale of alcohol alone could bring in up to two thousand livres a year, or twice the official pay. In the 1750s, the commanders of the Detroit and St. Joseph River posts received an extra three thousand livres a year, accepting bonuses and bribes in addition to their fixed remuneration.

Indian nations, enforce peace among them (the Pax Gallica), and keep the authorities informed of the movements of the different tribes and any conflicts that broke out. Inside the post, he was supposed to maintain order and discipline, settle disputes, distribute wages, and combat (or pretend to combat) illegal trading in furs or any other goods, particularly alcohol. In the spring, when the Indian trappers and North men returned with their furs, and the pork eaters arrived with provisions and news of the St. Lawrence Valley, he would supervise the trading sessions.

The actual trading usually took place outside the fort, with the gates closed. Because of the use of alcohol, which sometimes got out of control, the negotiations were often conducted in an atmosphere of intense nervousness and scarcely contained violence.

The officers' salaries were never very high. In the mid-eighteenth century, an officer received ninety livres a month, not much more than the steersman of a Montreal canoe or an interpreter. However, there was a fair bit of money to be made selling fur trade licences, alcohol, and gunpowder to the Indians. And nothing prevented a commander from doing a little fur trading on the side.

Life in the trading posts was terribly monotonous. Although the men were supposed to be there to collect furs, their main activity was actually gathering, processing, and preserving food to ensure the subsistence of the small community. With no bread, wine, or salt, the food tended to be very bland, especially in winter.

The men thus drank heavily to relieve their boredom. They also played cards, checkers, and dominoes, often for money, though gambling was officially forbidden. They told each other scary stories, and some did magic or conjuring tricks. Occasionally, the inhabitants of the trading posts would dance and play music consisting of a combination of French, English, and Scottish tunes, possibly accompanied by an Indian drum. A trading post that didn't have a fiddler was considered a sorry place indeed. Some had two or three fiddlers, and perhaps some fife players, and even a bagpiper. These luckier posts always held great feasts on Christmas and New Year's Day, widely announcing them long in advance. Men would sometimes walk from several days away to enjoy an evening's entertainment and the warmth of civilization.

THE DUTCH TRADERS

Rather than venturing
into the woods like the French,
the Dutch set up depots
on the coast and waited for the
Indians to bring them furs.

*In the hope of gaining access to
the furs of the St. Lawrence Valley,
they befriended the Mohawk,
who were bitter enemies of the French.*

The French were not the only ones to covet the rich resources of North America. In the first half of the seventeenth century, the Dutch, who had established posts on the eastern seaboard at the mouth of the Hudson, Delaware, and Connecticut Rivers, were their greatest rivals. The Dutch did not have grand missionary ambitions or dreams of empire like the English, Spanish, and French. They were attracted to America by the fur trade and by the hope of finding a passage to the Orient for the ships of the powerful Dutch East India Company, which at that time controlled a large part of European trade with Asia. With their high-quality trade goods, the Dutch soon developed a good relationship with the Indians on the coast. Rather than venturing into the woods like the French, they set up depots in the harbours and estuaries and waited for the Indians to bring furs to them.

Although the territory they occupied was never very large, it did give them access to good fur reserves and to an invaluable currency for trading with the Indians. Some East Coast tribes would string together polished shells to make wampum collars and belts, to which they attached great symbolic value but which they also used as money. The finest of these came from the shores of Long Island Sound near New Amsterdam on Manhattan Island. The Dutch encouraged the use of wampum, which quickly spread from tribe to tribe. When supplies ran short, they fabricated their own out of porcelain.

In 1624 the Dutch shipped a total of 7,246 beaver and 850 otter pelts to Holland; by 1633 the number had risen to 8,800 beaver and 1,383 otter. However, the resources of the estuaries were soon depleted. Pushed by the Dutch traders, whom they called *swannekens*, the Algonquian hunters from the coast moved up the Delaware River into Susquehanna territory and up the Hudson River into the land of the Mohican and Mohawk.

The Dutch no doubt realized that it was in their interest to win over these Iroquois nations, which were hostile to the French and had access to the rich furs of the St. Lawrence Valley.

Fort Orange (present-day Albany), located at the junction of the Mohawk and Hudson Rivers midway between Montreal and New Amsterdam on the Lake Champlain-Richelieu Valley route, became a very active trading centre where Mohawk hunters gathered to deal with Dutch traders. Acting as middlemen with the western Iroquois nations, the Mohawk soon offered significant competition to the French traders.

The Dutch traders had rarely gone into the woods themselves. It was only in the 1630s that a few Dutchmen came into close contact with Indian society. These *boschlopers*, like the French coureurs des bois, went up the rivers to seek out the Indians and offer them trade goods, guns, and a great deal of brandy in exchange for furs. They, too, came into conflict with the civil authorities, who deplored their disregard for established values and their "barbarian" way of life. Some of these

Dutch trade knives. The handle of the broken knife depicts a cavalryman carrying a woman, while the other one is decorated with a hunter.

The Dutch West India Company appointed Peter Stuyvesant director general of New Amsterdam in 1647.

young Dutchmen also married Indian women and had children with them.

One of these mixed-blood children, a red-headed Iroquois known as the Flemish Bastard, became a famous Mohawk chief. For thirty years, he served as an intermediary between the French in the St. Lawrence Valley and the Dutch and the English on the Atlantic seaboard.

In the 1640s, New Amsterdam was already a large, bustling town. Fort Good Hope on the Connecticut River, Fort Nassau on the Delaware River, and Fort Orange and Fort Amsterdam on the Mohawk River were also busy, well-organized trading posts. New Holland at that time had a population of four thousand, more than New France. For its English neighbours to the north and to the south down the Atlantic Coast, this was too many. For the Indians on the eastern seaboard, who found themselves dispossessed of their land, it was simply intolerable.

There had been a serious misunderstanding between the Dutch settlers and the original inhabitants. The Indians had an entirely different concept of property and ownership from the Europeans. They felt that no one could have absolute and permanent title to the land, any more than one could own the sea or the air.

Seeing the discontent of the Algonquian Indians on the coast, the Dutch stopped providing them with guns and ammunition, though they continued to give firearms to the Iroquois who lived inland, particularly their allies, the Mohawk. The Mohawk, in turn, armed their fellow Iroquois – the Seneca, Onondaga, Oneida, and Cayuga. They also spread Dutch manufactured goods as far as the Mississippi, destabilized the Huron nation, pillaged the Huron canoe brigades carrying furs from the Great Lakes to Montreal, and destroyed the

Armed and stirred up by the Dutch, the Iroquois destroyed Huronia and threatened New France.

commercial system of the Ottawa nation, completely upsetting the fur trade established by the French. On several occasions, they even attacked the St. Lawrence Valley settlements of Montreal, Trois Rivières, and Quebec.

In 1654 the Mohawk controlled the entire area south of the Great Lakes and the St. Lawrence Valley, from the land of the Illinois at the head of the Mississippi to New England.

For the French missionaries, converting the Mohawk was an exalting challenge that became a veritable obsession. The Jesuits who went among these Indians in order to evangelize them were practically assured of martyrdom. Jogues, Goupil, Lalande, Brébeuf, and quite a few others met a tragic and very painful death at their hands. The Dutch occasionally interceded with the Indians to save the missionaries, even though they were not of the same faith. The French adventurer Pierre-Espirit Radisson also found refuge with the Dutch when he fled the Iroquois family that had adopted him.

The Algonquian tribes on whose land the Dutch had established their trading posts and farms, and whom they still refused to arm, finally rebelled and were brutally put down. Already weakened by disease and alcohol, they were completely annihilated.

Thus, not long after the French colony's Huron allies had been decimated, the Algonquian tribes on the coast were also wiped out. In only a few short decades, the Europeans had radically altered the demographics of North America.

The English, who had assisted the Dutch in this destruction, especially on Long Island, conquered New Holland in 1664. Most of the Dutch living in America at that time remained and without too much difficulty found a place in the English institutions and businesses, which benefited from their knowledge of the country. The young society on the East Coast was thus imbued with the spirit of the Dutch *swannekens* and *boschlopers*.

When America Was French

The French managed
to control an immense territory
without settling it.

*Despite its small population,
Montreal dominated the continent
thanks to its intrepid explorers,
coureurs des bois, and voyageurs.*

By the end of the seventeenth century, the French were masters of most of North America, from the shores of the Gulf of St. Lawrence to the mouth of the Mississippi, as well as around the Great Lakes and on the Prairies. For a century and a half, they were almost the only Europeans to travel into the heart of the continent and become intimately familiar with its geography and its inhabitants.

It was Samuel de Champlain, founder of New France, who promoted the discovery of this immense territory in order to develop the fur trade, sending his interpreters to live with the Indians, encouraging exploration, and building trading posts and forts in strategic locations. By the time of his death in 1635, the French had a fairly good knowledge of the human and physical geography of the Great Lakes region. From there they spread out to the rest of the continent, except for the eastern seaboard south of Acadia and the shores of Hudson Bay, which were controlled by the English; a narrow strip along the coast of Alaska, where the Russians maintained a few outposts; and the Southwest, where the Spanish had been for over a century.

Within fifty years of their first winter in Quebec, thanks to their Indian allies, the French had discovered five routes to the great inland body of water they called the North Sea (which the English would later name Hudson Bay): via the Saguenay River, St. Maurice River, Ottawa River, Georgian Bay, or Nelson River. They then went on to explore the entire Great Lakes basin, crossed the Prairies, descended the Mississippi River, and climbed the Rocky Mountain foothills. Everywhere they went, they erected forts and established missions, around which

*This French-made
iron trade axe head
was discovered
in northern Texas.*

developed French settlements and villages, including Cahokia, Kaskaskia (near St. Louis on the Missouri River), and many others in present-day Arkansas, Alabama, and Louisiana.

The French territory of Louisiana, which Emperor Napoleon I would sell for $15 million to the young republic of the United States in 1803, was a vast area comprising all the states on the right bank of the Mississippi (Arkansas, Dakota, Iowa, Kansas, Missouri, Montana, Nebraska, and Oklahoma) in addition to the present-day state of Louisiana. In 1752 this area was home to some fifteen hundred Frenchmen and close to a thousand black slaves, who were engaged in farming, mining, and the very lucrative fur trade.

Other adventurers, missionaries, and coureurs des bois advanced into the Northwest, taking the very difficult Rainy Lake route to Lake Winnipeg and then ascending the North Saskatchewan River into the Rocky Mountain foothills and crossing the great divide to other rivers, such as the Athabaska, which flows into Great Slave Lake, which in turn drains into the Arctic Ocean through the mighty Mackenzie River.

The French were very familiar with the resources of all these lands and the various routes through them, which they dotted with their forts, missions, and trading posts, two dozen of them in the present-day United States. They explored,

*Jean-Baptiste Le Moyne de Bienville,
brother and companion of d'Iberville,
founder of New Orleans in 1718.*

and sometimes occupied, no fewer than thirty-one of the future American states.

Montreal, the commercial and cultural capital of this far-flung empire, was at that time the only major inland city. A number of its inhabitants, having made enormous fortunes in the fur trade, constituted a veritable colonial aristocracy. With its French culture and language, strong Indian influence, and importance as a cultural and commercial hub, Montreal would develop into a truly unique city with a character unlike that of any other city in North America.

From Montreal, voyageurs, missionaries, and soldiers fanned out across the continent, leaving French names on the lakes and rivers they travelled, the mountains and waterfalls they admired, and the Indian tribes they encountered. In so doing, they symbolically took possession of the territory for France.

However, these adventurous souls were not as numerous as one might think. Even in the mid-eighteenth century, at the height of the French presence and agricultural settlement, there were never more than a thousand white men in the entire Pays d'en Haut. And at least three-quarters of them were coureurs des bois who were only there temporarily or who had become assimilated into Indian society. Indeed, France's North American empire was born of a merging of races; its cohesion depended on the alliance that the French had forged with the Indians. As long as the Pax Gallica reigned, they remained masters of this vast territory, without ever needing to settle the land, as the English had done in the much smaller territory they controlled.

From north of the Great Lakes to the confluence of the Mississippi and Missouri Rivers, the Indians recognized their common identity: They were all children of the governor of New France. In 1673, when the Iroquois had petitioned him for peace, Frontenac had required that they thenceforth call him Father. Many Indian tribes thus found themselves obliged to

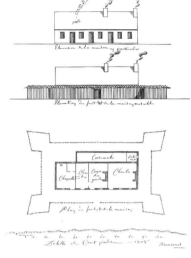

North America was dotted with French forts. Fort Pontchartrain in Labrador (pictured here) had the same name as the fort established at the site of present-day Detroit.

make peace among themselves since brothers don't fight. The representatives of French authority who came to the Pays d'en Haut, guided by the coureurs des bois, were charged with imposing this Pax Gallica, the essential cement of the French Empire, which was thus created not through settlement, but with the consent and co-operation of the Aboriginal peoples.

In 1669, in signing a treaty whose terms and scope they likely did not fully grasp, the Plains Sioux ceded their lands to France. Two years later, in June 1671 at Sault Ste. Marie, Simon-François Daumont de Saint-Lusson formally took possession of the entire Great Lakes region in the name of the king of France. The declaration was witnessed by some of the legendary coureurs des bois: Louis Jolliet, La Taupine, Largillier dit Castor, Bonhomme, Dupuis, Bidaud, and Nicolas Perrot. Some of these hardy adventurers also joined René-Robert Cavelier de La Salle on his exploration of the Ohio River and his subsequent expedition down the Mississippi to the Gulf of Mexico.

While it is true that La Salle was determined to make his fortune in the fur trade, he also had a vision. He dreamed of building a chain of forts in a giant arc from the St. Lawrence Valley to the Mississippi that would encircle the English clinging to the East Coast.

Even when France withdrew from the heart of the continent and fell back to the St. Lawrence Valley, its erstwhile empire remained imbued with the French spirit. For the Ojibwa, Mandan, Sioux, and Hidatsa, it would always be inhabited by the French adventurers who had built it.

Montreal, the capital of the continent, was connected to numerous trading posts by an extensive system of lakes and rivers, including the Mississippi and the Missouri.

NEW FRANCE

Thanks to a treaty signed in Montreal in 1701, France imposed peace on the Indian nations of North America for over a century.

This 1547 map reveals the extent of French explorers' knowledge, with which they were able to penetrate to the heart of the continent.

When France's North American empire was at its height, its influence extended from Hudson Bay in the north to the Gulf of Mexico in the south, and from Newfoundland in the east to the high plains bordering the Rocky Mountain foothills in the west. Before the Treaty of Utrecht, the only area not under France's domain was the narrow strip of land controlled by the British colonies along the Atlantic Coast. Although thinly scattered over this immense territory, the French dominated the political landscape of North America for many decades, owing in part to their knowledge of Indian customs and languages and to their mastery of the only efficient means of transportation in the seventeenth and eighteenth centuries: the birchbark canoe. A peace treaty that was negotiated by the French and signed in 1701 by forty Indian nations – including the Iroquois, the fiercest enemy of the French and their allies – favoured the continued expansion of New France around the Great Lakes and across the Prairies. Thanks to explorers such as Jacques Marquette, Louis Jolliet, Daniel Greysolon Dulhut, Pierre Le Moyne d'Iberville, and René-Robert Cavelier de La Salle, the Mississippi and its tributaries had already come under French control, making it easier for the coureurs des bois and other fur traders to penetrate to the heart of the North American continent.

While pushing ever farther south and west, the French also expanded their empire toward the north by capturing forts erected by the Hudson's Bay Company, the British fur trading enterprise that was founded at the instigation of two French adventurers, Pierre-Esprit Radisson and Médard Chouart des Groseillers, and that claimed all lands draining into Hudson Bay and James Bay, an area known as Rupert's Land. However, this immense, beaver-rich territory would be returned to the English, along with Newfoundland and Acadia (part of New Brunswick and all of Nova Scotia except for Cape Breton) by the Treaty of Utrecht in 1713.

Prior to losing these territories, New France was so large that it had been divided into two provinces, each under its own governor. The province of Canada comprised the land on both sides of the St. Lawrence River and the area around the Great Lakes, known as the Pays d'en Haut, while the province of Louisiana comprised the present-day state of the same name along with Arkansas, North Dakota, South Dakota, Kansas, Missouri, Montana, Nebraska, Oklahoma, and parts of Minnesota and Texas.

In all, thirty-one American states were discovered, explored, or settled by the French. It is thus not surprising

that the country is still liberally sprinkled with French names, including those of over five thousand cities and towns. Many of these names, often Anglicized or altered over time, honour explorers (for instance, Duluth, Minnesota, named for Daniel Greysolon Dulhut; Joliet, in northern Illinois, for Louis Jolliet, who explored the Mississippi with the Jesuit priest Jacques Marquette; and Vincennes, Indiana, for Jean-Baptiste Bissot de Vincennes).

Other place names, such as Bonnet Carré (Louisiana), Trempealeau (Wisconsin), and Culdesac (Idaho), are derived from French expressions. Certain French names evolved to the point of being unrecognizable: for instance, Cassatot (Arkansas), from *casse-tête*; and Ozark (Alabama), from the expression *aux arcs*.

Another indication of the extent of New France's reach is the surprising number of French terms that are still used in the United States to designate geographical features, such as prairie, bayou, coulee, butte, cache, and portage, to name only a few.

To control this far-flung empire, the French erected numerous forts, including a string of them to protect the trade route between Montreal and New Orleans. These forts, of various sizes and shapes (some based on plans by France's leading military architect Marshal Vauban), along with fortified trading posts and missions, served as stopping-off points for the voyageurs and as centres of commerce between the Indians and white traders. They also acted as a hub of attraction for French settlement. Many of these communities developed into lasting towns and cities (for instance, Fort Pontchartain, which became present-day Detroit).

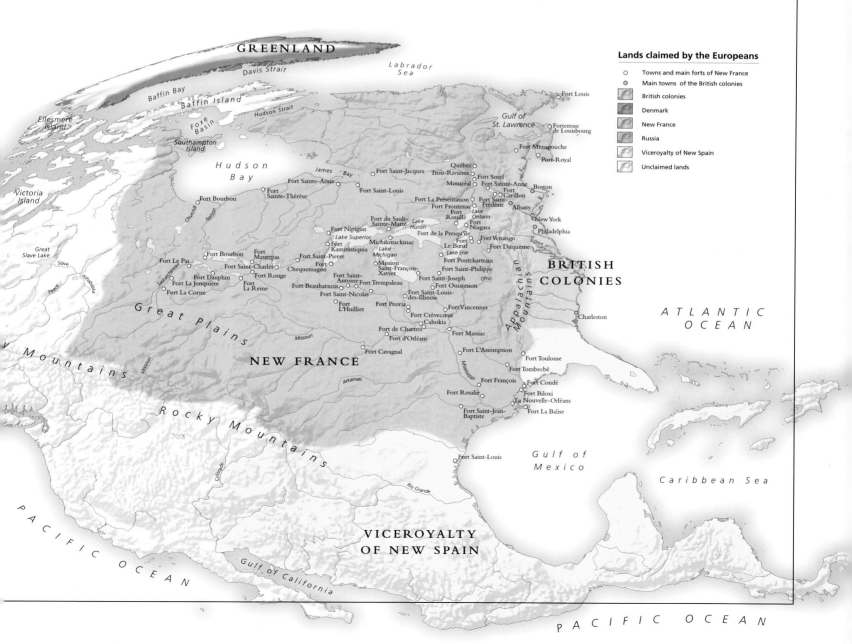

Lands claimed by the Europeans

- ○ Towns and main forts of New France
- ◉ Main towns of the British colonies
- British colonies
- Denmark
- New France
- Russia
- Viceroyalty of New Spain
- Unclaimed lands

Métis leader Gabriel Dumont spent his life resisting an alien system of law and order that white society wanted to impose on his people.

Part Four

ODYSSEY BEYOND THE MOUNTAINS

He knew that eventually the white men would come. They went wherever they thought they could find fur, minerals, whatever created wealth. He knew that sooner or later they would discover, on the high plateaus where the Yellowstone River had its source, the rough beauty of the land, pure and untouched. The scenery would take their breath away, even if they had seen Green Bay, the Prairies, and the Grand Coteau of the Missouri at sunset.

One day the white men would arrive. And they would be awed by the snowy peaks of the Rocky Mountains and by the glaciers pierced with fumaroles and geysers, by the furious torrents, the steel-blue and emerald lakes, and the canyons' precipitous walls. And, one by one, they would invade the valleys, whose rivers teemed with beaver and otter, the like of which did not exist in the St. Lawrence Valley or even in the Great Lakes basin. When the white men heard about it, they would come. He knew that for certain.

In the meantime, he thought of them only rarely. He had left so long ago that the faces and landscapes of his childhood were now too faded

for him to recognize. One of these days, the white men would come to him; but he would never live among them again.

Seven or eight years ago, he had left forever the soft Canadian countryside, had crossed one last time the Pays d'en Haut and the great Prairies. Two or three times he had run into white men – for example, when going with his friends the Crow to sell horses to the Mandan who lived on the Missouri. He had met three Canadians there, or rather three men like himself who had been Canadians during their childhood and youth and who had adopted Indian ways, even to the point of speaking Mandan among themselves.

With him, obviously, they always spoke French. They drank an excellent brown rum and laughed and smoked a good deal. He had found it amusing to speak French, which he rarely did, except sometimes when he was alone, or on a horse, or canoeing with his Indian wife, when he would sing old French songs at the top of his lungs, making her laugh. And it seemed to him that sometimes, though he wasn't sure, sometimes he even dreamed in French.

When he left the Mandan village a few days later, it struck him that neither he nor any of the

This woman is named Chan-Cha-Uia-Teuin, meaning Woman of the Crow Nation, likely indicating that she was a captive adopted by the Lakota tribe with whom she lived.

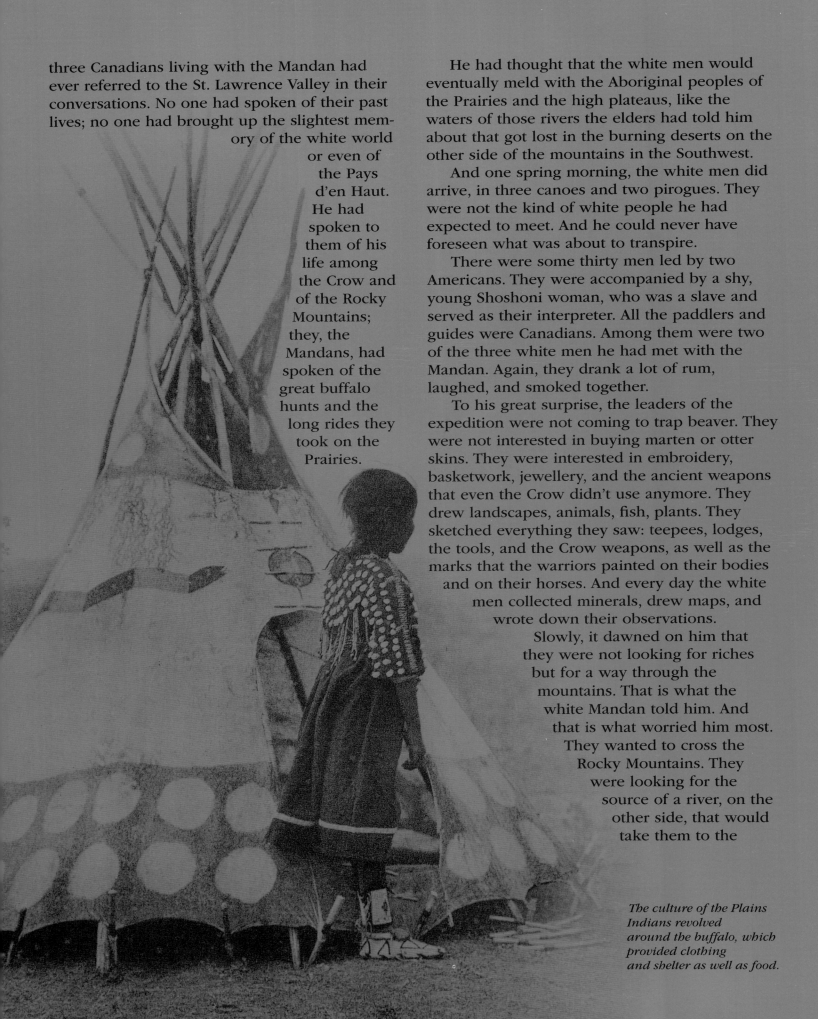

three Canadians living with the Mandan had ever referred to the St. Lawrence Valley in their conversations. No one had spoken of their past lives; no one had brought up the slightest memory of the white world or even of the Pays d'en Haut. He had spoken to them of his life among the Crow and of the Rocky Mountains; they, the Mandans, had spoken of the great buffalo hunts and the long rides they took on the Prairies.

He had thought that the white men would eventually meld with the Aboriginal peoples of the Prairies and the high plateaus, like the waters of those rivers the elders had told him about that got lost in the burning deserts on the other side of the mountains in the Southwest.

And one spring morning, the white men did arrive, in three canoes and two pirogues. They were not the kind of white people he had expected to meet. And he could never have foreseen what was about to transpire.

There were some thirty men led by two Americans. They were accompanied by a shy, young Shoshoni woman, who was a slave and served as their interpreter. All the paddlers and guides were Canadians. Among them were two of the three white men he had met with the Mandan. Again, they drank a lot of rum, laughed, and smoked together.

To his great surprise, the leaders of the expedition were not coming to trap beaver. They were not interested in buying marten or otter skins. They were interested in embroidery, basketwork, jewellery, and the ancient weapons that even the Crow didn't use anymore. They drew landscapes, animals, fish, plants. They sketched everything they saw: teepees, lodges, the tools, and the Crow weapons, as well as the marks that the warriors painted on their bodies and on their horses. And every day the white men collected minerals, drew maps, and wrote down their observations.

Slowly, it dawned on him that they were not looking for riches but for a way through the mountains. That is what the white Mandan told him. And that is what worried him most. They wanted to cross the Rocky Mountains. They were looking for the source of a river, on the other side, that would take them to the

The culture of the Plains Indians revolved around the buffalo, which provided clothing and shelter as well as food.

western ocean, the Pacific. This would mean that the white men would have charted a route from one ocean to the other. And that is why, guided by the white Mandan and the Shoshoni slave, they had climbed to the high plateaus of the Yellowstone River and called upon him and his Crow brothers. They felt that the Crow would probably know how to cross the massive barrier to the West. There had to be a pass somewhere and guides who would be willing to accompany them.

After grasping the white men's intentions, he explained to his brothers that the route the whites were looking for would eventually lead to their own downfall. "If they manage to cross once, they will cross as often as they want," he said. "And they will steal the wealth of our country."

They needed horses and supplies. The Crow gave them some wheezy old nags, pemmican, and rotten fish in exchange for their canoes, their pirogues, and a few muskets. As for routes, nobody seemed to know of any or even wanted to talk about them. If the Crow had been better armed, or more familiar with the few weapons that they possessed, they would certainly have forced the whites to go back or have annihilated them.

As for him, he had an idea that he kept turning over in his mind, a wicked, crazy idea. He was going to tell them that they would find a way if they went south, some fifteen or twenty days' walk from here. Once there, they would be up against very high mountains that were virtually impassable. They would have to abandon their horses because there would be nothing for them to eat on the inhospitable, sterile heights. And if, by some miracle, they did succeed in crossing the Rockies, and surviving the cold, and avoiding the precipices, and escaping the bears, and not dying of hunger, and if they found the

A Cree chief once told a North West Company representative that fathers often wanted their daughters to marry white men so that they would be better treated.

headwaters of the Colorado River, for example, it would take them through an incredible network of canyons towards arid regions where the great heat of summer would crush them, kill them. They would be lost forever in the burning deserts. No one would ever find their bones or even traces of them. And it would take years before the white men would dare return to this country.

He spoke of this plan to a few of his Crow brothers, who were just as determined as he was to push the white men toward their downfall. Confident of their support and pretending to translate what they were telling him, he described, in great detail, to the leaders of the white expedition, the countryside and routes that nobody had ever seen because he was inventing them. The Americans listened to him closely, taking notes, asking for details, which he would give them after consulting with his brothers.

He thought he had hoodwinked the white men. But when, a few days later, the Crow guides who had joined their expedition returned to the village, he realized that he had been tricked by the two Americans. No sooner were the latter out of sight but they had forced their guides, at gunpoint, to lead them not south but northwest, where there was a passable route, well-known and well-marked, that crossed the Rockies.

How had they known about it?

The little Shoshoni slave had told them. She knew this mountain country well. She had been born here. And she had become friends with two women from the Nez Perce nation that the Crow had taken as prisoners. With their help she had mapped out the itinerary that the expedition should follow.

It was only a matter of time now before the white men became masters of this country.

Chapter 6

THE WHITE INDIANS

As law and order advanced, the White Indians – a term that was used to describe those who were determined to live in the wild with the Indians – moved deeper into regions where they were not bothered. The expression "White Indians" was coined in the English colonies in the eighteenth century, followed by "Squaw Men" in the nine- teenth century, and enjoyed a certain vogue when settlers discovered that white men had deliberately chosen to live with the Indians. Toward the end of the eighteenth century, when the English and the Americans started to take an interest in the open spaces of the West, voyageurs, officers and explorers would encounter these men [or their descendants] within the tribes.

Through their work and relationships, the coureurs des bois lived in close contact with Indian society and often became assimilated.

The Rockies were one of many mountain ranges blocking the way west.

The Trappers

Almost completely abandoning
their former lives,
the trappers had only
increasingly sporadic contact
with white society.

*Refusing all authority,
some created veritable kingdoms in
the vast expanses of the West.*

The Canadian voyageur was only passing through, and the North man, though he lived in the Pays d'en Haut for several years, was bound to a fur trading company and remained in touch with the world back in the St. Lawrence Valley. The trapper, however, would spend the rest of his life in the farthest reaches of the back country, past the highlands and the Prairies, in the Rocky Mountain foothills, where the beaver were more numerous. The St. Lawrence Valley and the Great Lakes basin had been pretty much trapped out.

Between 1803 and 1806 the Corps of Discovery expedition, led by Meriwether Lewis and William Clark, crossed the Rockies and reached the Pacific Ocean. En route, they discovered the inexhaustible riches of those distant lands that had been almost unknown to the white men. Not long after their return to St. Louis, dozens of trappers, the famous "mountain men," made their way to the Rockies, going up the Missouri and its major tributaries, probing all the valleys of Montana, Idaho, and Oregon.

In this far country, they caught beaver, muskrat, and otter. Aside from increasingly sporadic contacts, they had nothing to do with white men. They lived with the Indians and soon came to think and act like them. In the English colonies of the eastern seaboard, where they almost never set foot anymore, these "white Indians" were contemptuously referred to as "squaw men" or by the more admiring term "free men."

They seemed to have no ties. Some were soldiers who had become so bored at the trading posts where they were garrisoned that they had ended up taking their rifles, stealing a few traps and perhaps a canoe or a horse, and going off to live with the Indians. Others had been guides hired to lead missionaries, explorers, or prospectors to some far-off spot, where they had more-or-less abandoned their employers. Or, more often, they had worked for a fur trading company but had become so indebted to it that they had seen no choice but to break their contracts and sever all ties with white society, going off to live with their Indian wives deep in the woods.

A trapper typically had a big beard and long hair under a wide-brimmed hat jammed firmly onto his head. The seams of his buckskin shirt and trousers were edged with long fringes that not only provided extra laces, but also drained off water in heavy rains or when fording deep rivers on horseback. He also travelled by foot or sometimes canoe.

On his feet, he wore moccasins decorated with beadwork and porcupine quills. He had a pouch containing bullets, an awl, a cloth for cleaning his rifle, tobacco, a pipe, and a small container (often the tip of an antelope horn) of castoreum to serve as bait for his traps, which were carried in a leather bag to keep them dry. His powder horn was hung around his neck, and his hunting knife and hatchet from his belt. Across the front of his saddle, or slung across his chest if he was on foot, or propped against the gunwales of his canoe, always within reach, always loaded and cocked, was his most prized possession: his rifle.

The mountain men never stayed long in one place. In winter, during the trapping season, they had to keep moving from valley to valley, from one beaver pond to another. Most, however, had homes and families to which they returned from time to time: Indian wives and children, who spoke Mandan, Ojibwa, or Shoshoni.

Some of these men lived with tribes that were hostile to the French. A few, such as those living with the Pawnee, had even been known to fight their European countrymen to defend their Métis families. When Lewis and Clark encountered the Mandan and the Hidatsa of Missouri in 1804, they met a number of Canadian trappers, including Toussaint Charbonneau and René Jussaume, who had been living with the tribes for many years.

Among themselves, these men spoke French, which remained the dominant language throughout the West until the mid-nineteenth century. At least half of them had been born in Canada or the French-speaking villages of the Mississippi Valley. Many, however, also spoke Chinook jargon, a trade language consisting of a simplified grammar with vocabulary drawn from several Indian languages along with a mix of French and some English words, often altered beyond recognition. From the Great Lakes and the Mississippi west to the Pacific, Chinook

The eighteenth-century trapper's preferred weapon was the long rifle, also known as a Kentucky rifle. It was often ornately decorated.

jargon long remained the lingua franca for tribes belonging to different language families.

The mountain men were free – to the extent that one can be in this world. But their freedom was often threatened. A trapper had to constantly defend his trapping grounds from other white men and Indians. He had to go farther and farther up the rivers and into the mountains. Over the years, the mountain men thus explored and trapped all the valleys on the east side of the Rockies.

By the age of thirty-five or forty, they would retire and settle near the places where they had spent their youths hunting, trapping, and trading. Chalifoux remained in Arkansas, and Robidoux and Charbonneau, in northern California. Papin cleared a patch of land on the Platte River. The Lucier and Gervais brothers settled in Oregon on the edge of what would become known as the French Prairie, a stretch of land along the Willamette River between Salem and Portland where, by the mid-nineteenth century, some 120 trappers of Canadian origin had retired.

Whereas the Lewis and Clark expedition had opened the West to the trappers, the influx of settlers in the 1830s and '40s led to their dispersion and rapid disappearance since settlers and trappers could not co-exist. They had completely different views of life, liberty, and property.

A trapper's deerskin jacket in a style common to the upper Missouri. The fringes helped channel off rain while also serving as a source of extra ties.

The settlers tried to take over the most fertile lands in the plateaus and valleys of the Rocky Mountains. They confronted the Indians, whom the trappers, having wed Indian women, looked upon as brothers. For decades, the West was wracked by conflicts triggered by the settlers. Their arrival in Wyoming, Missouri, Idaho, and Montana marked the end of the era of the trappers and sealed the tragic fate of the Indians.

The barefoot man with a trap in his hand is wearing a blue cloth cap with a wolf tail as well as an Indian jacket whose cut, like its heart and star motifs, is inspired by European traditions. His fellow trapper is wearing a coat made from a trade blanket; the three stripes woven into the blanket indicate its length and width and the weight of the wool.

THE TRAPPER'S WIFE

While voyageurs had only temporary liaisons with Indian women, the trappers tended to establish long-lasting relationships with their country wives.

Indian women who married trappers were expected to help them in all aspects of their work.

Typical of Plains Cree clothing, this dress is made of a deerskin folded and sewn along one side. The lower edge of the yoke, one of the shoulders, and the bottom edge of the dress are decorated with fringes and porcupine quills dyed red, blue, white, yellow, pink, and purple.

A good trapper could easily get by in the woods with little or no contact with other white men. But he had to have some kind of ties with the Indians among whom he had chosen to live. It was usually through the women that he could truly become part of the Indian world. Unlike the voyageur or coureur des bois, for whom Indian women were necessarily only temporary or seasonal partners, the trapper had a real wife, with whom he founded a family. The couple would share daily duties, he tending his traps and hunting; she taking care of the home, children, and domestic chores. In the fur trade, an Indian woman was much more suited than a white woman to play the role of wife and partner.

Some such unions lasted for years or even a lifetime. Like the voyageurs, the trappers married according to the "country" tradition. The trapper would present gifts to the family and ask the parents for their daughter's hand. In certain tribes, the elders would publicly remind the girl of her wifely duties, and then the trapper would simply go off with her. They would live as husband and wife for as long as it suited them both. A couple was considered legitimately married as soon as the partners had expressed their consent in front of witnesses. Divorce was equally simple.

The bride-to-be was sometimes "prepared" to please her white husband. The grease and paint she often wore would be removed and she would be dressed in a blouse, short dress, petticoat, and possibly long stockings and garters, more or less like a European woman.

The trapper adopted the manners and culture of his wife's tribe. She would not be just a sexual partner, but also an essential helpmate in his life. In the early years of their union, before he had mastered the language of the country, she served as his interpreter and guide. She also made or repaired snowshoes, moccasins, clothing, and fish nets. She would often maintain a small garden, prepare pemmican, grind cornmeal, gather firewood, prepare skins and meat, and hunt and trap small game. She would make dishes and containers out of birchbark, grain sacks out of skins, and mats out of woven reeds. But, most of all, she gave her husband the keys to a new world. Marrying an Indian woman meant establishing real ties with her tribe and becoming an integral

The Indians used whatever materials were available for making tools for scraping skins. The bottom two are made from elk antlers, the middle one from a moose bone, and the top one from a discarded rifle barrel.

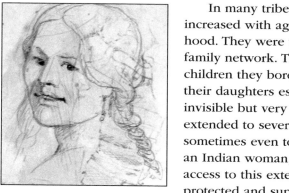

part of a society to which he otherwise would have had no access.

In Indian communities, the women often had more authority and influence than the men. Among the Sioux and Iroquois, they occupied functions that never would have been entrusted to a woman in France or any other European country. A young woman who married a white trapper did not lose any privileges; on the contrary, in most tribes her marriage brought her prestige and respect.

When her husband was off trapping, the wife took care of the material needs of the family. She raised and educated the children, whose first language was always that of her tribe. When they grew up, most of these children would consider themselves Indians. Through their father, they had easier and more direct contact with the white world and often acted as intermediaries, traders, or diplomats, but most of them saw themselves first and foremost as Indians.

At this time, the Europeans were exploring and claiming new territories on others continents as well. The relationships they established with the indigenous women were almost always tinged with violence. In New France, however, that had never been the case.

The women did not completely escape abuse, for trappers could be brutal husbands. Some white trappers, like Toussaint Charbonneau, who lived with the Hidatsa, bought female slaves or prisoners to serve as wives and treated them harshly. But in Indian society, women generally remained mistresses of their own bodies. Even a married woman did not belong forever to her husband; she could divorce easily and change partners without any problem. Indian women usually did not have many children – fewer, in fact, than white women because they nursed their children for two to three years.

In many tribes, the women's power increased with age, experience, and motherhood. They were the centre of a widespread family network. Through their marriages, the children they bore or adopted, and the ties their daughters established, they acquired an invisible but very real authority, which extended to several families and clans, sometimes even to distant tribes. In marrying an Indian woman, a white trapper gained access to this extensive network and was protected and supported in his various endeavours. It was in his interest to treat his wife well.

The country wife thus played a key role not only in the trapper's life, but also in the overall organization of the fur trade. The traders in Montreal and St. Louis were well aware of that and encouraged their men to take Indian wives. Similarly, for reasons of contacts, prestige, and power, certain nations, such as the Chinook on the West Coast and the Mandan, urged their daughters to marry white men. Many families in tribes of the Missouri Valley even reserved one of their daughters for possible marriage to a trapper.

In marrying an Indian woman, the trapper entered his wife's family circle. She, in turn, was received at the trading post, and her family benefited from this tie with the white world. It was a mutually advantageous arrangement.

This Plains Cree woman is tanning a deer hide on a European-style tanning frame. On her face, she is wearing tattoos made in part with vermilion, a fine red powder that was a very popular trade item. Although trade with the Europeans provided plenty of textiles for making clothing, tanned skins were still widely used, as can be seen in the works of Karl Bodmer painted during an expedition between 1832 and 1834.

SACAGAWEA'S STORY

The only woman
on the Lewis
and Clark expedition,
Sacagawea provided
invaluable assistance as a
guide and interpreter.

The presence of the young mother and child reassured the Indian tribes of the explorers' peaceful intentions.

Sacagawea was only ten or eleven years old when she was kidnapped from her Shoshoni tribe and adopted by the Hidatsa. The Shoshoni, known to Europeans as the Snake Indians, lived at the junction of three rivers that come together to form the Missouri on high plains where only a few white trappers had ever ventured. The Hidatsa lived lower down the Missouri River.

In the spring of 1804, when Sacagawea was sixteen, her adoptive family sold her as a wife, along with her younger sister, to a Canadian fur trader who had lived among them for some fifteen years. Nearly three times her age, Toussaint Charbonneau was a good talker and a skilful hunter and trapper, but no angel.

Charbonneau and his wives initially lived with the Hidatsa, at the confluence of the Knife and Missouri Rivers. It was lush, lovely country with a very pleasant climate. Within a radius of a few kilometres, there were

Necklace made of carved catlinite. Indian women came to prefer European glass trade beads.

five large villages, two Mandan and three Hidatsa, with a total of over four thousand inhabitants. Both tribes were prosperous horse breeders and buffalo hunters. The Hidatsa tended to be rather taciturn and undemonstrative, while the Mandan were very sociable. Their women were highly prized by trappers.

Sacagawea was six months pregnant in October 1804 when the Corps of Discovery, led by Meriwether Lewis and William Clark, arrived to winter in the region. The American president, Thomas Jefferson, had entrusted the two men with a mission to explore the Missouri River and follow its main tributary to its head in the Rocky Mountains, from whence they were to seek a river offering a practicable route to the Pacific "for the purposes of commerce." The underlying idea was to break the monopoly of the North West Company and the Hudson's Bay Company, whose continued presence in the Columbia Valley was confirming British sovereignty over Oregon.

The Corps of Discovery included a number of Canadians, experienced voyageurs who were used to life in the wild. Charbonneau, who spoke French and Hidatsa, offered his services along with those of his wife, who could guide the expedition to the land of the Shoshoni, her original people.

On 11 February 1805, Sacagawea gave birth to a baby boy and only a few weeks later set off on the long and arduous journey to the Pacific. For the first leg of the trip, up the Missouri River, they travelled by canoe and pirogue. There were thirty-one men, plus Sacagawea, the only woman, along with her baby, Jean-Baptiste, whom Clark nicknamed Pomp or Pompy.

The expedition lasted almost three years, during which time Sacagawea rendered invaluable assistance to the Corps of Discovery. She knew when and where to gather edible fruits, berries, and wild onions and how to hunt and dress small game, mend clothing, and repair the teepee. Just by her presence, she was often able to reassure other Indians of the party's peaceful intentions. One day, one of the pirogues was swamped. As the panicked men swam for shore, Sacagawea calmly plucked the explorers' journals from the water, thus saving one of the most precious artefacts of American national heritage.

Sacagawea guided the expedition to the country where she had spent her early years. Thanks to her, Lewis and Clark were able to establish valuable ties with the Shoshoni, exchange their canoes and pirogues for horses, and obtain provisions and information on what routes to follow through the mountains.

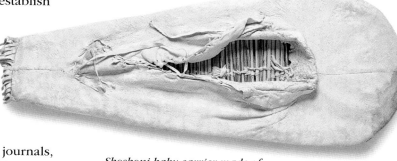

Shoshoni baby carrier made of deerskin over a willow frame. Willow could be bent into a curved shape without breaking.

In their reports and journals, Lewis and Clark do not draw a very flattering picture of Charbonneau. He was a competent guide and an excellent cook who could make a delicious buffalo sausage, but he was also sly and arrogant and would beat his wife severely at the slightest provocation.

From their journals, it appears that Sacagawea was reserved and uncommunicative. Even when she saw the Shoshoni faces and landscapes of her childhood, and was surrounded by her tearful family and friends, she never revealed her emotions. On more than one occasion, she saved the members of the expedition from serious difficulties, but she did it as her duty and with no thought of thanks or reward, in keeping with her status as a slave who had no rights, voice, or even name. In their writings, Lewis and Clark usually referred to her simply as "Charbonneau's squaw" or "the Indian woman."

Little is known about what happened to her after 1806, when the Corps of Discovery went back east. The reports make no mention of her ever being paid for her services. It is thought that she remained with her husband and son in the Hidatsa village on the Knife River and died around 1812 somewhere in South Dakota.

For a while Charbonneau worked for Manuel Lisa, head of the Missouri Fur Company. During the War of 1812, the American government entrusted him with a number of diplomatic missions with the Missouri tribes. After that, he traded with the Plains Indians. In 1834-35, when Prince Maximilian travelled up the Missouri River by steamboat, he served as an interpreter. He received a small pension from the American government until 1839 and lived into his mid-eighties.

Clark assumed responsibility for young Jean-Baptiste's education and brought him to St. Louis to study with the Jesuits. In 1823 Prince Paul of Wurtemburg, an amateur explorer, took him to Europe, where he stayed for six years, travelling and studying languages. In addition to Mandan, Hidatsa, and Shoshoni, Jean-Baptiste spoke French, English, Italian, and German. However, unable to forget the land of his youth, he returned to the mountains of Missouri and apparently adopted his father's wandering life. Sacagawea's son died in Oregon in 1866, at the age of sixty-one, on his way to Montana.

Today, near Three Forks in Shoshoni country, there is a lake that bears the name of Sacagawea in honour of the remarkable young woman who helped ensure the success of the Lewis and Clark expedition.

Acting as a guide and interpreter on one of his expeditions, Toussaint Charbonneau presents Prince Maximilian Wied-Neuwied to a Hidatsa chief.

The Trapper's Weapons and Equipment

Trappers had the combined benefit of Indian skills and know-how and European technology.

Trappers found that Indian trapping techniques did not damage the pelt.

The early-nineteenth-century trappers who went off to the Rocky Mountains, where beaver were still plentiful, were undoubtedly the best armed and the most experienced hunters ever to venture into the West. Not only had they learned invaluable skills from the Indians, but they also had the most sophisticated weapons ever produced by European technology, adapted to their specific environment and needs.

By the late eighteenth century, even before the white trappers had moved into the mountains, the long rifle, commonly called the Kentucky rifle, was in widespread use south of the Canadian border. This firearm was well suited to open terrain, where big game was rare and small game and deer or black bear had to be shot at fairly distant range.

But the Kentucky rifle was heavy and cumbersome; its .40- to .45-calibre barrel was over a metre long. And it was not very powerful or easy to handle, especially for a man on horseback or in a canoe,

or on foot when heavily loaded down with traps, tools, provisions, and possibly pelts. Some preferred the American army rifle, the M1795, though it was almost as heavy and cumbersome as the Kentucky rifle, or better still the Northwest rifle, which was distributed by the fur trading companies.

The American members of the Lewis and Clark expedition, which marked the beginning of the era of trappers and mountain men, were all equipped with Kentucky rifles. The Canadian guides and interpreters, however, used lighter

Trappers who obtained their supplies in Spanish-held territory often wore Spanish spurs, like this one dating from the 1790s.

weapons that were much easier to handle. Toussaint Charbonneau, for instance, had what Lewis called in his journal an "elegant fuzee," an English-made gun with a barrel less than a metre long, a practical, powerful, and accurate firearm that was light and easy to carry and could be quickly reloaded.

The American fur trading companies, which in the ensuing years sent trappers to the upper Missouri River and the valleys east of the Rocky Mountains, continued equipping them with long rifles. However, the American-made .52-calibre M1803 rifle, which had a shorter barrel than the M1795, was increasingly favoured by the mountain men.

Inspired by these various firearms, American gunsmiths created a rifle that was perfectly suited to trappers' needs and incorporated the new technologies then available. Perhaps most importantly, a new firing mechanism had been developed to replace the unreliable flintlock with a much more effective percussion system. The American gunsmiths also made their rifle both lighter and more powerful.

On the open, grassy plains of the West, where one could see and be seen for very great distances and where the targets were often large, heavy animals such as grizzly bears and buffalo, hunters needed a very powerful, long-range weapon. Mountain men were frequently on the move and could not encumber themselves with a rifle that was too long and hard to handle or that took too long to reload.

Around 1807 a young gunsmith named Jake Hawken settled in St. Louis where, with his brother Sam, he developed a rifle that would become the weapon of

California saddle, used in the 1830s; the mountain men had a preference for Spanish-made saddles.

Mountain men would carry a shot bag and a powder horn made from a hollowed-out buffalo horn.

choice for Western trappers. The Hawken brothers adapted the iron-mounted southern mountain rifle to meet the needs of buffalo hunters, making it more powerful, shortening the stock, and increasing the calibre, but without adding to the weight. Known as the Plains rifle, this robust firearm was immediately adopted by beaver trappers.

The Hawken rifle had a .50- to .55-calibre octagonal barrel slightly less than a metre long and rarely weighed more than five kilograms. Starting in 1830, gunsmiths in Pennsylvania, Ohio, and Missouri (especially St. Louis) started turning out thousands of Plains rifles, all more-or-less true imitations of the rifle created by the Hawken brothers.

With such a rifle, a man could kill a grizzly bear or stop a buffalo in its tracks from a range of two or three

hundred metres – and command the respect of any Sioux, Crow, Blackfoot, rival trapper, or white settler who encroached on his territory. The Plains rifle thus spread throughout the West within a few years.

The American Fur Company sold the Indians tens of thousands of trade rifles, which were similar to trappers' rifles except that they were not as well finished. Often the stock was barely polished and the screws were not properly sunk.

In the 1830s, trappers started using handguns, usually a pair of them and ideally of the same calibre as their rifles so that both could take the same bullets. They typically chose a .52 calibre for both their rifles and pistols. Thus armed, a mountain man was well able to defend his territory.

The mountain man was often alone. And sometimes, especially in the spring before the rendezvous, he carried a small fortune in furs. Even if he had ties to a trading company, which was supposed to ensure his safety, he could rely only on himself in the face of natural dangers such as wolves, grizzlies, and buffalo as well as accidents of various sorts. Conflicts with other trappers, white or Indian, were also not uncommon. They would fight over their territories, which no one actually owned or had a right to. The trapper, however, was a free spirit content to impose his own law.

This mountain man worked his huge trapping territory alone. He is riding a mustang and using a mule to transport his gear and provisions, leaving him free to carry only his Hawken rifle, made by the famous brothers who adapted the Kentucky rifle to meet trappers' needs. He is wearing a fur cap with a leather visor and a coat made from a blue trade blanket. Around his wrist is a whip with a handle carved from an elk antler.

THE HORSE

Introduced to North America in the sixteenth century by the Spanish conquistadors, the horse radically changed the culture and lifestyle of many Indian peoples.

Never having seen horses before, the Indians were terrified but soon learned to master these strange beasts.

It was from the Southwest, thanks to the Spanish, that the horse was introduced to North America, though they did their best to prevent its widespread use. The horses brought along on the expeditions of the early conquistadors (Hernán Cortés, Alvar Nuñez Cabeza de Vaca, and Hernando de Soto) in the first half of the sixteenth century did not survive long. Those that did not die of exhaustion or hunger were killed in combat. Injured horses would be finished off and eaten to keep them from falling into the hands of the Indians. Furthermore, it was practically impossible for the horses to reproduce since the Spaniards rode only stallions. In the herd of Francisco Vásquez de Coronado, who brutally conquered the Pueblo Indians in the early 1540s, there were only 2 mares out of a total of 552 horses.

The Indians were at first terrified of these large, unknown creatures. They believed that the horse and rider were a single, very fast, powerful animal, the most formidable enemy they had ever faced. In time, however, the horse would radically change their culture, lifestyle, and mythology – as much as, if not more than, the rifle.

The Indians occasionally saw runaway horses that had escaped from the Spanish ranches and haciendas. Once they had overcome their fear and awe, they began hunting these horses as food. Then they managed to capture a few of the animals alive.

This branding iron belonged to Pierre Chouteau, head of the American Fur Company.

On 13 August 1680, after 140 years of domination and exploitation, the Pueblo Indians rose in revolt and drove out their oppressors. The fleeing Spaniards left behind thousands of horses running free throughout the Southwest. When they returned thirteen years later, the Pueblos and their allies had mastered the horse. The small, light, high-strung Andalusian horses, descended from Arabian, Barb, or Numidian stock, were able to adapt to the extreme climate and terrain of Arizona and New Mexico much more easily than were the heavier horses that the English and French were importing from Europe.

Within a century, the horses of the Spanish conquistadors lost several centimetres at the withers and gained a new name: "mustang," from *mestengo*, meaning "ownerless" or "stray." The American horse, of European and North African origin, had returned to the wild before being domesticated again.

By the late eighteenth century, there were some two million feral horses roaming the prairies and high plains of the American Southwest. The Indians caught them in the spring when they were weakened by the privations of winter. But it still required great daring and ingenuity for a horse and rider to capture a mustang.

The presence of the horse gave rise to wars and tremendous upheavals among the Indian peoples. Thanks to the horse, certain Siouan tribes of sedentary farmers became nomadic and spread over a vast territory. Nations that had known nothing of each other

By the late eighteenth century, there were some two million horses running wild in the American Southwest.

suddenly came into contact. The nomadic Comanche of the Southern Plains soon mastered the horse and set off to conquer new territories, thus coming into conflict with other peoples, such as the Blackfoot, who became their worst enemy.

The horse transformed the culture and lifestyle of numerous Indian nations. The Ute of Colorado, for instance, were finally able to make their way down to the Great Plains to hunt buffalo – and to fight with the Comanche, Navajo, and Apache.

Nomadic tribes that had only dogs as beasts of burden were necessarily limited in the possessions they could amass and the size of their teepees. Whereas a dog could carry only about fifteen kilograms, a horse could pack up to eighty or ninety kilograms. A nomadic family who owned several horses could therefore carry poles and buffalo skins to put up a large teepee, as well as a good deal of food, clothing, tools and weapons.

The various tribes developed different breeds of horses depending on the types of stock they had captured or stolen and the grazing land available to them. In the cool, humid grasslands of Oregon, the Nez Perce and the Cayuse raised enormous herds. They would geld mediocre stallions to keep them from reproducing and, through this selective breeding, developed swift horses with great stamina, including their traditional battle horse, the spotted appaloosa, one of the first typically American breeds. The Indians applied war paint to their mounts as

Blackfoot saddle, made without a horn and cantle.

well as to themselves, painting red and yellow stripes on their horses' necks, dying their manes black and their tails red. The rider would wear vermilion paint.

Indian horses were used to the fresh prairie grass and did not like oats. They were frugal, hardy animals, well suited to the mountain men's environment. Hitched to a sled, they could pull up to a hundred kilograms of furs, in addition to traps, pots and pans, and other utensils, over almost any terrain.

In the eighteenth century, there was significant trade in horses between the Spaniards of New Mexico and the Plains Indians, especially the Comanche, Apache, and Ute. At trade fairs, such as the one in Taos, the Comanche would exchange slaves for horses.

In opening the great trails that in the nineteenth century crisscrossed the entire American territory, the horse played a role similar to that of the canoe in the eastern part of the continent. It was on horseback that the white men came to Colorado, California, Montana, and Oregon, opening the Jackass Trail (almost 2,400 kilometres long) from San Diego to San Antonio, the Butterfield Trail (almost 4,500 kilometres) from St. Louis to San Francisco, and the Oregon Trail (3,200 kilometres) from the former Jesuit mission of St. Joseph to Fort Vancouver on the Columbia River.

As the horse advanced from the Spanish-controlled Southwest across the Plains, the rifle was making its way from the English- and French-controlled East and Northeast. They met around 1790. And when they did, they gave birth to a completely new culture, that of the Plains Indians.

Trapping Techniques

Steel traps made
the trappers' lives much easier.
There were many different
models, some homemade, others
crafted by gunsmiths.

*When approaching a beaver lodge,
the trapper would wade
through the frigid water to conceal
his tracks and scent.*

Beavers like cold, moving water. They abound in the high, cool valleys of the Missouri, Yellowstone, and Snake Rivers, which rush down from the Rocky Mountains to the Prairies. In the seemingly dry grasslands of the West, beaver could be found simply by following the lines of willow trees and alders that grew along small streams. When he spotted signs of recent activity, such as beaver trails, gnawed branches, or dams, the trapper would approach, wading through the frigid water to conceal his tracks and scent. Beavers are wary animals; if they are disturbed, they will hide or abandon the area.

The trapper would position his traps near shore, approximately ten centimetres under water. He would choose a firm, flat surface, levelling off the stream bed if necessary or placing a flat rock on the bottom. He would then open the jaws of the trap with his foot or a pair of pliers made from a couple of sturdy sticks about thirty centimetres long and joined at one end with a leather strap.

Next, the trapper would take a strong chain about a metre long with a ring at one end and attach it to the trap. Once the trap was properly set, he would stretch the chain toward the middle of the stream or pond, where the water was deepest. Then he would take a stick – making sure to remove the bark so that it wouldn't look appetizing to the beaver – and shove it through the ring and firmly into the bottom of the pond or stream so as to anchor the trap.

On the shore, about fifteen centimetres above the immersed trap, he would stick a small branch dipped in castoreum, which the beaver could smell from a great distance, though it is not perceptible to humans. And then he would wade away through the water as quietly as possible.

*This Canadian trapper, named Antoine,
worked as a hunter supplying
western expeditions. Many of his fellow
Canadians also worked
as guides and interpreters.*

The beaver would swim toward the bait. In reaching up to sniff at the castoreum, it would step on the trap, which would snap shut on its paw. The beaver's natural reflex was to dive under water, dragging the trap along with it. The weight of the trap and chain would keep it on the bottom, where it would drown. When the trapper returned, he would locate the end of the chain by means of the stick and pull up the trap along with the dead beaver.

A good, hardworking trapper would catch a beaver in each trap he set. But he couldn't trap every day. Once a particular site had been trapped out, he had to gather up

*Beaver traps gradually
became lighter, enabling trappers
to carry more of them.*

his gear and move on to another valley or river, taking the time to set up camp there with his wife. He would carry along his pelts or cache them somewhere.

There were many different models of beaver traps, some homemade, others produced by professional gunsmiths in the East or the West. But whether the model was called Eclipse, Kagaroo, or Arros, and whether it came from St. Louis, Michilimackinac, or Fort Vancouver and was made by Lovell, Hawley, Sewell, Newhouse, or Victor, the principle was always the same: metal jaws that snapped shut on the beaver's paw.

In time, traps were made of steel weighing less than two kilograms without the chain. The trapper would go off with a half dozen or so traps in a waterproof bag made of buffalo skin. His traps were one of his most precious possessions, and he took good care of them. He would scratch or nick them with a knife to identify them as his. In the wilderness, it was easy to lose one's traps. The Indians did not have the same sense of property as the Europeans and had no compunction about taking them. The trapper would then lose several days trying to get them back, sometimes at the risk of his life. Around Bear Lake, they tell the story of a trapper who spent an entire day tracking the thieves who had stolen his traps, finally catching up with them at nightfall and demanding his traps at gunpoint. He finally made it back home after twenty-four hours of uninterrupted tracking and walking.

As soon as he had taken his traps from the water, the trapper would clean and dry them, apply a coat of grease to prevent rust, and wrap them up again in the leather bag, which he would hang from a tree. He would then skin the beavers, keeping only the pelt, castoreum, and a few tails for his evening meal.

This homemade trap was used for catching muskrat, which is found from the Gulf of Mexico to Alaska.

When he returned to camp, his wife would scrape the pelts to remove any remaining bits of fat, gristle, or muscle. Then she would stretch each pelt over a young willow branch, joining the ends to form a hoop. She would leave them to dry in the open air after marking each one on the edge or back with a knife, always using the same mark in the same place so that they could recognize their pelts at the trading post or identify them if they were ever stolen.

Once the pelts were dry, they would fold them in half with the fur facing inward, then pile them together and press them into forty-kilogram bales. They would sometimes make a crude press on site, using a good chain, strong hardwood branches, and leather straps. But it was easier to take the pelts to the trading post, which had powerful lever or screw presses. The bales, containing sixty skins each, were worth $300 to $600.

In the spring, the trapper and his wife would obtain horses and collect the bales of pelts they had cached in various locations during the trapping season. They would saddle up their horses, array themselves in their best finery, and head off for the rendezvous to do business and celebrate.

Each spring, the trapper and his wife would go to the rendezvous to sell their bales of furs.

THE RENDEZVOUS

These annual fairs for traders and suppliers also attracted magicians, charlatans, loose women, and all manner of adventurers.

Indian traders also flocked to the trappers' rendezvous, which soon developed into extremely popular fairs.

Long before European contact, the Indians had established an effective trading system between the Prairies, the Plateau, and the West Coast. The Lolo Trail, a highly frequented route across the Rocky Mountains from Idaho to Montana, had existed since time immemorial. With the arrival of the horse, exchanges became increasingly well organized. The Indians would put together impressive trading expeditions and would also hold huge trade fairs, some bringing together thousands of people for several days.

In the early nineteenth century, at the end of summer, some two thousand Crow would gather on the banks of the Missouri River to trade with the Mandan and the Hidatsa. The Crow raised horses and were great buffalo hunters. A proud, arrogant, and remarkably elegant people, they were dubbed "the Indian Brummels" by the French. After erecting their three hundred or so teepees near a Hidatsa or Mandan village, they would pass the peace pipe and then begin bartering. For instance, they might trade 250 horses and buffalo skins in return for 200 guns, ammunition, axes, clothing, and pots. They would have obtained the horses from the Shoshoni for half of what they were charging the Hidatsa and Mandan, who in turn would sell them for twice as much to the Cree and the Assiniboin of the Prairies in exchange for European goods from the Northeast. In this way, manufactured goods, produce from the land and the sea, fashions, and ideas circulated throughout the Indian world.

Another common rendezvous site at that time was The Dalles, situated on the Columbia River where it crosses the Cascade mountain range in Oregon.

Bowl of a Cree pipe carved with animal figures: a moose head for abundance and a turtle for long life.

There the Nez Perce and other Plains tribes would meet up with traders from the West Coast, usually in the fall.

When the trappers reached the mountains, they thus found trade routes and rendezvous that were already well established. The white traders took advantage of the Indians' existing network. Beginning in the 1820s, they opened trading posts along these routes and organized more rendezvous sites.

Pierre Chouteau, a rich entrepreneur from St. Louis, built a large complex on the Missouri River in southern Dakota. Fort Pierre, as it was called, attracted all the trappers of the region as well as horse traders and Indians along with their families – in short, all the various representatives of this new Prairie world. But as the new Rocky Mountain fur trade territory expanded, more places were needed for trading and receiving furs.

William Henry Ashley, a shrewd businessman who headed the Rocky Mountain Fur Company, had the idea of organizing annual rendezvous in different, easily accessible places. They were held in the summer and soon became very successful trade fairs, considerably enriching Ashley in the process.

The first such rendezvous was held in 1825 in southern Wyoming. The next year, it took place north of Great Salt Lake in Utah, and in 1827 and 1828, a little farther north, near Bear Lake on the border between Idaho and Utah. These get-togethers

Trade blankets were often cut up to make clothing.

were so popular that entire villages of Indian men, women, and children would turn up, bringing along hundreds of horses. The rendezvous thus had to be organized where there was sufficient water and grass for grazing.

The rendezvous were wild, unbridled celebrations, a welcome opportunity for the trapper to kick up his heels. He would have spent all winter in his distant valley, in a log cabin hung with furs, with only his wife and children for company. As soon as the warmer weather arrived, he would sell a horse, load up the others with bales of beaver, otter, and muskrat pelts, and set off, alone or with his family, for the legendary rendezvous.

In the 1830s the trappers would often meet around the Teton Mountains on the border of Wyoming and Idaho, just south of the Yellowstone Plateau, in Shoshoni country. Rising out of the Plains a little before the great wall of the Rocky Mountains, the Tetons can be seen from very far off and served as landmarks to those travelling in the region.

Each trapper would proceed directly to the company's trading post. In Jackson Hole, the Rocky Mountain Fur Company's agents would erect huge tents in which to do business. The clerk would inspect the pelts, compare them, and decide on a price for each. Once his pelts had been weighed, put away, and paid for, and his debts paid off, the trapper would obtain trade goods, gunpowder, bullets, and traps. He might also buy a few luxuries such as salt, a little flour, clothing, a bead necklace, or garters for his wife.

The rendezvous attracted traders and suppliers of various sorts, as well as charlatans, magicians, musicians, loose women, and a great many Indians.

The company's wagons would be drawn up near the camp. All around, Cheyenne, Ute, Gros Ventre, Crow, and Shoshoni, attracted by the possibility of good trades, would have put up their teepees and built makeshift

Pipe stems were as highly decorated as the bowls and were sometimes carved into a spiral shape.

corrals for the few dozen horses they had brought to sell. They might also be willing to sell, or to trade for a rifle, gunpowder, or alcohol, their black-haired daughters with their beaded dresses and winsome smiles.

Sharpshooting matches would often be held. One man might shoot out a candle from twenty-five feet; another might drive in a nail from a certain distance or slice a bullet on the edge of an axe. Many trappers rapidly squandered their year's earnings on women, gambling, and alcohol. The prudent ones would buy a better rifle, gunpowder, perhaps a few lighter, more powerful traps. But everything was overpriced at a rendezvous. Goods and provisions sent from St. Louis sold for at least ten to twenty times their original cost.

Isolated in his remote valley, the trapper would have lost touch with economic realities. And in the excitement of the rendezvous, it was hard to determine the true value of things. Some men were known to gamble away their new rifles, horses, and even their wives. The company's agents and clerk, however, always kept a cool head. They would give a ruined trapper enough credit to buy provisions, trade goods, firearms, and a horse. And the trapper would set off (with or without his wife) seeking another unknown valley, where he would spend the winter trapping beaver and looking forward to the spring and another glorious rendezvous.

The rendezvous was an occasion for wild partying, which sometimes degenerated into violence.

THE MIXED BLOODS

Many children of mixed parentage did not know their fathers. Raised by their mothers, they were entirely assimilated into Indian society.

Menominee chief Souligny bore the name of his great-grandfather, a member of one of the founding families of Green Bay.

Drawn to distant horizons, forever seeking new trapping and hunting grounds, the coureurs des bois, voyageurs, trappers, and traders spread throughout the continent, from the forests of the East to the prairies, deserts, and mountains of the West. And everywhere they went, they met, loved, and sometimes married Indian women – and, of course, had mixed-race children with them.

Their sons, in turn, usually married Indian women. While their daughters sometimes married white men, as their mothers had done, these white men were usually very assimilated into Indian culture. Most Mixed Bloods, both male and female, thus generally lived with Indian tribes and almost never with white people.

When the interpreters and coureurs des bois penetrated inland, they left numerous mixed-blood children wherever they went. The French, more than any other Europeans, had close relationships with Indian women, ranging from temporary liaisons to seasonal matches or lasting unions. An interpreter or clerk placed with the Indians by a fur trading company might have an Indian slave, a wife who had been purchased, stolen, or won through gambling, or even several wives. White men who were kept as prisoners or slaves of the Indians also had offspring who were adopted and raised as Indian children.

Scattered clusters of Mixed Bloods thus appeared very early on in the wake of the expeditions by Radisson and Groseilliers to the Great Lakes and by the Chevalier de Troyes and Sieur d'Iberville to the coast of Hudson Bay. But they were also to be found around the trading posts, forts, and missions – indeed, anywhere that white men came into contact with Indian society and women.

A very natural and prolific merging of races and cultures occurred between the French and the Indians. After the Conquest of New France, when the English moved more freely inland, they were surprised at the easy familiarity and close relationships that existed between the coureurs des bois and Indian women.

However, most children of mixed marriages or relationships likely never knew their fathers. They would be raised by their mothers, either in the mother's tribe or in the rather wretched communities that gravitated around the trading posts. In fact, so many Indian women with their mixed-blood children came to depend on the trading posts that in 1803 the North West Company required the fathers to pay part of the cost of their maintenance. But this order was never rigorously applied. First, it was not always easy to ascertain who the father was or, if the father's identity were known, to determine his whereabouts. If he could be located, he might refuse to have anything to do with the child or might

Military uniform given to an Osage chief and worn as a wedding outfit.

This fire bag, used for carrying flint, steel, and tinder, is made in the Cree style but embroidered in the Métis style.

not have any money. And, at any rate, the mothers of these mixed-blood children were often useful to the people in the trading posts since they provided a variety of services as well as serving as interpreters and intermediaries. They would hear of the Indians' intentions before the white men and often be able to prevent attacks.

Many mixed-blood children thus grew up in proximity to white society though they were never actually part of it. The situation was truly tragic if the mother no longer had ties to her own tribe, or if she herself were a Mixed Blood and didn't belong to any organized group. Her children had no roots, no sense of belonging. As adults, they would either live as poor, isolated nomads or exist on the fringes of white society, doing the most menial, worst-paid work.

The trading companies employed Mixed Bloods as guides, interpreters, and paddlers. They also relied on them to provide the posts with fish and game and other supplies. But they never really trusted them. When the Hudson's Bay Company organized hunting trips with Mixed Bloods, company officials insisted they be accompanied by officers with orders to act as strict masters.

Rather than accept these inevitable humiliations, many young Mixed Bloods preferred to sever all ties with white society and join the Indian world, which was much more welcoming. The Indians were always willing to adopt these children, whatever their origin, be they blond, brunette, or red-headed. Such children sometimes even had a

privileged status. Young Mixed Bloods, who would have lived as outcasts among the whites, were proud of their difference within Indian society.

The Mixed Bloods led a precarious, often parasitic existence. As long as they had no contact with other Mixed Bloods, they had no awareness of themselves as a distinct social group and had no way of acting together to improve their condition. They tended to be very timid and distrustful of white people, whom they disliked and feared and avoided as much as possible.

The best intentioned white men noted that even the poorest of the Mixed Bloods would not let anyone infringe on their freedom or treat them with contempt or abuse. They may have been timid and distrustful but they were never servile. If one spoke roughly to a Mixed Blood, one could be sure of never getting anything from him. "I am not a dog," he would reply. "Nobody speaks to me like that."

This Métis man on horseback is wearing a cap inspired by the Scottish tam-o'-shanter, like that worn by his companion. He is carrying a short rifle for hunting buffalo, and his saddle is stuffed with buffalo hair. The saddle blanket is similar to those used by the Lakota. The Métis man on foot is wearing leather leggings, like those used farther south to prevent rattlesnake bites. His leather coat is cut like a European frock coat.

Charles-Michel de Langlade's Story

His comrades in arms said that they had never seen a man so in control of himself and so courageous in battle.

Believing the boy to be inhabited by a protective spirit, his Ottawa brothers always held him in high esteem.

Charles-Michel Mouet de Langlade was only ten years old when his uncle, an Ottawa chief named Nissowaquet, took him along on a punitive raid against the Chickasaw. The Chickasaw were formidable warriors. As allies of the English, they played the same role in present-day Mississippi as the Iroquois did in the area south of Lake Ontario and in the St. Lawrence Valley. That summer, the

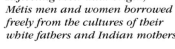

Pistol used circa 1745. Like army officers, trading post commanders carried such weapons for protection.

Ottawa managed to defeat the Chickasaw, something they had not been able to do in a very long time. Believing the boy to be inhabited by a protective spirit, they attributed their victory to him and subsequently held him in very high esteem.

Charles-Michel's father, Augustin, was a well-to-do fur trader from Trois Rivières who had settled in Michilimackinac with his wife, Domitilde, Chief Nissowaquet's sister, in the early 1720s. He worked in the fur trade in the upper Mississippi Valley and throughout Wisconsin, where he spent the rest of his life.

With his French and Indian background, and having travelled extensively throughout the Pays d'en Haut with his parents, Charles-Michel de Langlade understood at a very young age the major political issues of the day. Although he remained very attached to his Indian roots, he put his considerable talents to the service of the Europeans, partici-pating in many of the bloody conflicts that would shape the fate of North America.

When he was twenty-one, he led a small army of three hundred Indians and Frenchmen that routed the Miami from Pickawillany (present-day

Piqua), reasserting French control over the Ohio Valley and its peoples. During the raid, the Miami chief, Memeskia, or La Demoiselle as he was also known, was captured, boiled, and eaten by Langlade's Indians.

Langlade was promoted to ensign and played an active role in the Seven Years War, which resulted in France's ceding almost all of its North American possessions to the British. He was stationed at Fort Duquesne (Pittsburgh) with his small army of Indians and coureurs des bois and was instrumental in Captain Daniel Dumas's routing of the English at the famous Battle of Monongahela in July 1755. He spent the next two years fighting in upper New York State around Fort Carillon (Ticonderoga) and Fort George (Lake George), where he served under the Marquis de Montcalm, commander of the French troops in Canada. These skirmishes were intended to contain the English colonists of the eastern seaboard who wanted

Reflecting their dual origin, Métis men and women borrowed freely from the cultures of their white fathers and Indian mothers.

control of the Ohio Valley, New France's natural route to the Mississippi basin and Louisiana. Langlade conducted reconnaissance and drew up remarkably effective ambush maps, while maintaining close contacts with his Ottawa brothers and the large tribes west of the Great Lakes. No one else was as good at understanding and communicating with the Indians and rallying them to fight.

Nevertheless, the French Empire in North America was seriously threatened. Acadia had fallen, and the English were exerting tremendous pressure against New France in both the South and the East. In the summer of 1759, Langlade rushed with his Indians to the aid of Quebec, which was under siege by the young British general James Wolfe. On 26 July a detachment led by Wolfe was advancing up the Montmorency River, which flows into the St. Lawrence just below Quebec. Langlade proposed to attack it.

With his Indians and some reinforcements, he thought he could easily ambush the English detachment in the narrow valley and wipe it out. But Montcalm decided to recall his troops. Seven weeks later, at the disastrous Battle of the Plains of Abraham, during which two of Langlade's brothers were killed, Quebec, the capital of New France, fell to the English. Canada would soon become a British possession. Some historians believe that if Langlade's tactical advice had been heeded, the course of history might well have been different.

Langlade was not a man to nurse regrets. Like most of the inhabitants of the Pays d'en Haut, he accepted British domination without too much difficulty. After France's defeat, he took command of Michilimackinac until the arrival of the British commander George Etherington.

In the spring of 1763, he warned Etherington that the Ojibwa, whose chief, Pontiac, had remained loyal to the French, were planning an uprising. Etherington did not believe him. On 4 June, pretending to be playing lacrosse, the Ojibwa overran the fort and were about to kill its English inhabitants. At the risk of his life, Langlade saved the commander and his men from the stake and convinced his Ottawa relatives to deliver them safe and sound to Montreal. He then took command of the fort again until the British returned the following year.

In 1776 Langlade was in Green Bay when the commander of Michilimackinac, Captain De Peyster, recalled him to rally the Western tribes against the American revolutionaries who were threatening Canada. Langlade convinced the Indians to switch allegiance to the British, their former enemies during the conflicts with the French. All during the American War of Independence, Langlade and his men fought on the side of the British against the Americans in Vermont, Indiana, Illinois, and Missouri.

After the war, he returned to Michilimackinac, where he continued to work for the British Indian Department. He made frequent trips to Green Bay, where, like his father, he finally settled and became a fur trader. He had a son from a youthful relationship with a girl from the Ottawa tribe and two daughters with his wife, Charlotte Ambrosine Bourassa, whom he had married when he was twenty-five.

When he retired from the British army, Langlade was granted 3,000 acres (about 1,200 hectares) on the Thames River in Ontario. He died in 1800.

Toward the end of his life, Charles-Michel de Langlade claimed that he had taken part in ninety-nine battles and skirmishes. His comrades in arms said that they had never seen a man so in control of himself and so courageous in battle.

The Plains Cree maintained close ties with the Métis, many of whom were related to them through the "marriage" of Cree women with Canadian coureurs des bois or English or Scottish traders.

*At that time,
it was almost inconceivable
for a white woman
to go to the Pays d'en Haut
and live like the Indians.*

Part Five

ODYSSEY INTO THE FAR WEST

It was pitch black in the teepee. Marie could hear a low chanting sound near her. When she realized it was the Magpie – whom she called the old Magpie – she knew that she was either very ill or in danger of dying. Whenever the Magpie intoned her gentle chants in the night, it was to heal or to help someone die.

Marie wasn't about to die. She couldn't remember why exactly, but she couldn't die. Not now. The old Magpie must be chanting to heal her. She knew all kinds of chants, some of them capable of making a person fall madly in love, of giving death, or of healing the body and the soul. "If she's chanting, it is to heal me," thought Marie.

The old Magpie had always loved her. She was her second mother, her Indian mother. Her other mother, the white one, Marie hadn't seen since she left Berthier last spring. Maybe Marie would never see her first mother again, so sad, so angry, and so far away.

"You'll live like a Savage up there," she had said. "That's no place for a white woman. You won't even have a house. And no priest. And your husband won't even be around. He'll be with those Indian women."

But she had left regardless. And she had never regretted it, never. François had come into her life just in time. In less than four months she would have married another man, a good and courageous man who had his own farm. But François had arrived, just before Christmas, created quite a commotion in the parish, and set her heart on fire.

It was thought that he had come back for good. That he would marry and settle down on a piece of land, like his father and his uncles had done after a wild youth spent as voyageurs. But when Marie saw François in front of the church after Sunday Mass, she knew that he was not the type to stay around, and that sooner or later he would leave again. Just seeing his smile, and the way he looked at people, you could tell he wasn't the type to settle down.

"Drink, my little one," said the Magpie, lifting Marie's head and bringing to her lips a birch-bark container filled with a cold bitter liquid.

Marie had already told her Magpie the whole story. The old woman knew what had transpired in her young heart. Marie had described that Sunday afternoon when François had come to visit his aunt.

This Blackfoot woman is dressed in the typical Plains style: a deerskin coat and dress tied around the waist with a wide, colourful sash.

She was sitting apart from the others, with her cousins. She had eyes only for him, had ears only for him, and listened to him talk of the country that he had seen, the rapids that he had run, the Indians that he considered his friends, the wild horses, the buffalo herds.

"I don't know exactly how it happened, but our eyes met. And for a moment, he stopped talking, as if he had lost the thread of his story. And I didn't lower my eyes; I smiled."

The old Magpie's hand, so cool and soft, felt soothing on her forehead. Marie remembered her other mother's worried look that day in her aunt's kitchen.

Indian women married voyageurs "country style" and often ended up raising their children alone.

The men were whispering among themselves, and sometimes they laughed out loud and looked at the women to be sure that they were not listening. Marie's cousins said that a woman had to be crazy to marry a voyageur. "They already have Indian wives and children." Marie kept quiet. She wanted to go off with him, regardless. To be with him. But also to see these places with the magic names that he talked about – Lac Seul, Rainy Lake, the Assiniboine River, the Red River, Pembina.

Pembina! Suddenly she remembered why she didn't want to die. A woman who is carrying a child cannot die. Marie couldn't die because her son, the first white child in the Pays d'en Haut, would be born this winter in Pembina, in Dakota.

The Magpie had stopped her chanting for a moment, as though she were following Marie's thoughts, and she looked disconcerted. Her hand hesitated, and then withdrew. Marie looked for it in the dark. She turned her head and placed her burning forehead in the Magpie's hand, and the Indian woman resumed her slow chanting.

Marie continued to think of her white mother, the pain she had caused her when she told her that she was leaving with François. They were married in April. Three days later, François was hired by a Montreal trader. On the contract, which he signed with an X, he specified that there must be a place for his wife in the canoe. According to the notary, that had never happened before. "Never has a white woman gone to live with the Indians."

They left in early May. In the parish, everyone said that Marie was accompanying François because she didn't want him to fall into the hands of an Indian woman. It was true. But that wasn't the only reason. Marie wanted to see the country.

She did see a lot of country. And she would see even more. In the spring, they were going to hunt buffalo in Missouri with François's friends, the Métis and the Indians, and with their child.

It was at Rainy Lake, after a hard portage, that she told François she was expecting a child.

"He will be born in Pembina," he had said. "We'll spend the winter there." He was happy. He said that their child would be the first white child to be born in the Pays d'en Haut. "Nobody will have seen that before."

Marie had been an extraordinary attraction for François's friends. They would come to see her, to touch her blond hair, the skin on her arms, her face. They looked at her eyes as if they were rare jewels.

"He will have blue eyes like yours," he had said. "And he'll have your blond hair."

Marie touched her belly. She was not able to hold back a cry. Her belly was empty.

The old Magpie stopped singing. She lifted Marie, she put her arms around her and rocked her gently. Marie cried as though her heart would break. Just as daylight was entering the teepee, the memory of what had happened the night before came back to her.

"It's the Indian woman who poisoned me, I know it. She wanted to kill me, she killed my child."

"And it's another Indian woman who healed you," answered the old Magpie.

Marie had always known that there was an Indian woman in François's life. When they went up the Red River at the end of the summer, she had seen with what joy the men greeted the Indian women and how quickly they would disappear into the woods. And these women had stayed on with the men, night and day, until Pembina, and they were still there.

"Didn't you have a wife when you were living here?" she would ask François.

"You are my wife," he would always reply.

They arrived in Pembina at the beginning of October, at the same time that the bands of Indians and Métis were returning from Missouri, their Red River carts loaded with buffalo meat and hides.

Marie had quickly spotted her, the other one. The Indian woman who watched her constantly, darkly, with her persistent smiles and mocking expression. She was a lovely Assiniboin with a serious face and long, thick, shiny hair, very black. She was carrying a child on a cradleboard, which she would come and show Marie ten times a day. Marie, who didn't speak Siouan fluently, knew perfectly well what was going on.

"Is she the one, is she your wife?" she would ask François. "Is that your child she has in her arms?"

"You are my wife," François would answer. "You will always be my wife."

With the first snow, he left to go trapping on the Saskatchewan River, leaving Marie at Fort Pembina with the other women and children.

During the days following his departure, the Assiniboin woman would hang around Marie. She was all smiles, but without the child. She would do little things for her; she would bring her smoked fish, pemmican, moccasins decorated with porcupine quills; she offered her tobacco and sweet grass, which Marie accepted because she didn't know how to refuse. Little by little, she developed feelings of affection for the Assiniboin woman. And she was surprised, and sad, that the old Magpie didn't like the woman.

The family was the centre of Métis life. The semi-nomadic Métis trapper and hunter rarely went anywhere without his wife and children.

One day, Marie suffered a violent headache. The young Assiniboin woman offered her a herbal concoction that quickly relieved her. Several days later, the headaches came back. Again Marie accepted the woman's medicine. But this time, the pain grew worse. Marie felt dizzy and very nauseous. She lost consciousness. She vaguely remembered going out alone and walking in the snow. It was night, and she fell.

The old Magpie was no longer singing. She was rocking Marie in her arms.

"You will have other children," said the old woman. "I am telling you this. You will have many. I already have all the songs for them."

Marie knew that the woman was speaking the truth. She would have other children. She was well. François was coming back in a few days. In the spring, she would accompany him to hunt buffalo, like the other Indian women. They would make another child up there, on the Prairie.

"And the Assiniboin woman?"

"Don't worry about her," said the Magpie. "I have a song for her. She will never hurt you again."

Chapter 7

THE MÉTIS NATION

Their existence centres on nomadism, a tradition stemming from the distant origins of the Métis, whose ancestors were basically nomadic or who had long been detached from sedentary life. Hunting appears to the child as his natural vocation, as the "national" characteristic of the community to which he belongs. From the age of fourteen, he has been a fine horseman and remarkably experienced marksman. When he travels with the wagon trains, his long "fusil" across his saddle-bow, and with his shot bag and horn sling, he looks quite a little warrior. From this close contact with the untamed nature of the Western Plains, he gets the sharp memory and sense of direction [characteristic] of the Indian.

Combining different aspects of their Aboriginal and European backgrounds, the Métis created a new culture that was neither Indian nor white.

In the shadow of the foothills flowed lazy rivers that nevertheless often flooded the surrounding prairie in the spring.

THE WAGON MEN

The mixed-blood descendants of the coureurs des bois would constitute a powerful nation with its own democratic government.

Michel Rinville was one of those Métis who were said to be neither Indian nor white; indeed, they were part of a new nation.

Métis coats were made of tanned and smoked hides, often decorated with floral motifs.

They were known as Métis, or Mixed Bloods, because of their mixed parentage: their white father and Indian mother. Or as Bois Brûlés because their weather-beaten faces were tanned the colour of burnt wood by the sun and wind. They were also called wagon men because, for much of the year, they roamed the southern Prairies in long, noisy, dusty wagon trains. From spring till late fall, they would be seen with their families travelling across southern Manitoba, Dakota, and the Grand Coteau of the Missouri in hundreds of Red River carts, with their oxen, horses, and dogs. But their name for themselves was *hommes libres*: free men.

They were highly colourful characters. In addition to wearing colourful sashes and moccasins, they all seemed to be trying to outdo each other in their garb. They would deck themselves out in frock coats, plaid shirts, or blue topcoats along with wool or leather trousers and the most amazing hats: bowlers or top hats, soft or hard, straw, felt or leather, often adorned with a feather. Plus they had all sorts of accoutrements hanging from their necks or belts: a powder horn, a bag of bullets and shot, a pouch of tobacco, a hunting knife, a few medals and jewellery.

These free men and their Indian wives lived in small groups of two or three families, sleeping in the same teepee, hunting big game for food, trapping animals for their pelts, and trading with the big fur trading companies. Some might have had a small garden, a potato patch, and a few squash, but they were rather lackadaisical farmers. In 1827 chief fur trader Francis Heron wrote in the Fort Garry newspaper that the Métis refused to grow flax, even if they were provided with the seeds, and that some years their wives neglected to harvest wild rice.

Actually, what with battling drought and grasshopper infestations, the Red River Métis had other priorities and other aspirations. They were naturally more attuned to the realties of hunting and the nomadic life. They had developed their own identity, and their community was already attracting free men from other areas. Game was abundant, the fishing was good, and there were excellent natural pastures for their horses. And, most importantly, each spring there were herds of buffalo, which provided them with everything they needed to feed and clothe themselves and make a good living.

In 1807 there were forty-five free men on the Pembina River along with a few wives and children. Only seven years later, close to two hundred families wintered in the Red River Valley. Other small settlements grew up around Rainy Lake. A few small, more-or-less nomadic groups trapped and

The hunters used all parts of the buffalo, even braiding rope from its mane.

hunted here and there, near Fort Edmonton, Lac La Biche, and Lesser Slave Lake. By the mid-1800s, there were approximately five thousand Métis scattered throughout this vast region.

Within a few generations, they had grown into a flourishing community with a well-defined ethnic identity and an unquenchable taste for the wandering life. They had developed an entirely new lifestyle that was perfectly adapted to their environment. Without actually turning their backs on European civilization, they had embraced the Indian way of life and love of freedom.

Both women and men were excellent horsemen. By the age of twelve or thirteen, a young Métis knew how to handle a firearm and could catch a half-wild horse out on the prairie, throw a halter over its head, and ride it bareback or hitch it to a cart.

Descendants of the coureurs des bois and voyageurs, and of the French, Scottish, and English trappers and fur traders who had frequented the Pays d'en Haut for over two centuries, the Métis gradually formed a powerful nation with its own rules, laws, and culture. They had a true democratic government and a social structure largely inspired by that of the Plains Indians, particularly the Assiniboin and Nez Perce, who democratically elected captains to lead their hunting and war parties.

The Métis started cultivating land along the Red, Assiniboine, Saskatchewan, and Qu'Appelle Rivers. This land was divided into long, narrow strips

Fringes on the shoulders, down the sleeves, along the bottom edge of the coat, and even on the knife sheath were designed to channel off water.

running perpendicular to the river, as was the custom in Quebec. This system of "river lots" ensured that each property would have access to water, woods (for firewood and building materials), and the prairie, which was considered common property. The Métis considered access to pasture and water to be inalienable rights.

With their carts, they wore trails through this territory and established small villages and meeting places. The famous Red River Trail extended from Pembina to St. Paul, where trade was free and the Métis could escape the pervasive control of the Hudson's Bay Company.

The trail was their home. They literally lived on the trail, like sailors on the sea. On the move at least half the year, if not more, they spent less time in their villages of log houses than in their carts and teepees.

In the first half of the nineteenth century, this new nation was widespread enough that its young men and women intermarried, bringing in other influences and genes, creating a common cultural space and a new people. The French did not assimilate the Indians, nor were they assimilated by them; they merged with the Indians to form a new people.

The Métis now viewed themselves as an autonomous people, a true nation with its own traditions and culture. They had a legitimate desire to play a role in history and, most of all, to have a territory of their own.

Toward the end of the nineteenth century, the Métis gradually abandoned their traditional costume for a more European style of dress. This Red River cart driver displays some of the last signs of the typical Métis style: blue coat with copper buttons, moccasins, striped trousers made of buffalo wool, and the colourful sash favoured by the Métis.

FRANO'S BACK 03

143

GABRIEL DUMONT'S STORY

An excellent horseman and marksman, he took part in his first buffalo hunt at the age of fourteen.

Dumont was a man of action with a lifelong belief in the power of weapons and in the justice of the Métis cause.

In 1887, at the age of fifty, Gabriel Dumont toured the major cities of the eastern United States with Buffalo Bill's Wild West Show. He was an exile, a broken man, and a failure. Even his own people, the Métis of the Saskatchewan River Valley, who for thirty years had recognized him as their uncontested leader, no longer had faith in him. They too had been crushed and their dreams destroyed. His friend Louis Riel, leader of the Métis rebellion, had been hanged. His wife, Madeleine Wilkie, whom he had married at the age of twenty-one, died shortly after from tuberculosis. And he, once the most famous buffalo hunter in the whole wide West and the bravest of the Métis fighters, was now a sharpshooter in a circus.

Dumont's paternal grandfather had been an independent trader who occasionally worked for the Hudson's Bay Company. However, after the big fur trading companies had merged and rationalized their operations, they no longer hired the unpredictable free men. His father, Isidore, and his uncles therefore turned to buffalo hunting. The Dumonts became the leaders of an important clan.

When Gabriel was born in 1837, good trails were being opened up to the south, and large trading posts were being established, notably at Pembina, giving access to new markets for buffalo hides. It was a happy time, when the Métis truly believed they were a strong and free nation.

Gabriel Dumont was an excellent horseman and marksman and took part in his first buffalo hunt when he was fourteen. In 1851 his uncles and father had assembled some three hundred hunters at Pembina, along with their wives and children, and several hundred riding horses and draft horses.

A knife sheath with fringes like those on Métis coats and jackets, a tradition adopted from the trappers.

They proceeded to the Grand Coteau of the Missouri River. This region west of Saskatchewan along the American border was frequented by large buffalo herds, but also by aggressive bands of Sioux.

One morning, the party's scouts discovered an encampment of some 2,500 warriors. A confrontation was inevitable. The Métis drew their two hundred Red River carts into a circle, their wheels touching and their shafts pointing up and out. After piling all the baggage and bales of pemmican under the carts to reinforce this barricade, they dug trenches inside their ad hoc fortification to protect the women and children. Then they brought the horses inside the circle and dug rifle pits outside to provide the men with cover in the open terrain. Although there were only sixty-four men and thirteen boys, they inflicted such heavy losses that the Sioux were forced to retreat. The Métis lost only one man.

The Métis women wore long skirts all year round, along with long-sleeved, embroidered blouses and moccasins.

This incident certainly marked young Gabriel. All his life, he would believe in the effectiveness of armed combat, as well as in the justice of the Métis cause.

At age twenty-five, he was elected leader of a group of some two hundred families who lived in the Fort Carlton area northeast of Saskatoon. He knew the Prairies better than anyone and was renowned for his courage and generosity. Having no children of his own, he was devoted to his people.

The Métis of Saskatchewan thus naturally turned to him when they felt threatened by the policies of a government that seemed to completely ignore their claims and understand nothing of their way of life.

In 1869-70 the Red River Métis community had rebelled. They contested the Hudson's Bay Company monopoly and demanded to be allowed to trade freely. The insurrection was harshly suppressed, and some forty families sought refuge in the little community headed by Dumont, which was still enjoying a certain prosperity.

However, the buffalo herds were becoming smaller and rarer with each passing year. For good hunting, one had to travel farther and farther west. Some people even defied the sacrosanct traditional hunting laws.

The Métis had to accept that the era of the buffalo was over. Deprived of their means of subsistence, and with their territory threatened and their

By 1887 the most famous buffalo hunter in the whole wild West and the bravest of the Métis fighters was reduced to working as a sharpshooter in a circus.

rights ignored, the Métis were in serious disarray. Dumont had sent petitions to the federal government asking for representation on the Territorial Council, farming assistance, schools, and most importantly title to already occupied lands.

However, Dumont had difficulty making representations to an English-speaking government. While he was very familiar with the Indian peoples of the Prairies and spoke many of their languages, he did not have a good command of English. In March 1884, he therefore turned to Louis Riel, leader of the Red River community. He felt that Riel would be able to speak to the whites since he had studied with them and knew not only French and English, but Latin and Greek as well.

Riel, the man of words and vision, and Dumont, the man of action, would incite the Métis to rise up in revolt. Dumont was a fiery leader and an able commander. Although they won some good battles against the North-West Mounted Police and the Canadian army, they lost the war. Riel was arrested. Dumont and a few companions fled to Montana, whose Métis communities harboured a strong resentment against the Canadian government.

The following spring, Dumont was asked to join Buffalo Bill's Wild West Show, whose headquarters were in Staten Island, New York. Dumont contacted the French-speaking communities of New England and the nationalists of Quebec, who were outraged at what had happened to the Métis and invited him to come speak about the rebellion.

But Dumont, bitter and tactless, and no doubt too hot-headed, strongly reproached the clergy for not supporting their efforts. This, of course, did not go over well in Quebec, which was controlled by the Roman Catholic Church at that time. The lecture tour was cancelled.

Gabriel Dumont, the last of the traditional Métis leaders, went back to live on his old homestead. He died suddenly in Bellevue, Saskatchewan, on 19 May 1906 at the age of sixty-nine.

DESCENDANTS OF THE ENGLISH TRADERS

After their fathers left, many young Métis would break off all contact with white society.

The Red River colony was a cultural hub that held a strong power of attraction for the Métis, no matter what their origin.

In the early years of the Hudson's Bay Company (HBC), the men were officially forbidden to bring Indian women into the trading posts. This ban was ignored or lifted as the English bosses came to understand that there were numerous advantages in living with an Indian woman. However, their officers rarely mixed with Indian society in the same way as the French voyageurs – though that didn't keep them from having children with Indian women.

These children, like those of the French trappers, almost always remained attached to their mother's culture and world. There were, however, some notable exceptions. A few *bourgeois* and senior officers, such as Simon McTavish, founder of the North West Company, acknowledged and took care of the children they had with their country wives. When they retired and went back to live in Montreal or London with their white wives, they left a small nest egg to be administered by the company, which paid the children annual interest, usually in the form of goods.

Some of them had developed ties they were unable to break. When Edward Jarvis, commander of the HBC's

Albany Fort, was about to leave his post in 1783, he begged the company to overlook its policy and allow him to take back to England "this child, who is bound to me by the most tender ties ... Whatever the fault of his birth, I would not want to aggravate it by leaving him in this country an orphan and without assistance." In the account of his trek across the tundra from 1769 to 1772, Samuel Hearne speaks several times of those officers who, once their contracts had expired, asked to sign on again so as not to be separated from their children.

But only the HBC's senior officers had the financial means and moral authority to provide for their natural children and confer appropriate social status on them. Their sons received some education and could hold a permanent job in the trading posts. However, they rarely, if ever, were able to rise to their father's rank.

The vast majority of children born of English traders and Indian women formed a scattered world of poor, uneducated people. They may have been free, but they had no rights, power, or voice and were often looked down upon and exploited by the whites. After the departure of their fathers, many simply abandoned white society and returned to a nomadic existence.

In his *Observations on Hudson's Bay*, James Isham, governor of Fort Prince of Wales on the Churchill River, described these small communities, which also clustered around HBC trading posts such as York, Albany, and Moose Factory. Like most authors of such reports, he drew an unflattering picture of Mixed Bloods of Scottish or English origin. All noted that the girls were very beautiful. They also said that both boys and girls had an innate sense of direction in the woods and on open terrain, that they seemed to have a talent for

Jerry Potts, son of a Scottish clerk and a Blood Indian woman, understood several Indian languages and was highly respected for his talent as a guide.

learning languages, and that they all had a remarkable memory. But most of these authors judged Mixed Bloods in terms of the emerging capitalist values. They often mentioned their dissolute lives, immoderate taste for alcohol, inveterate laziness, and tendency to lie. And they deplored their lack of attachment to white society and values.

Unlike the buffalo hunters of the Red River, who had only periodic contact with the Indians and existed as a very autonomous community, the offspring of the English-speaking traders lived in smaller groups and only later gathered together into homogeneous communities.

Nevertheless, the fur trading companies depended greatly on the Mixed Bloods to supply their posts with fish and game. At Fort Edmonton, they also watched over the herds of horses, which could be a dangerous job since the animals were much coveted by the Indians. It was also the Mixed Bloods who carried the bales of furs and goods across the longest and most difficult portages. But they were never entrusted with work that was highly valued or well paid.

When the fur traders needed good canoemen and guides for travelling around the Northwest, in the area of Lake Athabaska and Great Slave Lake, they would hire Canadian Métis who had learned their skills with the French voyageurs of the St. Lawrence Valley and were experienced at navigating rivers.

The French-speaking Métis began circulating widely throughout the Northwest, coming into increasingly frequent contact with English-speaking Mixed Bloods at

This jacket is a fine example of Métis art, enriched by a melding of Indian and European traditions.

the major portages, such as La Loche and Assiniboine. In talking to the canoemen, the porters learned that there was a very strong and well-organized Métis community at Red River, where men and women led an easier and more agreeable existence than that afforded by the poor, semi-nomadic life to which they themselves were condemned.

Since the dominant language throughout the Pays d'en Haut remained French until the mid-nineteenth century, the offspring of English-speaking traders who did not become completely assimilated into Indian society often adopted French values and culture. English-speaking Mixed Bloods thus started gathering together into communities and villages where they too could hope to make a better life for themselves.

They did not become great buffalo hunters like the Red River Métis but instead trapped fur-bearing animals, fished, and did a little gardening. However, they too claimed it was their birthright to trade freely with the Indians and to settle wherever they wanted in the wide-open spaces of the West. The Hudson's Bay Company, which believed it held an absolute monopoly over the fur trade, did everything it could to discourage the development of the Mixed Bloods' settlements and especially any relations between the English-speaking groups in the West and the Red River colony.

But the ties that grew up between the two communities could not be broken. Their fates were linked. The children of the Canadian voyageurs and the descendants of the English-speaking traders were now united in the same struggle to defend their rights and way of life.

The Métis, from both the Red River colony and the small English-speaking communities, were often at war with the Sioux.

THE MÉTIS WIFE

The Métis culture found its most eloquent expression in the handcrafts of the women, which incorporated influences from their various native tribes.

The Métis women imitated European fashions in the clothing they made for themselves.

The Métis men usually married Indian or Métis women, almost never white women. Unless they were well brought up, educated, and very enterprising, it was nearly impossible for them to come into contact with a woman of European origin. The case of Jean-Louis Riel, father of the leader of the Métis rebellion, is an extremely rare exception. Jean-Louis was the son of a Canadian voyageur from the St. Lawrence Valley and a Métis woman from Île à la Crosse. He married Julie, the daughter of Marie-Anne Gaboury, the first white woman to live in the West, and Jean-Baptiste Lagimodière, a famous free man.

Through their wives, the Métis thus remained close to Indian culture and values. As with all the world's nomads, their lives centred around the family. A man almost never travelled without his wife and children, and his wife was involved in all his hunting and fishing activities. The children learned their mother's language before their father's.

The Métis and white men who settled in the Red River and Assiniboine Valleys married local women, especially Ojibwa women, who were known to be very strong and hardworking, and Cree women, who were renowned seamstresses and craftswomen. With their artistic abilities, they created an original material culture particular to the Red River region.

In addition to taking care of the home and children as well as helping out with skinning and butchering buffalo on the big hunts, Métis wives had numerous domestic chores: setting snares and traps; tending the garden, potato patch, and cornfield; gathering eggs of migrating birds in the spring; picking enormous quantities of wild berries; and harvesting tonnes of hops, which they sold to brewmasters at the fur trading companies. They also prepared venison, smoked fish, and made pemmican, which they stored in buffalo-skin sacks. The Métis' small barter economy depended almost entirely on the women, who traded sturgeon oil, moccasins, small game, and tobacco with the Indians and sewed clothing, leather bags, and saddles for the white men.

Sewing kit containing awls for making leather clothing and a French-made punch.

It was primarily through the women's handcrafts that the Métis culture found its expression. Down through the generations, they developed an original style of clothing and decorative art that harmoniously combined Aboriginal and European influences. All the materials, tools, motifs, and dyes were prepared by the women themselves.

After soaking the buffalo skins in the river, they would scrape off the hairs, then stretch the skins on frames. They would rub them with ashes and animal brains to polish and soften them. This lengthy handling would rid the skins of all impurities, making them very white, soft, and supple.

The women also tanned cowhide with lime water or by leaving it to soak for a month in a decoction of willow and oak bark. The leather would absorb the colour of the bark: red if they had used willow,

Métis women, like the men, sometimes smoked a pipe.

brown if they had used oak, or a combination of the two. The women used this leather to make moccasins. They also made *babiche*, or webbing for snowshoes, from buffalo or cattle sinew, and stretched hides over the sled frames built by the men.

They created very colourful heart-shaped or floral motifs with embroidery, beads, and porcupine quills to decorate the clothing they sewed as well as the horses' harnesses and saddles, moccasins, powder bags, game bags, and the famous octopus-shaped tobacco pouches typical of the Red River Valley.

Some women were renowned among the Hudson's Bay Company officers for their beadwork and feather arrangements. The finest leather coats were made on order for wealthy white men; the Métis had to content themselves with blue wool coats.

All these chores and the long hours spent doing needle and awl work enabled the Métis women to get together, talk, and transmit their precious skills from generation to generation.

Winter and summer, they all wore long skirts, long-sleeved embroidered blouses, and moccasins, using a brightly coloured blanket as a shawl. They did their hair in a long braid, often adorned with ribbons and beads, and always wore rings, necklaces, and earrings. The older women liked tobacco.

In addition to the local Cree and Ojibwa women, Indian women from other nations arrived later, when fur traders and winterers from the Northwest retired around the Red River with their country wives. Often knowing English better than French,

Fleshing tool for scraping the flesh and fat from hides; another type of scraper was used for removing the hair.

these women were naturally more drawn to Victorian fashion than were the French Catholic Métis women. But they too wore long skirts, the inevitable blanket, and moccasins. The Métis women subscribed to ladies magazines and followed European fashions in the dresses and coats they sewed.

A few families, such as the Riels, were able to send their sons to study in Montreal. Though they never sent their daughters, the girls were still generally better educated than the boys. When the Grey Nuns arrived in the region, it was the girls they first taught to read and write. The girls also seemed to pick up languages more easily. Sharing daily chores with their mothers, they had direct contact with the Indian cultures and languages. They lived happily in a very multicultural, multiethnic environment.

The gradual sedentarization of the Métis was due not only to the disappearance of the buffalo but also to the women. As they had more and more young children, they stopped following the men on their hunting and fishing trips and devoted more effort to furnishing and decorating their small log houses and to making them more comfortable. The gardens and vegetable patches also grew larger. And the women continued their handcrafts, which more than ever expressed the Métis culture and imagination.

This Métis woman is spinning buffalo wool, while her daughter embroiders a moccasin. Although the men's clothing was a flamboyant reflection of Métis culture, the women's clothing tended to be more sober, as though they were trying to dress like the white women.

THE RED RIVER CART

This strange vehicle could travel over any terrain and in any season.

No metal at all was used in making a Red River cart.

It was a terrible, shaky, noisy contraption, an amazing vehicle as much for its appearance and construction as for its operation and functionality. In seeing it approach, one had the impression that its various parts were about to fly off. Although it looked rickety, it had to be made with a certain give between all the parts so that they could absorb the bumps and shocks of the trails over which the famous Red River cart had to travel. The axle, hubs, side rails, and shafts were all fitted, pegged, or lashed together with leather strips.

The wheels were huge and dish-shaped, as high as or higher than a man. From a distance, they looked like two soup plates rolling on either side of the cart. The rims were wide (ten centimetres) to keep them from cutting into the ground and were made in six curved segments (called felloes) that were attached to each other with dowels and to the hub with spokes and further lashed together with leather strips. Some innovative cart-makers added iron tires, but the authentic Red River cart had not the least bit of metal on it, not even for the harness, the bridle, or the collar, which was made of buffalo hide stuffed with straw.

This strange vehicle could travel in any season over any terrain: snowy, icy, sandy, or rocky trails; fords; marshy ground; and mud holes. With its wheels removed, it could even float across rivers and lakes. Nothing, not even the spring floods, which some years covered vast areas of the northern Prairies, could stop the Red River cart.

A Red River cart could be made with the simplest of tools: a saw for cutting down trees, an axe for making boards, a knife for carving dowels and cutting leather strips, a hammer (or mallet, or the back of an axe head) for driving in tenons and dowels. And the necessary materials were readily found on the edge of the Prairies. Oak, if possible, especially for the hubs and axle – though maple or elm would do. Some carts were made completely of birch or ash, while others used half a dozen different types of wood. In Fort Garry, in the 1860s, the Hudson's Bay Company used large carts made entirely of oak, even for the platform and chassis.

If the axle broke, there were always extras (one or more carts in the brigade would be full of spare parts), or the men would go into the nearby woods and carve one out of green wood. It was attached to the body of the cart with strips of wet leather, which would shrink as they dried, holding the parts firmly together.

The platform or box was supported on two strong beams, three or four metres long, which were rounded off along approximately half their length to form the shafts. The other half was covered with planking or willow webbing in a rigid frame.

As it moved along, the Red River cart was an unbelievable sight and made an unbearable sound. No grease could be used on the hubs since it would have become gummed up with dust and mud. A brigade of these carts (sometimes hundreds travelling together) would never pass unnoticed. One could see the dust cloud it kicked up and hear its strange music for kilometres around.

The Red River cart brigades opened wide trails that descended the valleys of Manitoba and Minnesota and crisscrossed present-day North and South Dakota, Nebraska,

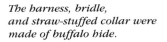

The harness, bridle, and straw-stuffed collar were made of buffalo hide.

and Wyoming, linking such places as Fort Laramie on the North Platte River and Fort Pierre on the Missouri, which were already beginning to be served by steamboats.

The first carts appeared in the Red River region around 1803. By the mid-nineteenth century, a Red River cart could be bought for ten dollars in Missouri, Mississippi, Illinois, and Saskatchewan as well as throughout Dakota and Minnesota.

It was likely modelled on a type of cart that was commonly used in the St. Lawrence Valley at the time and that Pehr Kalm described when he visited Canada in 1749. Before the development of the Red River cart, people on the Prairies had the Indian *travois*, a simple platform between two shafts, which was pulled by humans, horses, or oxen and used to drag heavy loads over the ground or snow.

The Red River Métis used oxen and sometimes horses as draft animals. Some carts had a single shaft and were pulled by a pair of animals, though usually one was enough. Horses were faster, but oxen could pull heavier loads over any terrain. The driver would sit with his legs dangling over the front of the cart. The carts would follow one behind the other, with each draft animal attached to the cart in front of it. On long journeys, the women and young children would sit or lie in the carts on blankets or buffalo robes. The older children, dogs, and tethered horses would run along with the carts.

At night, they would spread buffalo skins across the side rails and sleep under this shelter, well protected from the cold and rain. Since the carts contained no metal (other than rifle barrels, knives, and a few tools, which were stowed under the carts), they did not even have to worry about the violent thunder and lightning storms that swept across the open prairie.

The horses would graze a little way off, watched by the young boys and dogs. Everyone kept an eye on the horizon, eagerly looking for buffalo and watching out for the Sioux, who could appear at any time. No one ever knew whether they would be friendly or not.

Likely modelled on a type of cart commonly used in the St. Lawrence Valley, the Red River cart was made of oak, if possible, but maple or elm would also do.

THE BUFFALO

With no serious predators,
the buffalo was king
of the Prairies. It used
to roam the vast
grassy plains in herds tens
or even hundreds
of thousands strong.

*A source of clothing, shelter,
and food, the buffalo
was at the heart of Plains life,
culture, and spirituality.*

The North American bison, commonly known as the buffalo, is the largest mammal on the continent. It has a very broad forehead with short, curved horns buried in a thick, shaggy mane that covers its majestic head and extends down its massive neck. Its shoulders are higher and wider than its hindquarters and are topped with a large hump, which adds to its appearance of power and strength. The bulls weigh over a tonne and measure 1.8 metres at the hump. The cows weigh 650 to 800 kilograms and are faster runners than the bulls. The buffalo is a gregarious animal that lives in a well-organized, hierarchical society.

Male and female buffalo generally remain separate, coming together only during the summer mating season (early July to late September). During this time, the herd is very agitated, with the bulls engaging in head-to-head combat over the cows. The calves are born at the beginning of the following summer, after a gestation period of 270 to 300 days. Only half an hour after its birth, the baby buffalo is able to stand and within three hours is able to run and gambol about. It will remain close to its mother's side for the next two or three weeks and is usually weaned at about the age of seven months.

Before the arrival of the Europeans in the early sixteenth century, the buffalo was king of the Prairies. It roamed in gigantic herds totalling some sixty million head in all. When these herds passed by, the earth trembled, the grass was razed, and the mud was trampled rock hard. The animals were followed by great swirling clouds of dust and packs of wolves and coyotes, which did not pose a threat to the herd but merely picked off the sick or injured.

The buffalo had no serious predators. The only threats to its existence were the wildfires that raged across thousands of hectares of tinder-dry prairie in the late summer and fall and the heavy snowfalls that some years killed off tens of thousands of buffalo. Because of overgrazing, the herds were always on the move, constantly searching for new pastures.

The buffalo lumbered across the vast prairie, through the endless sea of grass that rippled from the Missouri River to the Red River and all along the upper Mississippi Valley, with the occasional salt meadow. The buffalo formed enormous, fiercely exclusive herds around these salt meadows each spring before spreading throughout the Prairies in the summer.

Unlike domestic bovines such as cattle, buffalo never grazed close to each other. The herd could thus spread out over thousands of hectares, covering the land as far as the eye could see in any direction. If they were threatened, however, they would come together into a dense, practically impenetrable mass. Before the introduction of the horse and firearms, neither man nor beast could approach a buffalo herd with impunity.

Grass fires caused by lightning or ignited by the Indians sometimes pursued the buffalo for days, until the animals reached moister pastures that stopped the advancing flames. In late summer, the herds thus often grazed on fresh grass on the

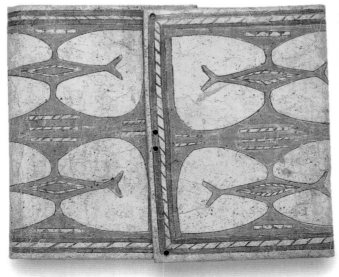

*This Cheyenne parfleche,
or untanned
buffalo-hide bag, was used
for storing meat.*

wooded slopes of Turtle Mountain, located on the border between Manitoba and Dakota, or around Devils Lake, a little to the southeast. They also wandered the grassy banks of the Assiniboine and Saskatchewan Rivers and throughout the flat Red River Valley. Some summers, such as in 1846, there were so many fires that all retreat was cut off and herds consisting of thousands of buffalo were decimated.

If the winter was extremely cold, with blizzards sweeping across the open prairie, the buffalo, like the moose and bear, would take refuge farther north where the prairie meets the boreal forest. This area, known as the parkland, consists of rolling countryside cut with ravines and dotted with small, densely wooded hills. There, the animals could shelter beneath the trees and find enough to eat under the shallow snow. However, they were much more vulnerable to hunters, who would take advantage of the tree cover and hilly terrain to approach them.

As soon as the weather let up, the buffalo would return to the treeless prairie out of reach of the hunters. Thus, for the Indians who lived in the parkland and around the Qu'Appelle, Saskatchewan, and Assiniboine Rivers, a mild winter was a calamity since the buffalo would remain out on the prairie, where it was extremely difficult, if not impossible, to approach

Springfield rifle with the stock sawed off to make it lighter and easier to handle with one hand when galloping into a buffalo herd.

them unless the winter was very snowy. Then, weakened by lack of food, the buffalo would flounder in the deep snow, making them easy prey. However, the hunters had to travel considerable distances in extremely difficult conditions in order to kill them and to carry home the meat and other parts of the carcass.

All western Indians thus experienced periods of great abundance alternating with extreme hunger and privation. The Indians of the Prairies were very dependent on the buffalo and followed its movements as best they could. The buffalo was the focus of their lives, their culture, and their spirituality.

The herd usually moved in a ponderous mass but could stampede off at speeds of up to fifty kilometres per hour if threatened.

THE HUNTING EXPEDITION

In organizing their
buffalo hunts,
the Red River Métis largely
modelled themselves
on the Indians of the Prairies.

*When the buffalo finally
appeared on the horizon, the hunters
would prepare to charge.*

The hunters never knew where the buffalo herds would be at any given time. They might have been driven much farther south by the huge grass fires that ravaged the Prairies for days or weeks at a time. Or they might have had to take shelter in the northern parkland to escape the heavy snows. Although they didn't know exactly where they had to go, the buffalo hunters always started off in a south-westerly direction through Dakota to the rolling, grassy plateau known as the Grand Coteau of the Missouri.

In organizing their buffalo hunts, the Red River Métis largely modelled themselves on the Indians. Because of their hunting way of life and frequent wars with other tribes, the Indians of the Prairies had developed a strong social structure and rigorous discipline that subjugated individual desires to the good of the community.

The Blackfoot, who lived surrounded by enemy nations, had a very strong and highly structured government based on the family unit. For each hunting or war party, they democratically elected a leader, whose authority was based not on force but on his courage and wisdom. He had to be able to consult and heed the advice of the other warriors and leaders with whom he shared his authority when necessary. His role was one of convincing others rather than commanding them.

The Assiniboin, who were great buffalo hunters, had a sort of police force that was in charge of supervising preparations for their hunting and war parties and organizing ritual dances and religious ceremonies. It would also intervene in disputes and ensure public order, give the charge signal on a hunt or in battle, and impose sanctions, such as confiscation of meat, corporal punishment, or destruction of the offender's weapons, in the case of infractions.

It is not surprising that the Métis took their inspiration from these models of social organization. They lived in the same environment, had a similar lifestyle, and hunted the same animals. And they, too, lived under constant threat. They had to be numerous enough and particularly well organized to cross the Prairies, which were infested with hostile tribes, approach a herd of tens

Sold by the Hudson's Bay Company, this type of knife was highly prized by the Métis for cutting branches and butchering carcasses or for hand-to-hand combat.

of thousands of buffalo, kill hundreds of animals, selecting those with the best skins and the tastiest meat, and bring back tonnes of food and buffalo robes. They also had to be able to organize transportation, food, and shelter for the hunt. All this required a code of conduct, clear rules, an executive body, and a leader.

Each spring and fall, Métis scattered for hundreds of kilometres around would gather for the buffalo hunt, initially at St. Boniface. Men, women, and children would go along on the expedition, which sometimes had over 1,500 participants and, starting in the 1830s, included a chaplain as well. The party that set off in June 1840 included some 400 hunters, 200 men to look after the horses and draft animals, and almost a thousand women and children, who made the trek on foot or in Red River carts. All around ran the dogs, spooked by the squeaking and squealing of the 300 carts, the neighing and mooing of the animals, and the cries of the drivers.

Mounted on their fastest and freshest horses, a loaded musket at the ready, the hunters awaited the captain's signal.

The Métis used the buffalo's woolly underfur for padding their saddles.

Each family had several carts, sometimes as many as ten, pulled by horses or oxen. Some carts carried firewood for heating and cooking (since none was to be found on the Prairies), some held poles and skins for teepees, while others contained spare hubs and axles, food, and ammunition. Where the terrain permitted, they would proceed three abreast so that they could quickly repel any attack.

They first went to Pembina, 120 kilometres away in Dakota, just south of the American border. There they would erect a tent city consisting of 50 to 75, or even 100, teepees, with the carts drawn up in a defensive ring around them. A little ways off, they would build a corral for the horses and oxen, which would be watched over by the young boys. The men would take turns as sentries, scanning the horizon day and night. A leader and ten captains would be elected to ensure that everyone obeyed the hunting rules and to mete out appropriate punishment if they were broken.

For instance, no hunting was allowed on Sundays for any reason whatsoever. Everyone had to stay together; it was not permitted to go off looking for buffalo on one's own or to charge into the herd or start shooting before the leader had given the signal. For a first offence, the offender's saddle and bridle would be cut up. For a second offence, his coat would be cut up. For a third offence, he would be flogged. If anyone stole anything,

be it only a leather strap or a buffalo tongue, he would be led to the centre of the camp, where the others would cry his name followed by "thief" three times.

Each day, the hunting expedition would penetrate deeper into the Prairies, always in a southwesterly direction, toward the Grand Coteau of the Missouri. Scouts on swift horses would ride ahead each morning and come back before nightfall to report. One might have found fresh buffalo tracks and droppings, the remains of a calf eaten by coyotes, or a few old lone bulls. Another might have spotted a large group of buffalo in the distance. The leader and captains would decide on their strategy for the next day, and each captain would be given an itinerary and schedule.

Gradually they would close in on the great herd until finally one day they would see an endless, undulating mass on the horizon, as if the land itself were moving. They would prepare to charge.

To spare the horses, they would walk them as close to the herd as possible, always downwind. Buffalo did not have good eyesight so hunters could get within a few dozen metres before they were noticed, whereupon the great bulls would slowly close ranks. Snorting, pawing the ground, and raising great clouds of dust, they would form a rampart of horns between the cows and calves and the hunters.

The hunters would mount their fastest and freshest horses. With a loaded gun in their hands, their mouths full of musket balls, they would wait, silent and immobile, for the leader's signal.

THE BUFFALO HUNT

The charge lasted only
a few minutes.
The effort was brief
but extremely intense, and the
danger was considerable.

*Before the advent of firearms,
hunters mounted on horses killed
the buffalo with spears
or with bows and arrows.*

The leader would give the signal at the last possible moment, just before the buffalo stampeded. The men thus had time to get in close to the herd, with their fresh, well-trained horses. They would aim for the cows since their flesh was much more tender and tasty. But the cows were also faster than the bulls, which would run behind them in a seething torrent of muscles, hooves, and horns, which the hunter had to get through on his horse, guiding it with only his knees.

Dropping the reins, he would charge into the maelstrom of hurtling bodies and pounding hooves kicking up a suffocating, blinding cloud of dust. In his hand was his loaded musket; around his neck, his powder horn; in his mouth, a dozen musket balls. After threading his way through the bulls, he would kill his first cow with a shot behind its hump or between its ribs. Without slowing down, he would pour more powder into his gun barrel, spit in

another ball slippery with saliva, give it a couple of seconds to slide down the smoothbore barrel, approach another cow, shoulder his weapon, and fire again.

Some hunters could kill as many as a dozen cows in a single charge. But the average for a good hunter was three or four, possibly five, depending on the size of the herd, the lay of the land, the strength of the horse, and the skill of the hunter.

In 1840, during a ten-day buffalo hunt, a party of fifty-five Métis killed a total of 1,776 cows, or an average of 32 per hunter. The total value of the animals was estimated at £1,700 sterling, while the cost of the hunt, including the wages of the men hired to take care of the horses and butcher the kill, was no more than £200. The hunters thus divided up £1,500, taking home almost £30 each, which in those days and in that environment was a tidy sum.

The charge lasted only a few minutes. The horses would be exhausted, some wounded, their flanks gored by buffalo horns. The men, too, would be dead tired. The effort was brief but extremely intense, and the danger considerable. A hunter who was thrown or whose horse was injured could be trampled to death by the herd unless he managed to grab one of the animals rushing by and pull himself up onto it long enough to slow it down and allow the herd to pass.

As the herd thundered off toward the horizon, the dust would settle and silence return to the prairie. Slowing to a walk, the hunters would finish off any wounded buffalo. The women and children who had watched from afar would come rushing up. After binding any wounds and saying a brief prayer, they would begin to skin and butcher the animals.

Using ropes and leather collars, they would spread the rear legs of the buffalo so that it lay flat on its belly. After skinning the animal, they would remove the "boss," a small fatty hump weighing about one and a half kilograms located at the base of the neck, just under the big hump, which was also considered a great delicacy. The stomach and udder, too, were much appreciated. But best of all was the tongue.

To keep up their strength for butchering, the Métis would gorge on the fresh meat, especially during the first days of the hunt. The resulting indigestion was known as *mal de bœuf.*

The women would slice the meat into narrow strips, which they would spread on wooden slats laid across a trestle. After it dried in the sun, they would roll up the best pieces in forty-kilogram packages.

*Mallet used for pounding dried
buffalo meat and saskatoon
berries to make pemmican,
the staple food of
the coureurs des bois.*

The skins would be stretched on frames to dry, and the women would scrape the inside surface with a flat, sharpened bone. Meanwhile, the men would smash the larger bones so that the children could extract the marrow, which would be stored in the buffalo's bladder for later use in cooking and frying.

Scraper for removing hair from buffalo skins, used by the Plains Indians and the Métis.

Much of the buffalo was wasted. It took eight to ten buffalo to fill a single cart. One cow would produce barely twenty kilograms of pemmican, enough for only half a *taurau*, and some fifty kilograms of lesser-quality meat.

Before they had firearms and horses, the Indians were unable to kill many buffalo, though some tribes did develop highly effective hunting techniques. They would drive the animals into pens, where they could be surrounded and killed. In the foothills, they would stampede the buffalo over a cliff and then finish off the injured animals. These sites were known as "buffalo jumps," and some were used for thousands of years, right up till the 1870s. The most important was Head-Smashed-In Buffalo Jump in present-day southern Alberta.

The buffalo provided the Indians not only with food but also with materials for making their teepees, clothing, tools, weapons, and jewellery. They fashioned shields from the thick hide of the shoulders, hardening it with glue made from the hooves. With the finer leathers, they sewed clothing, moccasins, blankets, and teepees, using the brains to soften the hides. The shoulder blades served as shovels, and other flat bones as scrapers, while the skulls were used as bowls, the horns as cups, and shards of the larger bones as awls. The ribs were made into tomahawks or canoe ribs. The Indians also crafted small tools and jewellery from the teeth and dice from the vertebrae. They used the intestines as strings for their bows and the long hair of the mane as padding in saddles. The tail served as a flyswatter, while buffalo chips (dried dung) made excellent fuel. Sleds had even been made from a buffalo's rib cage.

With the introduction of firearms and horses and the opening of good trails providing access to new markets, a veritable buffalo industry developed. After the first steamboats made it up the Missouri River as far as Fort Pierre in 1831, transportation costs declined considerably. In the 1840s some 100,000 buffalo robes were shipped to St. Louis from the upper Missouri, and 25,000 from the Southern Plains. Tens of thousands were also shipped overland to St. Paul. These robes, dressed by the Indian women, were bought from the hunters for $3 apiece, then resold for $5 in St. Louis and $10 on the East Coast retail market.

The buffalo hunt gave rise to a way of life characterized not only by a vibrant and distinctive material culture, but also by legends and heroes that are a fundamental part of North America's history.

Anyone who fell off his horse during the charge was in danger of being trampled to death by the herd.

THE REBELS

From the harmonious meeting and merging of very diverse cultures, the Métis created an autonomous society founded on tolerance, equality, respect for the individual, and collective values.

The Métis never hesitated to take up arms to defend their values and freedom.

At a time when relations between Indians and whites on both sides of the Canadian-American border were marked by conflict and bloody battles, there were a few thousand men and women in the heart of the continent who had managed to create a unique nation from the harmonious meeting and merging of very diverse cultures. The fiercely independent Métis were almost the only people to voluntarily achieve this ideal fusion of races, forging a distinct, mixed society founded on tolerance and equality. This revolution in human relations required great openness of spirit and, at least in the beginning, a certain sense of adventure.

It was an innovative attempt to find a new way of living together in a more just world – a world in which each man, woman, and child would have access to nature's bounty, enjoy freedom of expression, and be able to seek his or her own place in the sun, while respecting the rights of others.

In reconciling the fundamental values of two civilizations and in welcoming men and women from sometimes very distant, rival or enemy cultures in a spirit of great tolerance, the Métis were building a new society, a nation of free and equal individuals the like of which had never been seen before. Though people have aspired to a better life since time immemorial, they have almost invariably created oppressive, exclusionary societies that are suspicious of outsiders and rarely capable of compassion.

The Métis, however, were by their very nature open to a variety of influences. They spoke French, English, Siouan, Algonquian, and a jargon combining all these languages. Their religion was Catholic, Protestant, or animist. They lived on both sides of a border that the Canadian and American governments had sliced through their territory. They belonged to neither France nor England, nor to

Ambroise Dydime Lépine was one of the thousand French- and English-speaking Métis who stood up against eight thousand powerfully armed troops.

the United States. They were a proud, sovereign people. Everything about them was mixed: their ancestry (as they had descended from different races on two or three continents), their accents, their cultures and customs, their ideas and beliefs, and their history.

Their society was, of course, greatly inspired by the European and Aboriginal cultures from which they originated. From the Indians of the Prairies and Plains, with whom they always remained close, they borrowed a very democratic social structure. While the Métis were not against private property, they did own much collectively and shared the work and the riches of the soil. Even their land-holding system was based on sharing and on an equitable division of

Though vastly outnumbered and outarmed, the Métis put up a strong fight at Batoche.

resources: Each property had water access, and each family had the right to pasture for its horses and to wood for heating and building. All individuals benefited from the assets and power of the collectivity. Helping those who were less fortunate was a duty profoundly ingrained in Métis culture.

These men and women loved the life they had chosen and were deeply attached to their land, but above all they cherished their freedom. They enjoyed absolute independence, sincerely believing that they didn't have to answer to anyone. They had their own government, elected their own leaders, and made their own laws. They recognized no superior or authority outside their community.

Their leader was democratically elected by the people – and, if necessary, democratically removed from his position. He was expected to consult his captains, also democratically elected. His mandate was limited to specific activities. For instance, the leader of the buffalo hunt would be in charge of organizing the hunt, directing the hunting and butchering operations, and ensuring that the meat and hides were equitably distributed. Once those activities were accomplished, his mandate was over.

The Métis took up arms to defend their freedom when outside authorities tried to impose other laws, other leaders, and a land-holding system that was incompatible with the Métis way of life, blocking water access for some and access to grazing land for others.

Some four hundred Cree under Chief Poundmaker (pictured here) and Chief Big Bear fought on the side of the Métis.

It was inconceivable that anyone would attempt to deprive them of their freedom. Such a loss would kill their soul, threaten their very existence. The Métis had no choice but to rebel, despite the overwhelming odds against them.

So they fought, defending themselves whenever they felt their freedom was at stake. It was always outside threats and pressure that stirred their national consciousness and strengthened their feeling of solidarity, to the point of uniting the French-speaking and English-speaking Métis communities of Manitoba, Dakota, and Saskatchewan in a common struggle.

The Métis were rebels not only because they took up arms against the British Empire and the Protestant royalists of Ontario, but also, and most importantly, because they refused to adopt the social models that others wanted to impose on them and that were contrary to their concept of social justice. They insisted on seeking another way, on trying to create the ideal new world of which everyone dreamed. Their efforts in this regard were exemplary.

In the long history of humanity, it was the Métis who gave us the model of an egalitarian and tolerant society founded on respect for both individual and collective values. Their life was a creative act. The social model they developed is still alive – and still eminently worthy of emulation.

Illustration Credits

Abbreviations
NAC: National Archives of Canada
LAC: Library and Archives of Canada
BM: Bibliothèque de Montréal
BNQ: Bibliothèque nationale du Québec
JAM: Joslyn Art Museum, Omaha, Nebraska
CMC: Canadian Museum of Civilization
MHB: Musée d'histoire de Berne
MFT: Museum of the Fur Trade, Chadron, Nebraska
NL: E.E. Ayer Collection, The Newberry Library, Chicago

t: top; **b**: bottom; **l**: left; **r**: right; **c**: centre

6: I-60004.1, Notman Photographic Archives, McCord Museum, Montreal
7: Cree Woman (detail), K. Bodmer, watercolour, JAM
8: E97.32W r28, Minnesota Historical Society
9: PA-74670, NAC
10-11: © Richard Hamilton Smith/Corbis/Magma
11: b PA-038139, NAC
12: Vaisseaux appareillant Le Havre (detail), A. Willaerst, Musée André Malraux
12-13: © Francis Back
13: t Private collection
14: tl BM; **tr** S. Poulin, MFT
15: Sauvage Nepisingue en Canada, photo, Bibliothèque nationale de France. Of 4a
16: t Recueil de Proverbes (1657-1663), J. Lagniet; **b** Louis XIII (detail), Pierre Paul Rubens, Sipa-Icono
17: t op.cit., J. Lagniet; **b** Le quai et le pont de la Tourelle [...] (detail), c. 1640, attr. T.D. Matham, © PMVP/Toumazet
18: t A.J. Miller, C-000422, NAC; **b** VIII-F-14789, H. Foster, CMC
19: t Young Blackfeet-Assiniboin Girl, captive (detail), K. Bodmer, watercolour, JAM; **b** (detail), A.J. Miller, C-000430, NAC
20: l pl. 24, La Floride française (1562-1565) (detail), Lemoyne de Morgues, LAC; **tr** © Erwin and Peggy Bauer; **b** © Erwin and Peggy Bauer
21: t © Erwin and Peggy Bauer; **b** © Joe McDonald/Corbis/Magma
22: l Les Indiens d'Amérique du Nord, E.S. Curtis, H. Foster, CMC; **r** Ihkas-Kinne, Siksika Blackfeet Chief, K. Bodmer, watercolour, JAM
23: t Pachtuwa-Chta, Arikara Man, K. Bodmer, watercolour, JAM; **b** op.cit., E.S. Curtis, H. Foster, CMC
24: tl pl. 23, op.cit. (detail), Lemoyne de Morgues, LAC; **tr** VIII-F-2063, H. Foster, CMC; **b** X-A-438, X-A-439, H. Foster, CMC
25: t VIII-F-14828, H. Foster, CMC; **c** XI-A-557, H. Foster, CMC; **b** VIII-F-8569, H. Foster, CMC
26: tl BM; **tr** S. Poulin, MFT; **b** S. Poulin, MFT
27: t J. Verelst, C-092418, NAC; **b** Private collection
28-29: © David Muench/Corbis/Magma
29: b NA-726-30, Glenbow Archives, Alberta
30: t Voyages curieux et nouveaux [...] (detail), C. Le Beau, Amsterdam, 1738, BNQ; **b** S. Poulin, MFT
31: t (detail), T. de Bry, NL 22261, LAC; **b** © Francis Back
32: l (detail), C.J. Sauthier, C-007300, NAC; **r** III-G-823, H. Foster, CMC
33: BM
34: l Jardine's Naturalist's Library, 19th century, Dover Publications Inc.; **r** S. Poulin, MFT
35: t © Bruno Petrozza, Courtesy of the Fur Council of Canada; **b** Treasury of Animal Illustrations, 18th century, Dover Publications Inc.
36: l (detail), W. Hollar, P/P1951, The British Museum; **r** Chapelier, pl. 5, Encyclopédie Diderot; **b** S. Poulin, MFT
37: (detail), W. Hollar, P/P609, The British Museum
38: l C-123411, NAC; **b** III-C-596, H. Foster, made by: William Mathieu Mark, 1993, CMC
39: © Erwin and Peggy Bauer
40: t (detail), A.J. Miller, C-000402, NAC; **b** pl. 25, op.cit., Lemoyne de Morgues, LAC
40-41: t III-X-249, III-X-260, H. Foster, CMC; **b** (detail), A.J. Miller, C-000403, NAC
42: tl (detail), C. Krieghoff, C-146152, NAC; **tr** III-J-45, H. Foster, CMC; **b** Chesterfield Collection L-36, Queen's University Archives
43: t op.cit., C. Le Beau, BNQ; **b** III-G-413, M. Toole, CMC
44: tl Carte de l'Amérique septentrionale, 1688 (detail), J.B. Franquelin, Collections du ministère de la Défense, SHM; **b** S. Poulin, MFT
45: t S. Poulin, MFT; **b** Canoes in a Fog, Lake Superior (detail), 1869, F.A. Hopkins, Glenbow Museum
46-47: © Gary Braasch/Corbis/Magma
47: b NA-3471-32, Glenbow Arch.
48: tl Jésuites martyrisés par les Iroquois (detail), 1664, F. du Creux, LAC; **tr** S. Poulin, MFT; **b** R. Lochon, C-021404, NAC
49: © Francis Back
50: tl op.cit., F. du Creux, LAC; **tr** III-X-236, H. Foster, CMC; **b** S. Poulin, MFT
51: H. Beau, C-011988, NAC
52: tl pl. 42, op.cit. (detail), Lemoyne de Morgues, LAC; **tr** III-I-1323, H. Foster, CMC; **b** V-X-401, CMC
53: © Francis Back
54: tl S. Stretton, C-014827, NAC; **tr** S. Poulin, MFT; **b** CII A1. (detail), document held at Centre historique des Archives nationales, Paris
55: Encyclopédie des voyages [...], vol. 5 (Paris, 1795), J. Grasset de Saint-Sauveur, C-003164, NAC
56: t (detail), A.J. Miller, C-000419, NAC; **b** VIII-E-13, M. Toole, CMC
57: t op.cit. (detail), F. du Creux, BNQ; **b** © Francis Back
58: tl (detail), A.J. Miller, C-000439, NAC; **tr** S. Poulin, MFT; **b** III-X-237, H. Foster, CMC
59: © Francis Back
60: l (detail), op.cit., F. du Creux, BNQ; **c** Neville Public Museum of Brown County and the Catholic Diocese of Green Bay, Wisconsin
61: F. Remington, NA-1406-55, Glenbow Arch.
62: t (detail), A.J. Miller, C-000427, NAC; **b** R.F. Kurz, Inv. 1894.404.57, MHB
63: t S. Poulin, MFT; **b** The Trapper's Bride (detail), A.J. Miller, oil on canvas, JAM
64: 1-20027, Notman Photographic Archives, McCord Museum
65: Cree Woman, K. Bodmer, watercolour and pencil, JAM
66-67: PA-045620, NAC
67: PA-059559, NAC
68-69: © Michael S. Lewis/Corbis/Magma
69: b PA-041367, NAC
70: t No. 41, p. 122, F.B. Mayer, NL
70-71: © Francis Back
71: t III-X-262, H. Foster, CMC; **b** S. Poulin, MFT
72: t No. 44, p. 63, F.B. Mayer, NL; **b** S. Poulin, MFT
73: t S. Poulin, MFT; **b** T.G. Anderton, NA-935-1, Glenbow Arch.
74: tl BM; **tr** S. Poulin, K. Matthes; **b** S. Poulin, K. Matthes
75: b © Francis Back; **tl** S. Poulin, K. Matthes
76: tl No. 44, p. 22, F.B. Mayer, NL; **tr** III-P-1 a-b, H. Foster, CMC; **b** III-I-1328, H. Foster, CMC
77: © Francis Back
78: t (detail), C-150336, NAC; **b** PA-125409, NAC
79: t No. 40, p. 49, F.B. Mayer, NL; **b** S. Poulin, K. Matthes
80: tl (detail), F.A. Hopkins, C-002772, NAC; **tr** S. Poulin, MFT
80-81: (detail), F.A. Hopkins, C-002771, NAC
81: t W. Armstrong, C-019041, NAC
82: tl (detail), F.A. Hopkins, C-002773, NAC; **tr** S. Poulin, MFT
82-83: © Francis Back
83: tr S. Poulin, MFT
84: tl Ex-voto of Pierre Lemoyne d'Iberville, 1994X.029, Musée de Sainte-Anne-de-Beaupré; **tr** 1998.1130, Château Ramezay Museum; **b** 1998.890, Château Ramezay Museum
85: t W. Berczy, C-132756, NAC; **b** S. Poulin, K. Matthes
86: tl (detail), R. Dillon, C-189402, NAC; **tr** S. Poulin, MFT; **b** S. Poulin, MFT
87: t III-G-838, H. Foster, CMC; **b** (detail), J. Peachey, C-150742, NAC
88: HD2.3 r7, Minnesota Historical Society
89: Mandan Indian Woman (detail), K. Bodmer, watercolour, JAM
90-91: C. Horetzky, PA-009169, NAC
91: Chesterfield Collection W-5, Queen's Archives
92-93: © Richard Hamilton Smith/Corbis/Magma
93: b PA-019631, NAC
94: tl B. de La Potherie, C-113193, NAC; **b** III-C-687 a-b, H. Foster, CMC
94-95: © Francis Back
95: r S. Poulin, MFT
96: tl A. Heming, NA-1185-6, Glenbow Arch.; **tr** V-A-237, H. Foster, CMC
97: PA-066528, NAC
98: tl Fort Clark on the Missouri, February 1834 (detail), K. Bodmer, aquatint, JAM; **b** op.cit., R.F. Kurz, MHB
98-99: III-C-589, H. Foster, CMC
99: b The Surveyor: Portrait of John Henry Lefroy (detail), c. 1855, P. Kane, Glenbow Museum
100: tl Kitchie-Ogi-Maw, 1845, P. Kane, oil on canvas, 912.1.11, Royal Ontario Museum; **tr** III-X-239, CMC; **b** S. Poulin, MFT
101: t Making Presents to Snake Indians (detail), A.J. Miller, watercolour, gouache, pencil and inks, JAM; **b** III-X-247, H. Foster, CMC
102: t 1998.838, Château Ramezay Museum; **b** Two of the Companies' Officers [...], 1823 (detail), P. Rindisbacher, watercolour with pen and black ink over graphite, No. 23007 © National Gallery of Canada, Ottawa
103: t C-008711, NAC; **b** P. Rindisbacher, C-001934, NAC
104: tl Interior of Fort Laramie (detail), 1858-60, A.J. Miller, watercolour, 37.1940.150, The Walters Art Museum, Baltimore; **tr** S. Poulin, MFT; **b** S. Poulin, MFT
105: t No. 42, p. 78, F.B. Mayer, NL; **b** (detail), A.J. Miller, C-000426, NAC
106: tl Amérindiens vendant du tabac [...] (detail), 1982.162, Collection of the Stewart Museum at the Fort on Île Sainte-Hélène; **tr** S. Poulin, MFT; **b** Portrait of Governor Stuyvesant, c. 1660, attr. H. Couturier, No. 1909-2, New York Historical Society
107: (detail), J. Verelst, C-092421, NAC
108: tl (detail), G. Heriot, C-010682, NAC; **tr** S. Poulin, MFT; **b** 1998.816, Château Ramezay Museum
109: t Plan du fort Pontchartrain, Labrador, 1708, H4/350, NMC 2299, LAC; **b** (detail), Paul Sanby (Junior), C-151295, NAC
110: l © Sipa-Icono
110-111: © D-K Images
112: T.G. Anderton, NA-935-1, Glenbow Arch.
113: Chan-Cha-Uia-Teuin, Teton Sioux Woman, K. Bodmer, watercolour, JAM
114: op.cit., E.S. Curtis, C-024489, NAC
115: O.J. Murie, PA-136025, NAC
116-117: © Sheldan Collins/Corbis/Magma
117: b PA-018000, NAC
118: l op.cit., R.F. Kurz, MHB
118-119: © Francis Back
119: t S. Poulin, MFT; **r** S. Poulin, MFT
120: tl op.cit., E.S. Curtis, H. Foster, CMC; **tr** V-A-439, R. Garner, CMC; **b** S. Poulin, MFT
121: t op.cit., R.F. Kurz, MHB; **b** © Francis Back
122: tl A.J. Miller, C-000438, NAC; **c** VIII-F-14817, H. Foster, CMC
123: t S. Poulin, MFT; **b** The Travellers Meeting with Minatarre Indians near Fort Clark (detail), K. Bodmer, aquatint, JAM
124: tl La chasse au cerf, Les voyages du Sieur de Champlain, 1620 (detail), BNQ; **tr** S. Poulin, MFT; **b** S. Poulin, MFT
125: t S. Poulin, MFT; **b** © Francis Back
126: tl (detail), A.J. Miller, C-000406, NAC; **tr** S. Poulin, MFT
126-127: b Thomas Wiewandt © Corbis/Magma
127: t V-B-424, J. Soublière, CMC
128: tl Setting Traps for Beavers (detail), A.J. Miller, watercolour, gouache, pencil and inks, JAM; **tr** Antoine – Principal Hunter, A.J. Miller, watercolour, gouache, pencil and inks, JAM; **b** S. Poulin, MFT
129: tr S. Poulin, MFT; **b** Captain Walker (detail), A.J. Miller, watercolour, gouache, pencil and inks, JAM
130: tl No. 41, p. 120, F.B. Mayer, NL; **tr** S. Poulin, MFT; **b** S. Poulin, MFT
131: t V-E-276, CMC; **b** (detail), A.J. Miller, C-000424, NAC
132: tl Souligny, WHI-1868, Wisconsin Historical Society; **tr** S. Poulin, MFT; **b** S. Poulin, MFT
133: © Francis Back
134: tl No. 41, p. 65, F.B. Mayer, NL; **tr** 1973.5.1, Coll. of the Stewart Museum at the Fort on Île Sainte-Hélène; **b** P. Rindisbacher, C-046498, NAC
135: G. Moodie, NA-3811-12, Glenbow Arch.
136: Frances Anna Savage, c. 1850, MP-1985.52.4, Notman Photographic Archives, McCord Museum
137: Piegan Blackfeet Woman, K. Bodmer, watercolour, JAM
138: PA-034102, NAC
139: PA-050799, NAC
140-141: © ML Sinibaldi/Corbis/Magma
141: b PA-074674, NAC
142: tl No. 41, p. 48, F.B. Mayer, NL; **tr** LH997.115.1, H. Foster, CMC; **b** V-X-409, H. Foster, CMC
143: tr No. 44, p. 15, F.B. Mayer, NL; **b** © Francis Back
144: tl NA-1177-1, Glenbow Arch.; **tr** S. Poulin, MFT; **b** No. 44, p. 22, F.B. Mayer, NL
145: NA-3432-2, Glenbow Arch.
146: tl (detail), A.J. Miller, C-000427, NAC; **b** NA-1237-1, Glenbow Arch.
147: t S. Poulin, MFT; **b** (detail), A.J. Miller, C-000434, NAC
148: tl No. 41, p. 102, F.B. Mayer, NL; **tr** S. Poulin, MFT; **b** H. Julien, C-061461, NAC
149: t V-D-117, H. Foster, CMC; **b** © Francis Back
150: tl C-081787, NAC; **b** op.cit., R.F. Kurz, MHB
151: t NA-1709-35, Glenbow Arch.; **b** 988.36.1 a-g, H. Foster, CMC
152: tl (detail), A.J. Miller, C-000436, NAC; **b** S. Poulin, MFT
153: t 988.8.1, H. Foster, CMC; **b** © Erwin and Peggy Bauer
154: tl Half Breeds Travelling (detail), P. Kane, oil on canvas, 912.1.24, Royal Ontario Museum; **r** S. Poulin, MFT
154-155: b (detail), A.J. Miller, C-000417, NAC
155: t S. Poulin, MFT
156: tl (detail), A.J. Miller, C-000401, NAC; **b** V-A-332, H. Foster, CMC
157: t VI-D-73, H. Foster, CMC; **b** Half Breeds Running Buffalo (detail), P. Kane, oil on canvas, 912.1.26, Royal Ontario Museum
158: tl (detail), A.J. Miller, C-000435, NAC; **tr** NA-2631-6, Glenbow Arch.
159: t O.B. Buell, C-001875, NAC; **b** (detail), Grundy, C-002424, NAC

Printed in Spain